Table of Contents

Warmup

My purpose in writing this book is to give you an accurate picture of the sports broadcasting profession, whether you're a sports fan who is curious or an aspiring sportscaster.

Many teachers and broadcasting professionals unselfishly gave strong assistance to me in my 50 years in the business. It's impossible to repay them for their devotion to the profession, but it's possible to help the next generation. Hopefully this book will serve that purpose.

To those who have allowed us in your homes via radio and television, we thank you for your hospitality and your kindness through the years. The thrill of being a sportscaster has lived up to all expectations for me. But only because of a strong family who understood what the job required, and many relatively unknown men and women. Thanks to the statisticians, spotters, media relations people, players, coaches and managers who took time to help along the way.

Time now for me to step aside, except for a few personal stories along the way. The storytellers of today will take you on a journey of passion for a craft, pursuit of an education and a place in a broadcast booth. Their lives are fascinating. The lengths to which they have gone to put themselves in a position to be broadcasters will leave you in appreciation of them.

Batter up!

Brownie

Mark 9:23: Everything is possible for him who believes.

CHAPTER 1
STARTING LINE

Are you the type who reads, watches and discusses sports constantly? Do you remember meaningful games, plays and controversies? Any sportscaster who doesn't love, love, love sports is in for a tough time in the profession. Some of us are not encyclopedic in our knowledge of sports. That's not a necessity, but it helps. Many of us have a passion for one particular sport only. That's limiting in the career path it offers. But if you're content to pursue that one favorite sport, realize that you are reducing your employment options.

At the top of the pyramid is the professional soul of the broadcaster. Is he or she a tireless worker at his or her craft? Is the broadcaster a historian, storyteller and tireless researcher? Is this person capable of solid judgment and being a team member? Does he or she have a sense of fairness and at the same time a passion for the presentation of a game? Work ethic, as with almost any profession, plays a large role in the success or failure of a broadcaster. An attention-getting voice is simply not enough. You don't have to be able to name the winners of every Super Bowl, but that knowledge might come in handy. An interviewer might just be impressed enough with your knowledge that you get the job over other candidates.

P *resident Calvin Coolidge said,*
"Nothing in this world can take the place of persistence. Talent will not;nothing is more common than unsuccessful men with talent. Genius will not; unrewarded genius is almost a proverb. Education will not; the world is full of educated derelicts. Persistence and determination alone are omnipotent. The slogan 'Press on!' has solved and always will solve the problems of the human race."

Fortunately, a broadcaster's task is not that weighty! Nonetheless, the ability to bounce back from a lackluster performance is a necessary part of the equipment of a good broadcaster. Just as a golfer who starts the round with a triple bogey, the broadcaster must be able to focus on what is next rather than dwelling on an early mistake in the broadcast.

Rules of the Game

You don't take off on a thousand-mile driving vacation without checking a map. And you shouldn't begin your career as a play-by-play broadcaster without knowing the rules of the sport. Your time spent in the rulebook will bail you out of many potentially embarrassing moments on the air. There are classes available for people who officiate each sport, but when considering them make sure you're headed to the right place.

Once I took a baseball umpiring class, but it was for high school umpires. High school rules in baseball are quite different from professional rules. It was a waste of time and confusing to be studying rules that aren't used in the major or minor leagues. A few days at Harry Wendelstedt's Umpiring School in Daytona Beach, Florida one year provided an eye-opening experience and a much better place to hang out.

There are young people who are willing to pay to attend schools like that and pursue a very low-paying job in the minor leagues. Even the Class A umpiring jobs are very tough to land.

Tough travel by car late at night and low pay are in the future of those umps, and very few make it to the major leagues. But they pursue their dreams.

One night some of the students at the Wendelstedt school were cooking a pot of spaghetti for their dinner in an apartment they shared in the area during the eight-week school. While they were fixing dinner after all day at the school, they had their rule books open and they were quizzing each other. That's dedication!

Broadcasters not only need to know the rulebook; they need to understand that beyond the rulebook there is a casebook for umpires that explains the rules much better than the rulebook.

The casebook is a much better resource for a broadcaster, because it uses sample situations and applies the rules to them. Brushing up on the rules before the season starts is a solid plan. Baseball rules are more complicated than rules in other sports, but no matter what sport is in front of you it's a necessity to know the rules.

The infield fly rule in baseball is one of the most confusing in any sport. Some players panic and start running toward the next base if the ball is not caught, but they don't have to run. The broadcaster needs to know that so he can explain what the player might have been thinking. In basketball, there's a charge-block call and a sportscaster has to be able to explain that rule.

These situations might not come up for months, but a broadcaster has to be ready for them when they happen. It's a good idea to get to know coaches and officials and occasionally ask them about their experiences with confusing rules so you'll be ready when the time comes.

Develop a Code of Ethics

If a manager, coach, front office executive, player or anybody you rely on for information gives you information "off the record," your responsibility is to keep it quiet. Betraying a confidence can get you in a lot of trouble. It's not the same as a reporter for the *Washington Post* getting background information from somebody at the Defense Department, but it's important to your career to keep a confidence. It may seem small in nature to you, but if someone asks for your cooperation, your word should be your bond.

There's a saying in broadcasting: "You're only as good as your last game." It can be an insecure profession at times, if not at **ALL** times! The point of the saying is that a career can be meteoric one day, headed perhaps to the national network level, only to get derailed the next. The thought behind the saying above is that a broadcaster needs to stay focused on what is next rather than feeling great or terrible about the most recent broadcast. It's not unlike a game of golf. One young female golfer was asked how long she thought about the previous shot, whether it was a great one or a disastrous one. She said, "No more than ten seconds for either one." Here's a promise that there will be no more golf analogies!

You'll work with many people in broadcasting if you have a lengthy career. Word travels quickly in the business about people who spread rumors and bad-mouth their associates behind their backs. If you never speak in critical terms about any of your fellow employees behind their backs, you won't have any worries about acquiring that type of reputation.

Throughout the book we'll have some fun with broadcasting mistakes on the air. Let's face it, some days our minds and mouths are not on the same track. We all say things on the air that are embarrassing. Some of these quotes are from good friends. This is not an attempt to embarrass them. They would not mind, because they would tell you that sometimes we just have to be able to laugh at ourselves. If this happens to you, roll with it and have some fun!

Jerry Coleman, Hall of Fame baseball broadcaster

"Winfield goes back to the wall, he hits his head on the wall and it rolls off! It's rolling all the way back to second base! This is a terrible thing for the Padres!"

Pedro Guerrero, Los Angeles Dodgers

"First I pray that nobody hits a ball to me; then I pray that nobody hits a ball to Steve Sax."

Bill Petersen, Football Coach

"Three things are bad for you. I can't remember the first two, but doughnuts are the third."

Joe Torre, Baseball manager

"I'm not sure whether I'd rather be managing or testing bulletproof vests."

CHAPTER 2

EDUCATION
High School Years

If you have a good idea that you want to be a broadcaster at an early age, you can get started by training yourself on a small tape recorder or the voice memo on your smartphone. Hop on the internet and grab the rosters of the teams playing a game on TV, sit down with them and do your play-by-play on tape. Practice doing the game the way you have heard announcers do it, taking commercial breaks when they do. Turn down the sound and provide your own commentary without listening to them. After the game, listen to the tape and make notes on your thoughts. How did you do? It's common to be disappointed. If that's the case, try another game. And another. And another. When your work improves, have your parents or another family member listen to your tape and offer comments. Keep practicing and see how much you improve. High school games provide excellent opportunities for training as a broadcaster. It's easy to take a tape recorder or smartphone to the corner of the bleachers and practice doing the games. While you're at it, keep a scorecard while you announce. That's one of the most difficult aspects of learning to broadcast baseball. Writing in a scorebook while talking on the air does not come naturally, and the sooner you start practicing the more naturally it will become a part of your experience when it counts on the job.

Those who know in high school that they are interested in journalism can get an early start. Any sportscaster can benefit from taking classes that emphasize writing and working on projects that involve storytelling and collaboration with fellow students on text and pictures in a publication.

Bridgeland High School journalism teacher Samantha Berry in Cypress, Texas is the president of the Texas Association of Journalism Educators. She's taught for ten years at the high school level. She said a class in news writing and news reporting at Texas Tech changed her life. She followed the career of Diane Sawyer of ABC News. The news magazine show 20/20 was her favorite.

Some of her students take her class as freshmen. Many of them are attracted to podcasting now. "What's really important for me as an educator is teaching them how to be a responsible consumer of the media, and that involves long discussions about the history of journalism, about bias and fake news, how to be a conscientious consumer," says Samantha. "For us, bringing kids into that class really starts with that. Then we start to get a lot more specific. News, editorial, sports, entertainment."

Areas of Interest

She steers students into their areas of interest, which might include writing, photography, design or – yes, even play-by-play. She points students into curriculum at the *New York Times* learning network, *The Newseum* in Washington, D.C. and other sources. One of her students, a senior, is researching colleges for journalism and would love to be a play-by-play basketball broadcaster.

Selecting a college can be daunting. This book offers much more on that important choice. Although broadcasters come in many shapes and sizes and from diverse backgrounds, their choice of a college can be one of the most decisive factors in how their career starts. And it goes beyond the classes offered at the college, as you'll find out on page 205.

College Years

For decades, some of the top universities in the U.S. for broadcasting training were Syracuse, Missouri and Northwestern as well as a few others. All of those universities offer excellent facilities for students, including radio and television studios. There they receive training on the air and behind the scenes. More than 50 years ago the University of Missouri School of Journalism had a class titled "Broadcast News and Film." Videotape had not been pioneered at that time, leaving film as the primary visual source for portable cameras for covering news and sports. Students could deliver newscasts and sportscasts on the air live at that time. They also could get training in writing in broadcast style as well as shooting and editing film. They were used as cameramen or camerawomen in the television studio on live programs.

Syracuse University was a pipeline for several top play-by-play broadcasters who reached high levels. Notably, Syracuse sent many graduates directly to ESPN for entry level jobs. In recent years, Ball State has been a solid breeding ground for play-by-play jobs. In Texas, Sam Houston State in Huntsville has a strong Mass Communication school and has trained several sports broadcasters. Dan Rather, the longtime CBS anchorman, is a graduate. Sportscasters such as the late Bob Allen and Randy McIlvoy, Steve Sparks of the Houston Astros, Mike Capps of the Round Rock Express and Michael Coffin of the Corpus Christi Hooks also were trained at Sam Houston State.

You'll be reading about the college experiences of the broadcasters throughout the book. Peter Roussel passes along advice from his career on page 205. He's gone from the White House to a communications program at a Sam Houston State University.

It's a profession! Be ready for some bumps along the way. In my first job after college, the news director wanted me to do weekend TV sportscasts. But he said I looked too young and because of that I didn't have credibility with the viewers. I commented that the audience age 18-34 was the one TV ratings experts constantly talked about targeting. He asked if I could grow a mustache. The answer was no. But my wife and I bought a fake mustache and tried to trim it to fit. That project wound up in the wastebasket, and so did my chances of doing sports on camera at that station!

CHAPTER 3

Gifts

"Talent" is a generic word used to describe "on air people," or broadcasters. It's not used as widely any more. It's a strange term, although those of us who are blessed to be on the air have been gifted by God with a voice that is at least pleasant enough to be a guest in someone's game room or car for a few hours. And we're fortunate to have the ability to speak, describe and entertain. But, as important as the quality of a broadcaster's voice is, it is not nearly enough by itself for excellence at the top level of broadcasting. Articulation, vocal range, pacing and mastery of pauses and changes in pitch all factor in when a listener determines that a broadcaster's voice is acceptable if not pleasing. And, above all, opinions about broadcasters are subjective. We could all debate for many days why certain broadcasters are more popular than others.

Reporter? Artist?

Are you a reporter? That's a basic question for any broadcaster. Any play-by-play broadcaster can work on skills by practicing any type of description as it occurs. It's vital, especially for radio broadcasters, to describe what is happening. One veteran radio broadcaster friend feels that today's young broadcasters missed the training on the art of description that older broadcasters received because previous generations grew up listening to radio before television became abundant in homes. Al Michaels described his mother going to the refrigerator as a kid. Radio is "the theater of the mind." Although an event may be televised as well as broadcast on radio, the radio broadcaster is responsible for describing, and the commonly used phrase is "painting a picture on a blank canvas."

The more vivid the description, the better the listener understands what the picture looks like. The best radio broadcasters give the listener a verbal picture of what is happening.

Example: "Trips right with a split backfield. Here's the snap. Brady rolls right and loops a throw toward the goal line. Jones reaches up and snags it, falling backwards into the end zone. The Patriots take a 6-0 lead!" As radio listeners, we are all blind, in a sense. None of us can see the game. The broadcasters bring the picture of the game to us.

You or Ernie Johnson?

How do they prepare for that commentary? Most grew up listening to a broadcaster they respected and attached their dreams to his style. But at some time in their development, they realized they must break away and used their own distinctive talents to find their own way in the booth.

At one point in my career, my favorite broadcaster was Ray Scott. He used words sparingly on the air. He was the play-by-play broadcaster on CBS for many Green Bay Packer games. They were the best team in the NFL. A typical Ray Scott call on TV was, "Starr to Dowler on a slant-in… TOUCHDOWN!" When I tried to broadcast more like Ray Scott, it didn't work for me. That style on a baseball game for a team that lost 101 games and didn't have much excitement was the wrong choice. I was fired after that season. Takeaway? Don't be Ray Scott. Be you.

Hopefully you will gain an understanding of what sportscasting involves through this book. By reading about professionals who tell you what they experienced and what you're likely to find out, you can prepare yourself better for an exciting journey that can be challenging and also humbling as your career progresses.

VOICE

Often someone asks of a broadcaster if his or her voice came naturally or whether it could be developed. The Kalas family handed down some of the best voices heard by many of us. Hall of Fame baseball broadcaster Harry Kalas was the Voice of NFL Films in addition to his legendary career as a play-by-play broadcaster for major league baseball, the NFL, college football and basketball. His father was a minister with an equally attention-getting voice. Harry's son Todd, featured on page 79, who is now a Houston Astros TV broadcaster, inherited that same powerful voice. The gene pool was very strong in that family! Often the voice is a God-given gift, but it can be enhanced. Whether a person's voice is considered to be professional in quality or not, it can be improved.

In ancient times, the Greek orator Demosthenes was an orphan at the age of seven and he wanted to take his guardians to court because they were spending all the money he inherited from his parents. To prepare for speaking in court, he practiced speaking in front of a large mirror with pebbles in his mouth! He had a stammering problem, and the practice solved it. He became a great speaker and leader.

Opera or Jazz?

Singing is one avenue to strengthen a voice and broaden the range of the voice. We can all sing, although not always on key! It's not necessary to sing well to create the desired effect – making the voice stronger. Singers are taught to care for their voices the way a baseball pitcher cares for his arm. Years ago, pitchers were taught never to rest their pitching arm near an air conditioning vent. Is that scientific? Perhaps it's not a good idea to take a chance by resting your arm next to a steady stream of cold air.

In your area of expertise, experts can aid your performance when it applies to your voice.

Singers are taught by their voice coaches never to raise their voices when they're not singing. They're also taught never to clear their throats. Oddly, many broadcasters do that all the time. If a radio personality plays a song and is about to come back on the air, it's common for that person to make a sound before speaking into the microphone so there won't be a throat issue. Actually, that's not a good idea. It can cause wear and tear on the vocal cords. A broadcaster has to rely on that "instrument" for a paycheck. No voice, no job! Drinking water constantly keeps the vocal cords hydrated properly. Caffeinated drinks are to be limited.

Singers, like athletes, warm up before their performance. It's not a good idea to come out of the bedroom for breakfast and yell something to begin the day! Voice coaches can be extremely helpful to a broadcaster. The technique of using the diaphragm to create the proper timbre for the voice is of the utmost importance. Using your voice for a period of approximately three hours per day requires some understanding that your voice is a muscle and it responds to exercising it and preparing it for the types of use you will need. It's not uncommon to have a sore throat after using your voice in a more strenuous way than normal.

How the Superstars Did It

Hall of Fame broadcaster Jack Buck told broadcaster/author Tom Hedrick in *The Art of Sportscasting* about strengthening his voice and learning to project it by yelling at potential customers as he sold newspapers on the street corner all day; Marty Brennaman took acting lessons for ten years because he wanted to act on Broadway; Jim Nantz spent two years with a speech therapist to rid himself of problems pronouncing words with "l" sounds.

When a broadcaster is preparing for a season that lasts several months and it's been weeks since he or she did a game, it makes sense to build up the voice by using it.

Let's say that you've been doing a two-hour talk show in the summer and now it's time to begin a season of doing play-by-play hockey. Hockey is a grueling sport for the voice. It will put many more demands on your voice than a talk show, and you can prepare for those demands.

Air from our lungs creates sound waves, or vibrations, when the vocal cords meet in the middle of the opening and touch each other. Controlling the balance of the air and the adduction, or touching, of the vocal cords determines how the sound is transmitted through our voice.

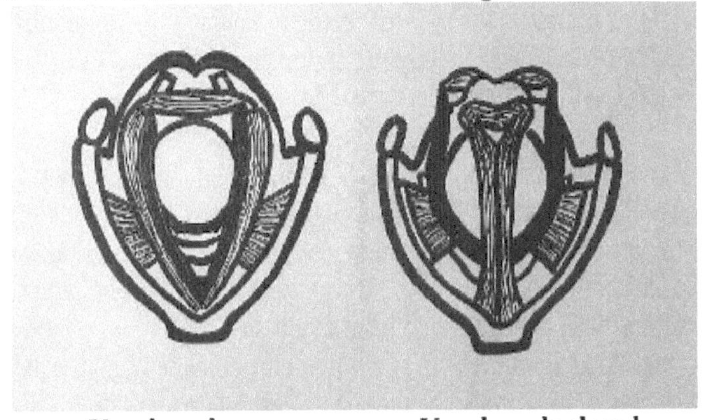

Vocal cords open   **Vocal cords closed**

A strong voice comes from the diaphragm. Being in a proper posture and breathing from the diaphragm allows us to project air through the lungs from a more powerful starting point. In the photo above, the vocal cords are open and air is passing through the opening. When you speak, they meet in the middle of the air passage.

From time to time, a broadcaster will have to undergo surgery on the vocal cords. Singers also have to go through that surgery at times. Understanding how the voice works can help you to use it properly so it serves you well. If you have a voice problem and you're worried about getting through a game, try sipping warm cranapple juice. It really helps! That advice came from network broadcaster Marv Albert's voice coach. He probably paid quite a bit for it, but it's free to us now!

It's a logical approach to do more talking as your first game approaches, maybe even working on a play-by-play practice period or an entire practice game. Broadcasters usually consider that type of approach to be boring, unnecessary or a waste of time. But to those who are students of preparation, paying attention to the voice makes sense. After all, how many broadcasters can have a good broadcast without a voice? Your voice may be fine for two periods of a hockey game but then it may be raspy for the third period because it's not strong enough. How will your call sound if there's a game-winning goal in overtime? Will you enjoy hearing your voice crack over and over on the highlights? That could be the outcome if you don't do your due diligence on the most important tool you have! Standard advice for good health applies to all people who depend on their voices: stay out of the cold, especially without a head covering; avoid the rain; find what medication you need to use when allergy season arrives; keep yourself in good physical condition; avoid late nights and long hours if you can. Boring? Yes.

"The Rain in Spain Falls Mainly in the Plain"

The line above is from a song in the musical "My Fair Lady." Eliza Doolittle was taking voice lessons to speak proper English. It's a sound plan to enroll in speech and debate classes in high school and college. This type of training is extremely beneficial. The use of the voice in these types of public speaking formats strengthens it. The coordination of mind and voice, the essence of broadcasting, is benefitted by these classes.

A Voice and Articulation class in college can be exceptionally helpful. Diction is extremely important in the broadcasting profession. Speaking clearly and distinctly is a must. Slurring words and using sloppy speech is unacceptable. Sometimes names in sports are difficult to pronounce. You may not be able to pronounce a long name of a foreign player without some practice.

It's critical to pronounce names properly. Someone will notice if you don't, and eventually it could work against you if you struggle in this area.

Taking classes in Spanish is a solid idea. Learning another language requires discipline and much practice. Speaking that language takes you a step further. It's extremely helpful in today's world to be able to speak Spanish. It allows you to have a conversation with a Spanish-speaking athlete and shows that athlete that you are making the effort to relate to him or her. It also places you in a favorable position when it comes to pronouncing Spanish names.

Thinking and speaking on your feet trains your mind and your mouth to react quickly to a comment by an adversary in a debate or a broadcast colleague on the air with very little time to craft your response. That's what broadcasters do.

Screaming

A play-by-play broadcaster needs to have as wide a vocal range as possible and some expressiveness in order to keep from sounding monotonous. On a game-winning home run in baseball, the announcer might say, "There's a deep drive to left field and it's going, GOING, GONE!!!"

As that simple call unfolds, the announcer increases the volume and also reaches a higher pitch. The combination of the two helps to portray the excitement of the home run.

It's much easier to make a call like this if there's a sellout crowd and the crowd provides a crescendo of background cheering, forcing the broadcaster to top it with his or her own climactic tone of voice. If the game is a high school game with 30 people in the stands, it's much more difficult and challenging to "sell the call." But the broadcaster is charged with portraying the proper amount of energy on the field with the proper vocal effort in the booth.

We all need to develop polish in this area. Find a room or an area where you can practice and listen to tapes of yourself telling a story with expression. Work on making your voice softer and then firmer as called for during the story. Use pauses and questions if they work for your style. Concentrate on drawing the listener into the story by using these techniques, including changing the pacing of your speech. Ask friends and family members to listen to your tapes and offer you their critiques. When they give you positive feedback that you consider to be honest, move on to critiques from professional media people. The best critiques are ones that have a fair amount of "constructive criticism," giving you specific areas of improvement for you to target.

Your improvement may be dependent on your ability to self-critique and also to separate valid criticism from comments that are beyond your ability to create significant change in your performance.

A Talk in the Park

We remember the famous game-winning calls, but not the quiet chatter during the routine moments of a game. But often how a broadcaster handles the unexciting times of the game can determine how successful the broadcast is.

Is it time to tell a story? Is something odd happening in the stands that bears mentioning?

Maybe the analyst will find it humorous and chime in with a comment that is entertaining. These challenging lapses in the action are uncomfortable to some sports broadcasters. Others relish the opportunity to divert from the game and create a different dialogue off the beaten path.

But there is always the responsibility to come back to the game, at least momentarily, before launching off onto some tangent that has no value to the listener.

Years ago, we were doing a baseball telecast in San Diego when the game was stopped because a swarm of bees gathered on a ball girl's chair in foul territory outside the left field line. The bees were stinging some people nearby. There was a 52-minute delay in the game while a beekeeper could be located! No broadcaster is prepared for this type of interruption. Since there was no break in game action, no commercials were scheduled. Where is a commercial when you really need one? They're always hounding us when we really don't want them! Somebody brought the president of the Padres into the TV booth and we interviewed him for several minutes about the bees and their efforts to remove them from the field. My TV partner, Jim Deshaies, was on the internet googling "bees" and he kept us entertained with various bits of information.

We were far from doing a baseball game, but occasionally this sort of interruption causes a mild panic in our minds because it is not anything anybody can prepare to handle. It's helpful to have a working knowledge of many different topics in case you find yourself in a "bee" game! But you're probably not going to be an expert on bees, so be ready for an occasional challenge in the booth.

ABC-TV commentator Howard Cosell had perhaps the most extensive vocabulary of any sportscaster. Cosell was an attorney, and he loved to toss around words that most in his audience could not define and hadn't heard many times in their lives. It was impressive. If you try it, it probably will not score many points for you. People check out of your broadcast if they sense you are trying to impress them with your knowledge. They want the score and the facts about the game first and foremost, not the number of your IQ.

Hockey broadcaster Mike Emrick has perhaps the best vocabulary of any current play-by-play broadcaster. He has developed a remarkable ability to express a simple play in different terms. Emrick keeps interest in a broadcast with his colorful terminology interwoven with his passion for the sport.

Throws, Tosses, Lofts and Lasers

There's every reason to make your vocabulary more versatile. You'll read later about how some sportscasters keep a list of synonyms they use for each sport. It's helpful to change your action verbs on the air so you can avoid being monotonous. You can describe how a quarterback "fires" a laser over the middle. Another time he may "zip" the pass. Or he might "force" a pass into heavy traffic over the middle.

On another occasion he might "loft" a high pass into the back of the end zone. Command of the English language is critical in this job. Those who don't strive for variety can be considered dull. When a broadcast is three hours long, the listener or viewer will notice if there's a tiny vocabulary in the booth. It's not harmful to have an extensive vocabulary, but keeping the rare lengthy words in your back pocket usually is a solid plan. Using the proper syntax is also one of the responsibilities of the job. Improper grammar may prevent you from getting jobs.

It's hard to visualize a broadcaster keeping a job by saying things like, "Jim and me went to a game last night." Another difficulty that may arise can be prevented by being precise with your vocabulary. If it's your choice to call a mistake on the field "a bonehead play," you should be comfortable that you've chosen the right words or be prepared to be confronted by somebody. But it's better to use those words than to say of the player, "He's a bonehead." Those are fighting words! If a running back spikes the football before he crosses the goal line, you're on solid ground. But if he tripped and fell before he could score, your choice of words should reflect exactly what happened.

Knowing and using the English language should be high on your list of priorities and always in your toolbelt when you do a game. There's every reason to correct yourself immediately after a mistake. That's not a weakness unless it happens often.

Ready to Jump In?

If you're ready for a play-by-play assignment now, there are openings at SHN Sports. "The first thing I ask anybody is 'Why do you want to do this?' says Rob Hipp, who teams with Karl Schoening to run the company. If you've never done a game, you submit a short tape of yourself doing play-by-play to start your broadcasting journey.

SHN Sports is a national live streaming company based in Austin, Texas that features live internet broadcasts for sports of all levels. Wherever you live, you can become a network affiliate at no charge. You handle your plans to broadcast games of your local high school, college or sports league. SHN Sports will send you the software and equipment recommendations to broadcast the games on their preferred platform, which as of this writing is currently YouTube.

If you want to do a coaches' pregame show 15 minutes before kickoff, that's your call. Hometown flavor is important to SHN Sports.

"We don't dictate how they run their broadcast; we want them to have control of how they run their business," says Hipp. You can attend the online SHN Live Academy for a minimal investment to get professional instruction and polish your skills.

Is It Show Time Yet?

With affiliates in six states, the current SHN load of 20-30 football games on Friday nights has plenty of room to grow. You can sell advertising and game content if that is of interest to you. SHN offers a product called "Broadcast-in-a-Box." The most difficult part of self-producing your own broadcasts is setting up and tearing down the equipment. SHN offers instruction in the fundamentals of those duties, emphasizing that broadcasters need to sound their best and present the best video possible. This cannot be done if the equipment is not set up properly.

"We're in the broadcasting business to tell a story. It's not about us. I think a lot of young broadcasters have this idea about getting to be on radio on TV, but it's not about them. It's about who we broadcast for," summarized Rob Hipp. "If they want to do live stream, they have to do it themselves, with our guidance," said Karl Schoening.

"It's more possible and more accessible than ever for someone who wants to sell a broadcast themself. The future and the present of broadcasting sports is no longer limited to people who have media outlets covering them or producing the content because of a contract exchange.

"It's just a stockpiling of equipment," Schoening explained. "If you're going to invest $1,000 a year to get equipment, within four years you may have something that looks like an ESPN broadcast more or less pretty easily. We're just here to guide people and make sure that they don't spend money where they don't need to and they get the critiques that they deserve."

You can visit SHNLive.com for more information on how to start or expand your broadcasting career, learn tips and tricks in live streaming and much more.

Assume the Mic is Open!

Rule number one of broadcasting is: Assume your microphone is live at all times. By doing that, you will avoid embarrassing moments such as the story below provides.

I had a whole team mad at me one time because I made a stupid mistake and forgot my microphone was on. Actually, it was left on during a commercial and only a few people could hear it. When you're training to go on the air, the rule of thumb is that any time you are within range of a microphone, assume it could pick up what you're saying. At times we all ignore that rule. And at times we get burned.

During a baseball game we were in commercial break. We wear headset microphones and usually leave them on during breaks, because sometimes the producer will want to have a conversation with us between innings. During this break, the Astros had put a new player in the game at third base.

I mumbled to myself, half joking to my partner, "----------- can't play third base!" Little did I know the players were listening in the clubhouse. After the game, the general manager of the team had been in the clubhouse and was aware of the problem.

He warned me that the players were upset about something I said. At first I couldn't understand what they could possibly have heard that caused that reaction.

When he told me it involved this player, I finally understood that this was not from a remark I'd made ON the air, but OFF the air!

Oh brother! We have enough problems trying not to alienate people with our comments ON the air. That's when I first discovered that the audio specialist in the production truck did not turn off our mics during the commercial breaks. When the players walked past me on the airplane after that game, they stared daggers through me. A voodoo doll would have felt more comfortable than I did at that moment. This player happened to be the most popular guy on the team, and he was sensitive.

I was squirming all during that flight before finally cornering him at the airport and apologizing to him. Lesson learned.

Byrum Saam, baseball broadcaster
"Playing second base for the Mets is Felix Millan. He's a Puerto Rican,
but he's a good hitter."
President Gerald Ford
"I watch a lot of baseball on the radio."
George Brett on teammate Jamie Quirk
"He looks like a greyhound, but he runs like a bus."
Bobby Robson, soccer coach
"We didn't underestimate them. They were better than we thought."
Terrell Owens, NFL
"Don't say I don't get along with my teammates. I just don't get along
with some of the guys on the team."

CHAPTER 4

The Gateway Guys

We'll hear from two young professionals in this chapter who have "checked all the boxes" when it comes to training, education and work ethic. They have placed themselves in an excellent position to advance because their resumes have been built on a strong foundation. What's ahead of them? It will be interesting to follow their careers, because they've stamped themselves as two broadcasters to follow in the same way we follow young athletes.

Coincidentally, they both grew up in St. Louis. Both did play-by-play for the Gateway Grizzlies, an independent baseball team. Coincidentally, they're friends. In fact, one helped the other get the job with the Grizzlies. Thus, they become the Gateway Guys.

Adam Young
TV & Radio Play-by-Play for NM State Sports Properties

Adam Young is the 31-year-old voice of New Mexico State sports, as well as other freelance assignments. The 2010 graduate of Southern Illinois University-Edwardsville is a shining example of a rising star in the sportscasting profession who has followed the advice given by many of his predecessors. His career track began early. Adam was on the air a few weeks after his high school graduation. He was focused all along on being a sportscaster. Basketball was his favorite sport because that was his first love. He played basketball and thought he might go into coaching if sportscasting didn't work out.

His sportscasting idol was Dewayne Staats, longtime sportscaster who also graduated from SIU-Edwardsville and went on to the Houston Astros, Chicago Cubs, New York Yankees and Tampa Bay Rays in baseball as well as other sports assignments. Another reason Young chose SIU-Edwardsville was the program's connection to major league sports in St. Louis. Students could get media passes to St. Louis Cardinals, Rams and Blues games as a part of their education.

He described his first job on the air. "Well, it was the campus radio station for SIU-Edwardsville where I went to school. They produced some other play-by-play guys over the years besides Dewayne Staats." Adam realized the value of the connection to major league sports.

Making a Big Leap

"I figured I could be in big league clubhouses at an early age and rub elbows with some people that could help me later on in life," said Adam Young. "The news director at the campus radio station let me on the air the summer before I even started college, so I had a high school graduation and a few weeks later I was doing a news update and a sports update on a 50,000 watt station just outside of St. Louis, which was a little crazy. But I think it helped me grow early on when I was working out kinks while I was still young. So whenever I did get out of college, I was ready to go and had a pretty good idea of what the business was about.

"But I was so naïve to everything, too, that I didn't really think a whole lot of it whenever I was on the air at 17 years old. But I think it was faster than most."

Was Adam intimidated by being at a large station because of the philosophy that a young broadcaster needs to start at a 1,000-watt station and make mistakes there?

"Honestly, I don't think I ever knew what 50,000 watts meant at that point. I think it took a little while for me to kind of understand how many people could listen. Over time, I think especially since it is a campus radio station and students are doing the news and the sports, I would hear the phone ring and the news director would answer it and he would be telling people, 'Look, these are younger men and women who are learning on the fly. Understand they might have screwed up that news report a little bit, but just keep in mind they're learning."

Trimming Mistakes

"I understand this is the number one jazz station in St. Louis, which it was, and a lot of people can hear it and a lot of people listen to it, but as far as the news, the sports, the reporting side of it, we did news updates and sports updates at the top of the hour, the bottom of the hour, morning and afternoon. People had to realize that these are younger people, just getting started in the business and trying to figure out if they're actually going to stay in this business. The school I went to wasn't exactly the most competitive for on-air opportunities, so I got to do everything. I would sit in the production studio when I wasn't on the air and I would read off the teleprompter and just practice. I knew I wanted to do it, but there were a lot of other people that were kind of on the fence – 50-50. Our news director was an intimidating figure who told you how it was and I loved that and we had a really good relationship. But it scared some people off, because they saw what it could be and how hard it was gonna be. I don't think they really wanted to put in the time and the effort to get to where they wanted to be."

How were his classes in college? "Honestly, I didn't learn a ton in the classroom. I remember thinking that right when I got out of college. I learned a little bit. There were some teachers that I had that were still in the business. I recall one of the teachers that I had for television was actually still a reporter at KSDK-TV (NBC affiliate, Channel 5) in St. Louis. I watched him a little bit growing up. Knowing that he was the professor, I think I really focused a little bit more on him, knowing that he was still doing it, had a really long career, but I just don't think you can learn this in a classroom per se."

Looks Good on Paper

"There are certainly things I think you can pick up on, and some universities do a really good job of examples, maybe showing play-by-play, examples of what people are really doing, in the business," said Young. "I think visually, audio-wise and all that kind of stuff really helps. Because you can write down all your goals and all your dreams and all that kind of stuff and write a report on what you want to do, but you have to do it. I believe my work experience, which the college that I went to helped me get, I think that was the most beneficial part of my four years of college. I remember when I went into college I said, 'Look, I just want to get the most experience possible so when I leave here after four years I'm ready to go.' And I felt like I was, but I think a lot of it was - I just got out there and did it. Whether it was play-by-play or public address announcing or reporting, or just learning how to handle yourself in a professional environment at the age of 18, 19, 20, 21. That can be a little daunting, especially when you're rubbing elbows with people that you really looked up to when you were growing up. I think the work experience, especially in college...you just can't leave with only a diploma. And I tell young broadcasters that all the time.

"If you just think that you're gonna go to college, major in Mass Communications or Television-Radio or whatever your emphasis is and you think the piece of paper is good enough, whether you go to Syracuse, or any other college around the country, it's just not good enough.

"People are gonna say, 'What did you do when you were in college?' Because just going to classes is not gonna get you through. I realized that early but I know there's a lot of younger people I'm sure still but especially when I was in college that didn't quite realize that it's not just a piece of paper.

"This is a profession where you need to get hands-on experience, because once you leave college it'll be as competitive as anything you've ever seen." Young stepped out of college and landed a job doing play-by-play for an independent baseball team in the St. Louis suburbs, the Gateway Grizzlies.

Gateway to Success

"Most of us have funny stories in this business where you probably shouldn't have gotten the job, but you found your way into it," Young explained. "I actually interned with them the summer before my senior year of college. I was the number two broadcaster, which meant I got the middle innings of play-by-play, did the color for the other innings and did everything else that they needed me to do – team notes, releases, pregame interviews, postgame interviews - that kind of stuff. So, I had a previous relationship with the organization. I didn't know much about independent baseball and I didn't know there was a huge difference between independent baseball and affiliated baseball, to be honest.

"It was an organization that would draw about 4,000 fans a night. So it was an unbelievable atmosphere. I loved it. It was the best summer of my life when I was in college.

"Then I leave college. I get the number one job at a summer collegiate league in North Carolina. So I go out to Fayetteville, North Carolina and broadcast a summer out there. I come back to St. Louis because I had a bunch of college stuff lined up. I come back, and the man who was the number one, his name is Joe Pott, had spent ten years with the team. He was leaving, so he notified me and he said, 'This job is gonna be open.' But he didn't say, 'Hey, this is your job' or anything."

Time to Step up to the Plate

"I knew I had to work for it," remembered Young. "I contacted the general manager. He said, 'Hey, come to the ballpark tomorrow and we'll talk.' Fortunately, I had been following the team the entire summer in the little off time I had when I was still doing the games in Fayetteville. I had a pretty good understanding of the team and league still, so I go to the ballpark, I meet the general manager and he's a little quirky. He and I had a great relationship, but he's the kind of guy who will make you do some stuff you never thought you would do. I meet him, he's, 'Okay, I can't really talk. But how about you go up to the team shop, grab a scorecard. You've got the fifth inning of play-by-play tonight.' I said, 'What?' He said, 'You've got the fifth inning of play-by-play.' I said 'Okay.' So I go up to the booth and they have me do the top of the fifth inning. And I hadn't been on the air for them since the year prior. So I did that. I got done and contacted the GM and it went weeks and weeks and weeks. And he said, 'Hey, send me some of your most updated stuff.' I sent him that. And then he responded and said, 'The team coming into town doesn't have a broadcaster. I want you to sit on the visiting radio side and do the whole series and send me all the innings.'

"This went on and on and the season ended. A couple of weeks after the season, they started the interview process."

Why You?

"I went into the interview and he flat out told me, 'Look, we've got guys that are much more experienced, much older, much more seasoned, better than you right now. Why should you get the job?' I went on this rant about, 'I will do anything possible if you just let me broadcast your games. If you just let me do this, I will scrub toilets. I will wash dishes after the game.' He looked at me like I was crazy. I said, 'You think I'm crazy? I did that when I was at Fayetteville,'" said Young.

"After the game was done and I was off the air, I went down and I helped out the kitchen staff because it's a small, little deal and that's what I thought was right to do. Look, I'll do anything, I'm telling you. I'll scrub toilets, I'll sweep out the concourse during rain delays if you want me to.'

"I went through that little spiel and about a week later I got the job and I stayed there for four years. I'm certain if I didn't have that job, I wouldn't be where I am today, because I grew the most I've ever grown on the air. I was calling over 100 games a season, running my own network. All that kind of stuff really, really helped me. It's a long story, but I know that's what got me the job."

Now What Do I Do?

The art of getting the job is important. So is the art of keeping the job! This job was a way of life. "Especially if you're going to do baseball at the lower levels, you're everything," said Young.

"I remember I ran the website, I ran the media relations department, I did all of our social media and when I was with the Grizzlies that's when video was starting to really become a thing, where you did video and ran features that included sponsors. You did player spotlight interviews and it was sponsored by somebody. And then social media has taken over. Twitter was a big thing, Instagram, all that kind of stuff.

"I remember I got pretty good at multitasking. I'm calling a game and saying, 'Here comes the 3 and 2…ball outside…ball four.' And I'm tweeting on the computer about a score update. It's not ideal. I know when you get to the higher levels, the general manager doesn't want you tweeting during a game, or writing your press release during a game, but it's part of it. Honestly, I always thought that if I was doing game notes it was part of my prep.

"I'm trying to find out little nuggets about the team and the players and I wrote the bio packets and the roster bios on each player. So that was part of my prep as well. It certainly helped me call the game. But I loved doing road games because you didn't have all that other stuff kind of becoming a problem. I'd have sales people come up to me during a commercial break in the third inning saying, 'Hey, where did you put this?' Or 'Did you contact this sponsor?' So your mind was everywhere I think during home games. But on the road you could focus on the broadcast and obviously select sweet stuff like that."

Is That All?

"I remember at one point during I think it was my first season the general manager called me into his office after a game and said, 'Hey, your press releases have to be longer for game recaps.' I said, 'What do you mean?' He said, 'Look, it's very basic. I would like a quote or two from the manager if you can after the game.'

"I said, 'Steve, I'm writing those game stories as the game is going on.

The deadline for newspapers is like 10:15 and we're playing a 7:05 game. If the game goes to 10:10, I'm on my postgame show emailing off the game recaps to the local media.' So your hands are kind of tied in that area where you're doing your best but you are literally writing the game recap as the game is going on. You learn how to multitask. Engineering the broadcast is part of it too. I've heard from a lot of people who are decision-makers in the business, and Tom Bowman's one of them, who is the broadcast manager at Learfield IMG College.

"He said he loves to hire minor league broadcasters because of what they do and they also engineer their broadcasts. They're not used to having somebody right there connecting the equipment and going through a troubleshooting problem if something arises. That's what you do. I know that's helped me a lot in my career.

"I've filled in on occasion at different colleges or when I came out here (New Mexico State) and they basically just gave me the equipment and said, 'Here you go.' And hopefully you know how to use it, which I did because it was the same stuff I used in baseball with the Grizzlies. I think that's a huge part of it too. And that's something that you don't learn in college. You do not go in a rack room and have the engineer tell you how to use stuff. I know doing baseball with the Grizzlies really helped me learn how to utilize the equipment, use it properly, go through issues with stuff that comes up. And you're also learning how to format a broadcast. How do you want your pregame show to go? And how do you want your postgame show to go? I've taken that with me throughout the years."

Not the Road to Relaxation

In baseball, there are two different worlds – home games and road games. There tends to be a more relaxed situation on the road because the ball game is the focus and there are few demands on a broadcaster's time compared to home games. At home, there are sometimes family schedules and concerns. The baseball front office can have duties waiting for the broadcaster after a road trip, including some appearances, meetings and other obligations. But in the minor leagues, travel is absolutely brutal.

"It was awful," remembered Young. "We bussed everywhere. We never flew. We went from St. Louis to Travers City, Michigan which I think was 11 hours. We went to Canada. There was a team from London, Ontario in the league and we had to bus to Canada. Guess who the traveling secretary is? The broadcaster.

"I don't know how I got that dubious honor, but I was the traveling secretary. I was the one who went into customs and got us into Canada.

"The word was from our general manager before we left, 'Hey, if you guys have any arrests in the last seven or eight months for anything, let us know because there could be an issue getting you into Canada.' Sure enough, we're crossing the border and I'm inside going through the list and they said, 'Hey, we need so-and-so to come in here.' I said, 'Is there a problem?' They said, 'There could be.' So I had to go on the bus at 4 a.m. and get one of our pitchers because he had a traffic ticket and got it taken care of and we eventually got there.

"The travel was crazy," said Young. "That part of it, too is…you have to learn how to prepare on a bus. You have to learn how to sleep on a bus, because if you don't you're gonna be in big trouble. Because sometimes we arrive in a city at 10 a.m. or 11 a.m. or noon and you have to be at the ballpark at 3 o'clock. Travel was a very underrated part of it. In the first year I thought it was the coolest thing ever because I was seeing all these new ballparks. After a couple of years, it became more of a nuisance than anything."

Rigid Test

Although baseball was not initially Young's favorite sport, he's glad it became his first job. "I think baseball was just what I got into first and I'm glad I did, because I think a lot of people will tell you if you can call a baseball game effectively, you can call pretty much anything else. Especially if you are doing it solo, and I did that pretty much for four years. I was number two at home, but on the road it was just me. You're calling 100 games in 110 days and it's grueling. You see a lot of different situations and you learn how to react to them on the air. You're traveling with the team and you're learning how to conduct yourself.

"When you're younger than some of the players, are you gonna be the guy that goes out and has some beers with the players after a game and takes it too far, and then the next day you can't effectively call a game? Stuff like that that I don't think a lot of people think about, but you're in those types of situations. But baseball – I always loved baseball. I didn't play it after grade school. I didn't play in high school or college, but I thought I knew the game pretty well."

, **Wow!**

"I'll never forget the first time I actually did a game when I was the broadcast intern with the Grizzlies I remember looking at my broadcast partner, who had been the voice there for ten years and was a pretty seasoned broadcaster and I thought to myself, 'There's no way I can do this,' thought Young. "The way he was weaving stories in and out of his play-by-play and he looked so comfortable, and for me that first year especially and really the first three or four years everything happened so fast. The game was way faster for me than it was for anybody else, it felt like. I couldn't learn how to prepare effectively early on. I was preparing hard but I wasn't preparing for the right stuff. I realized over time that being around the batting cage is more essential than digging into *Baseball Reference* and trying to find everything about this guy's stat line the last five years. That's how you get your stories. The players talk to you. They respect you. They see you at the cage every single day. If you just say hi to them, maybe over time that could be beneficial down the road. I learned a lot by doing baseball.

"I knew I could do basketball pretty effectively just because I'd played it and at a pretty high level. If I wasn't doing this, I'd probably be a basketball coach, so I knew that sport pretty well and it came easier to me.

"But baseball was tough early. I'll tell all the young broadcasters, 'If you want to do a sport the first five years or so that'll help you develop in the business, I think it's baseball.' Being on the air for three, three and a half hours and trying to fill that time is very, very tough.

"It looks easy to people from the outside. When I got into it, I thought it was going to be a lot easier that what it was."

Now that he's immersed in his career, Adam has proven himself capable of handling assignments in various sports on both radio and TV. He's in an enviable position. What is on his wish list?

What's Next?

"After hard work and constant studying of tapes and watching people that I respect in the business and just trying to find out how to do this and how to do it effectively, I've been able to grow a lot the five years that I've been here," analyzed Adam. "That's the scary part of the career – when you don't know what your next step is. I don't think you ever know what your next step is gonna be, but I do believe in past years, past experience, past jobs that I've had I kind of knew where the next opportunity could be or where I thought it would be. But right now, it's just like a point in your career when you think, 'Well, I don't know if I'm ready for this particular level…I think I am but I don't know if employers think I am.' I don't want to make a lateral move per se in my career. It's a lot easier to look at that and try to digest that when you do have a job that you love and you're getting these opportunities and you're getting seen and that kind of stuff. That's exciting and also a little scary when you don't know what the next step is gonna be."

Nate Gatter

Big Ten Network and SEC Network Plus

Nate Gatter's first memory of deciding to be a sportscaster was somewhere between the ages of four and seven. A Notre Dame football game was on TV. "There were some guys on the screen holding microphones and talking and I asked my dad if they were getting paid or if they do this for fun as a hobby. And he said, 'No, that's their fulltime job. That's what they do for a living.' And I said, 'OK, then I'm gonna do that.'

Nate's family moved from Milwaukee to Harrisburg, PA to St. Louis. The little kid who decided to do play-by-play became an athlete, playing baseball, football and basketball. He was an above average player on an above average team at Clayton High School, a 4A high school. But he didn't think he was good enough to play at a Division I college. At age 18, he focused on broadcasting. Then he plunged in with both feet!

"The first game I ever did was on my 18th birthday. I graduated high school two days before. In my second semester of high school I remember a good friend of mine showing me a website for this sort of a fledgling summer college baseball league in St. Louis. As I remember it, it was more with the mindset of 'This could be a fun thing to do over the summer when we have nothing to do. We could go do these games. They're not charging anybody to watch them. We could go down one day and see what's what.' Then in the course of clicking around the website, I noted that they had a broadcast tab on the top and I clicked on it and it was just blank in the way that a developing league that has a plan and an idea but hasn't had the time to get around to it yet. A blank page on their website. And I thought, 'OK, that's interesting.'"

Free Is Me

"I found the email for the guy who was the president of the league," recalled Nate. "I sent him an email that said, 'Look. I have no experience. But I've wanted to do this for a really, really long time, I think I'd be good at it, and I will work for free.' He emailed me back the next day and said 'Let's talk.' And that was that! I talked to him briefly and he said, 'Sure. You've got the job.' And I ended up doing over 100 games that summer because I was the only guy for this whole league. I would set up in a field and I would do three or four games in one day.

"As the summer went on, it also became an enormous responsibility for an 18-year-old because we had no staff, no budget, nothing.

"It was the president of the league, VP of the league and their wife and girlfriend respectively and that was just about it.

"On some days I was literally lining the field before the game. I called up umpires. I filled up Gatorade jugs. I confirmed that the Jimmy Johns was gonna come between games of the doubleheader. All sorts of stuff like that. Most games I would keep the official scoring on an iPad while calling the game and doing the walkup music and some games I would turn down my headset mic, grab the PA mic, announce the batter, then turn the headset mic back up and go back to doing the play-by-play. It was terrible! It was not like I was doing all of these things well. I was doing none of them well. But it gave me a feel for, if you're going to make this happen, you'll be doing a bunch of different jobs in the minor leagues that you don't really want to do and didn't necessarily know you were gonna do at the outset. Over the course of three months I ended up with a great taste of what was gonna be waiting for me over the next few years if not the next decade if I was really gonna be serious about this. And I was largely undeterred, thank God. I stuck with it and ended up here slowly but surely."

No Irishman

His college choice was supposed to be Notre Dame, because his mother and brother were passionate Golden Domers. But it was not his destination. "In the interests of full disclosure, I didn't want to go to Mizzou (Missouri). I grew up planning on going to Notre Dame," summarized Gatter. "I was raised to be crazy about Notre Dame." But he was "not one to apply myself a whole lot in the classroom."

He thought about North Carolina. Financial reasons were a factor. He wanted to broadcast in the Cape Cod League. That meant working for no salary and paying for housing for ten weeks in the summer.

He needed a used car to drive from Columbia, Missouri to Jefferson City and Fulton for his college play-by-play jobs at Division II and III schools.

He struck an agreement with his parents to attend Mizzou, where the in-state tuition and scholarships he could attract made college more affordable than Notre Dame.

Although the Missouri School of Journalism is one of the finest in the country, it doesn't give students many opportunities to do play-by-play. Nate understood that he needed to pursue those jobs outside of the college curriculum, and his success really got his career jump started. His experience is an important one for aspiring play-by-play students to understand.

> "My freshman year I sat down with my journalism advisor and she said, 'What do you want to do?' I said, 'I want to do play-by-play.' She said, **'What's that?'** That's not her fault. At the time I thought, 'How do you not know that?' In retrospect, I don't feel that way. It was more about my naivete and not fully understanding how much of a niche play-by-play was and how I was gonna get better at it."
>
> **Nate Gatter**

What's That?

"As much as I appreciate Mizzou, and as many opportunities as Mizzou ended up giving me, the vast majority of play-by-play work that I did in college, the vast majority of the improvement that I did, the vast majority of the important things that happened for me in my professional development from age 18 to 21, happened independently of any curriculum I was going through at Mizzou," said Nate Gatter.

Mizzou's program offers students just a few games of play-by-play experience because of the need for students to share in those experiences equally.

Pile It On

"You're not gonna get much better doing six games a year," advised Gatter. "You need more repetitions than that. So, I ended up going out to D-II and D-III schools and then, as it worked out, getting some digital TV stuff at Mizzou later on. What I wish I had been more aware of going in is: what places could I get more reps as a student?

"I would have looked somewhere like Ball State, where they have this really, really robust student-centered sports network. They're developing broadcasters and lots of people behind the scenes as well. And they're doing an incredible job with their sports link program, which I think is on the cutting edge and in my opinion, twenty years from now we'll talk about Ball State in the same breath as maybe not Syracuse when it comes to play-by-play guys but in the same breath as Fordham and Arizona State and Northwestern. I would have explored any and all Big Ten schools as opposed to the SEC, because they're committed to their digital arm and they're committed to using students on their digital TV broadcasts for soccer, for volleyball, for women's basketball, for hockey, for baseball-softball.

"You can get way more reps on TV as a student at Maryland, at Indiana, at Wisconsin, at Michigan State than you can at Mizzou or any number of traditional broadcasting schools. My awareness of what place has a good broadcasting school was basically Syracuse is number one and then after that you just look at the top journalism schools. And in retrospect, I would have done that totally differently."

> *"My number one takeaway was, and my number one piece of advice is, it's always about creating opportunities for yourself. If you're looking for the school to help you in some way, I think the best journalism school is not a priority. The vast majority of my experience was coming from working for other schools or working for baseball teams in the summer. I was doing between 50 and 80 games per year as an undergrad."* **Nate Gatter**

Help Yourself

One asset to attending major university journalism programs such as Missouri and Syracuse is the reputation of those universities. Some of the top media companies in the U.S. interview on those campuses and choose summer interns. Internships can turn into jobs, as they did for some of us. But those jobs may not include play-by-play. Nate's focus on that direction drove him to gain valuable experience, but his degree was in Political Science rather than journalism because he realized that he could graduate sooner in Poli Sci and get into the job market quicker.

His play-by-play at Lincoln University and Westminster College made him a more attractive job candidate than a journalism school graduate with 12 games of play-by-play on his resume. Nate worked over 100 games his senior year due to his own initiative in hustling for work.

Adam Young and Nate Gatter both had the same job with the Gateway Grizzlies in the summer, learning all the skills that propelled them to their next opportunities. Nate has moved on to SEC Network Plus TV play-by-play of women's basketball, volleyball, soccer and softball as well as baseball. He also works men's and women's volleyball at Ohio State on the Big Ten Network and handles football play-by-play for the Western Kentucky University Hilltoppers.

He was the 2017 Jim Nantz Award Winner from the Sports Talent Association of America as the top collegiate play-by-play broadcaster.

Tough Competition

"My 2018 – first 12 months out of school – was very comparable portfolio-wise to my 2017," Gatter stated. "In 2017 I did well over 100 games while doing my last year of college. I try to remind myself of that. I've been out of college 2 ½ years and in general it's been much more difficult than I expected, especially a college experience in doing games on TV, in getting a pro baseball job before I graduated, in winning the Jim Nantz Award, I felt like, **"I'm God's gift. I'm the next big thing. Clearly everybody loves me. Everybody loves my work. I'm doing great stuff."**

One of Many Jobs

"Minor league GMs are interested in a lot of things that have very little to do with play-by-play," advised Nate Gatter. "Most of them care about it to some degree, but they care way more about whatever the other parts of the position are – usually media relations stuff. Now there's a lot of social media content. Can you produce media content for us? Can you do graphic design? And then there's Old Reliable, which is 'Can you sell?'

"And all of those things are important, and cumulatively they become, in my opinion for most minor league GMs, much more important together than play-by-play is. The quality of your play-by-play tape is probably 20 per cent of what they care about, if that. I always explain it to people as if I have a 9 to 5 when I go into the Grizzlies as Director of Media Relations.

"I do the game notes, I handle press releases, I pitch stories to the media, I handle a lot of videos for us, that kind of stuff. Then at 5 o'clock I get off that job and I start my side gig, which is as a play-by-play broadcaster. That's when I flip into that mode.

"Then I'm able to prepare for the game, do the pregame, call the game, do the postgame, get off. Then I do a little more media relations stuff."

Familiar Refrain

"Then I go home and do it again," said Gatter. "It all happens in the same place for the same employer, but it's almost like I have two different jobs. I think many GMs look at it that way. The 9 to 5, whether it's ticket sales, ad sales, whether it's media relations, content production, graphic design or some combination of all those things – that's where you're making money for the ball club.

"In most cases, certainly at the low levels of the minor leagues, the broadcast is losing money. The broadcast is secondary. The quality of the broadcast is important.

"But what separates an 8 out of 10 play-by-play guy from a 4 out of 10 play-by-play guy in the eyes of most A ball GMs? I don't think very much."

"That's the kind of thing that kicks me in the teeth a little bit, and I'm hopeful that I've been able to turn that into a positive in that I was arrogant," analyzed Gatter. "I hope it was not outwardly arrogant at that time. Certainly, I was inwardly arrogant, which is a lot better than being outwardly arrogant, but I think I had very high expectations, which really at the end of the day only ends up hurting me. Because at the end of the day I'm only giving myself unrealistic expectations about how things are going to go and then as a result being disappointed or upset at myself or whatever, ending up in a bad place because I'm not getting XYZ, I'm not making this amount of progress, I'm not taking these steps. That doesn't really end up serving anybody's best interests.

"Hopefully now I've been able to take some good things out of those experiences and understand that this is a long process and it's not going to be easy, and there are lots of things that come into play aside from broadcasting.

"This is still an industry where you're going to hear 'no' way more than you're going to hear 'yes' and it's not going to get easier necessarily to hear no, but you can prepare yourself to handle it differently. Hopefully I've made some progress in that regard that will serve me.

"I've become much more fluent in TV play-by-play. I've gotten more experience. I've enjoyed it much more than I thought I was going to. I think I've adjusted to be more interested in network television as a result of getting my foot in the door there.

"I think that's where versatility is worth more there than almost anywhere," explained Gatter. "If you're trying to get your foot in the door at the Big Ten Network or an ACC Network or an SEC Network, or even smaller regional outlets, it's not gonna be because you're hired to do the number one football game every Saturday."

Soccer or Field Hockey?

"You're not going to be on the 'A' team," stated Gatter honestly. "They have guys for that. They have guys with experience, notoriety and all that. They're going to be bringing guys in to do kind of a smorgasbord of soccer, field hockey, lacrosse and women's basketball and softball and maybe college baseball. Having that fluency in all the different sports is really important because then it's realistic for them to bring you in on a fulltime basis. I've become a fan of softball and soccer. To be honest with you, I still don't particularly like volleyball but I've learned to enjoy certain parts of it and I've developed at least an adequacy.

"So, if the Big Ten Network says 'We need somebody to do soccer and volleyball in the fall,' I say, 'Great. I'm your guy.' Broadcast as many sports as you can. Learn those sports and it can be an enormous advantage for you way down the line."

Both Nate Gatter and Adam Young agree with me that the top network play-by-play broadcasters in the nation with names like Joe Buck, Jim Nantz, Mike Tirico, Al Michaels and Mike Emrick are the "unreachable stars" for the rest of us – at least 98 per cent of us! It's great to aim high in your professional dreams, but if you truly enjoy your craft there's no reason to be discouraged if you're not in some Hall of Fame when you're 40!

George Rogers, NFL running back
"I want to rush for 1,000 or 1,500 yards, whichever comes first."

CHAPTER 5

STAA

Jon Chelesnik

Founder/Owner/CEO of Sportscasters Talent Agency of America

In 2003, Jon Chelesnik was at a crossroads in his career. He had played basketball at Kansas State and, "When I realized the NBA had no interest in slow guards who can't shoot," moved into sportscasting for 14 years. He worked for ESPN radio and did some college football broadcasting.

Chelesnik started Sportscasters Talent Agency of America "out of necessity to pay my bills. I had lost two sportscasting jobs in the course of six months and quickly realized that all I know is sports broadcasting. I also enjoy helping people, so the genesis of STAA is to take the only expertise I have and share that to help people and also to pay my bills. It's grown beyond my wildest expectations, to be honest." His agency charges a small initiation fee and a monthly membership fee. He works with broadcasters to match them with job openings and improve their craft and their marketability.

"The most valuable part of my STAA membership is my access to Jon Chelesnik," says Alex Gold, sportstalk host of SB Nation Radio Network. Chelesnik is known for his faithfulness to his clients and his timely responses to calls, emails and texts.

How did Chelesnik develop the contacts to start his business?

"They started through my own experience in the industry, and as you know sportscasting is such a small industry. The people that you meet today are likely going to cross your path down the road, so that was the foundation for my own contacts within the industry.

"In the time since starting STAA, my contacts have grown exponentially with employers, with talent and in some cases talent that went on to become employers."

Q. What are the most significant changes since you got into the talent business?

"The Internet. The job market is now digital. It's changed how demos are presented to employers. In my career, it started off on cassette tapes or VHS cassettes if you were a television personality. Then it progressed to CDs. Now you go online. Even the application process is online. Long ago, applicants no longer had to put their home address on their resume. "Employers are not going to mail them because today's job market is digital. All contact is going to take place that way, including requests for phone numbers if necessary."

Q. What do employers say that they want today?

> "Personality. That becomes especially important the higher you climb up the ladder. The most interesting part of that is that the personality extends off air. Regardless if you're a TV sportscaster, reporter, a talk show host or play-by-play broadcaster, your employer wants you to be accessible to your audience beyond the hours that you're on the air. Having a social media presence and sharing your personality on those platforms is of great importance to employers today." Jon Chelesnik

Q. So, it's not enough just to be a solid broadcaster who knows the facts, who broadcasts well, who speaks well. That's simply not enough

anymore?

"No. And the other huge part of it, especially for play-by-play broadcasters who are going to likely have to work their way up through minor league sports, is media relations, graphic design and sometimes sales.

"Those kinds of ancillary skills are the largest part of the job in minor league sports. You have to do those things, which you might not be as enthusiastic as you are about broadcasting, to get the jobs."

Q. Do you think the business is more competitive than when you got into it?

"It is certainly more competitive, because it's easier to find the jobs now. When I was coming out of Kansas State, you had to mail or subscribe to *Baseball America* to find out where openings in minor league baseball might be. Now the openings are so much easier to find that people who might not otherwise have had enough ambition to do the legwork to find them are applying. With the advent of the Internet, there are also infinitely more opportunities than there were before."

Q. At what age should a young person get in touch with your agency to establish a relationship?

"Anybody at any level or any step of their sportscasting journey can contact me for suggestions and advice. If anybody is ambitious enough to ask me for guidance, I'm eager to share it with them. It wouldn't benefit them to become a paying member, at least until they're in college and seeking some internships or wanting additional resources to help and improve their craft. Or if somebody is at a stage in there where STAA wouldn't be a good fit for them, I'll tell them that."

Q. If you're talking to a young person who's 16 years old and wants to do play-by-play in sports, what is your advice?

> "Go to a college that has a campus radio or television station. Getting reps is going to be the absolute most important thing. You don't have to go to one of the high-profile schools as long as you get the reps and you find people to critique your work, provide some

Q. When you hear from guys putting together tapes for critiques and you listen to tons of these tapes and critique these people...is there a common shortcoming or need to develop in some particular area?

"As far as the construction of the demo, yes. Don't send just highlights. My mailman can sound great doing ten-second highlight clips. You need to send longer, extended segments for employers to hear all the different things they're listening for in evaluating you.

"I would suggest that while time and score and description are important for obvious reasons, the number one thing a play-by-play broadcaster can do to make their call great is to turn the broadcast from a narrative into a story.

"Every game has something that one team is trying to accomplish and the other team is trying to keep them from. What's at stake for both teams if they win? What are the consequences if they lose? And then within the game, what are the subplots? Things like scoring runs, or a key player going to the bench in foul trouble. If you can turn the broadcast into a story, you'll make the listeners who don't otherwise have a vested interest in either team care about the broadcast and they'll stay tuned." Jon Chelesnik

Check out staatalent/jobs.com to see current job listings. It's the best website in the industry for young broadcasters to get a free service about what jobs are currently open.

Jon Chelesnik also offers a wealth of resources at this website for no charge. If you want to become a paid member, the services will be more extensive.

The STAA play-by-play pyramid, shows you the breakdown of essential ingredients for a good broadcast and a detailed explanation of each component.

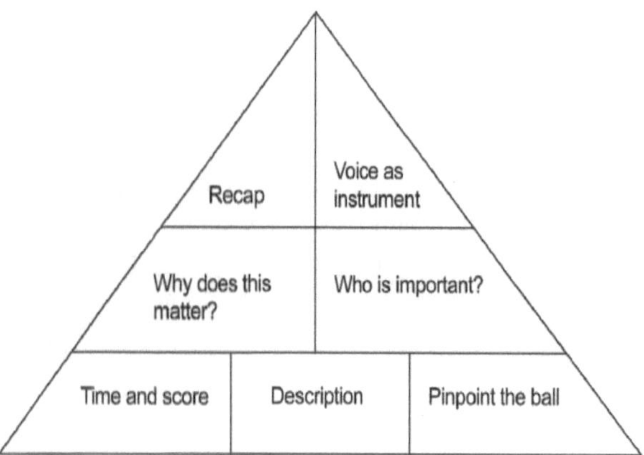

1. **Time and score:** New listeners don't want to wait. <u>At least</u> every :90.
2. **Pinpoint the ball**: Where exactly is the ball? Use both vertical <u>and</u> horizontal reference points.
3. **Description:** Relevant action, movements, behaviors, sights, sounds, smells & emotions of players, coaches, fans and atmosphere.
4. **Why does this matter?** Turns your broadcast into a story. Explain what's at stake in this game, this moment, this possession, this play, this at-bat.
5. **Who is important?** Develops the characters (teams, players & coaches) in your story.
6. **Recap:** Tell new listeners how the game got to this point. Every 8-10 minutes.
7. **Voice as instrument:** Match your pacing to the speed of the action. Use inflections and pauses for emphasis and dramatic effect. Be appropriately energetic & excited but never scream.

CHAPTER 6

Play-by-Play

For those who want to target play-by-play for their careers, the path might be a jagged one strewn with boulders! After completing your education, it's time to assess the job market. That will give an early picture of the industry as it applies to you. First and foremost, most need to earn a paycheck. That requirement may override waiting for your dream job to materialize. In fact, it may NEVER materialize!

What Path Should You Choose?

Take it from a guy who was married and needed income: getting a job somewhere trumps waiting for your fortune to drop from the sky! Some of us put our number one desired destination on the back burner and settle for what's available and achievable. Especially if a spouse has to be considered and if she's willing to sacrifice her own career wishes to take that path. At that point in life, anchoring the Masters golf coverage or doing play-by-play of the Stanley Cup Finals is not in the picture. Low-hanging fruit is fine for this initial stage of proving ourselves. One route is a small market opportunity, such as a play-by-play opening at a 1,000-watt radio station in a small town. Surprisingly, those jobs are incredibly difficult to land. There may be somebody at that station who is a good professional entrenched in that job, and the only way he's leaving is for a better job.

What job offers can you attract? With the clock ticking on those paycheck requirements, it makes sense to seriously consider anything in broadcasting that will provide for your financial needs while building your resume. In our case, it was an offer from a big station in a medium radio/TV market where I had been an intern.

There was nothing available in sports, but a news reporter/cameraman opening was what I took. My wife got a job. My schedule was Wednesday through Sunday nights. Dianne had weekends off and worked the normal 9 to 5 hours. We only saw each other Monday and Tuesday nights. That's common for young married couples with one having a broadcasting job. The idea of being a sportscaster was far from a reality. The closest I could get was writing and preparing the TV sportscast on weekends and handing it to the news anchor to read. He had a full plate and didn't want to do sports, but the news director did not think I was ready to go on camera in the studio because I looked too young! Frustrating! Nonetheless, that was the situation and I had to be content shooting film of car wrecks, shootings and stabbings and an occasional on camera film report from a visit to town by a dignitary or some other such story.

Hindsight

In retrospect, would it have been better to pursue a minor league baseball play-by-play job? Yes. But even those are sometimes a pipe dream for a recent college graduate. There's no guarantee that that approach would have paid off. Luckily, the play-by-play came much later. But at least it came! More on that later.

If the job does become a reality for you, this next section of the book will give you a chance to get some insight into what it's like to be at the microphone doing play-by-play for each different major sport. You'll hear from professionals who have made careers of describing the action in a variety of situations, including radio and television. You'll see how they prepare and perform on the air in a job many people consider one of the best in the world.

For those of you who are doing play-by-play as a hobby and have a "day job," there is a chance to read about somebody in your situation later in the book, such as the stories on page 189 in Chapter 21.

From people who were "locked" in before the age of ten to those who didn't start in broadcasting until late in life, there are many stories and many avenues to these highly-valued jobs. There may be someone who serves as a role model for you. If so, search out information about that possible role model and see if you like what you find. Quickly you can reach out via Facebook, Twitter or Instagram to see if you can get some pointers from that person. Nothing ventured, nothing gained.

CHAPTER 7

Baseball Basics

It helps to have played baseball at some level, but it's not totally necessary. If you haven't played or you haven't played at a high level, it's going to take a good number of conversations and research to understand the responsibilities and the demands on a player. Managers and coaches can be some of the best resources available. Their explanations and stories from their playing days or coaching and managing days can help you understand the game and how to present it.

Entry-level professional baseball

We got some schooling in independent baseball from Adam Young's story. In many ways, being able to handle that Herculean load of work is far tougher than doing baseball at the top level. The experience of that type of job transfers to anything that may follow in your life.

"Good evening from Gorgeous Park in Salem, Oregon. I'm Jim Smith with Rockhounds baseball. Tonight the Rockhounds take on the Saratoga Warbirds. It's a clear night, 73 degrees and sunny….." And you're off and running with another night on the air. Once you get through a pregame show that usually includes a brief interview with your manager, the game starts. After setting the scene, the starting pitchers become your focus. You'll have research on what pitches each pitcher throws and you'll have his statistics written on your scorecard.

As each batter comes to the plate, you reference his statistics and describe the action.

What are your tools of the trade? In this era of computers, you can have the key players on each team tiled on your laptop from a website and click them as they come to bat.

RADIO: All Listeners are Blind

In the 1970s at spring training in Tampa, Florida, a blind man named Wayne Ryan was enjoying the sunshine at Cincinnati Reds games at Al Lopez Field. We struck up a friendship and he asked if I was driving to the next day's game in Clearwater. He rode along with me and we sat together in the stands. From time to time, he asked me to describe what had just happened on the previous play. As we got to know each other better over the years, I realized the responsibility of a broadcaster to deliver that picture of the action to the listeners. But, in reality, we are all unable to see the game on radio and we depend on the broadcaster to give us the description. It's up to the broadcaster to decide what's relevant and interesting about what he's seeing. On a radio broadcast, mentioning whether a batter is a right- or lefthanded hitter is a must. Some broadcasters go into detail on his stance early in the game, some save that for later.

As the game moves along, you're writing on your scorecard to keep a record of the game. We are all different when it comes to keeping score. It's standard to write down the defensive players on a diagram of the diamond. If you don't remember who the centerfielder is, his name is written at that position on the field. The general rule of thumb for a broadcaster is to keep his or her eyes on the field as much as possible. If not, when you look up again, the ball might be caroming off a player! Confusion in a broadcaster's mind is never good. Check out this scorecard from Adam Young:

* Series Opener   * Gm1 of a 4gm Weekend Series   * Looking to stay undefeated @ Home

| Visitor Mastradons | W-L 3-4 | (7-45/season) GB | Home | Road | Streak 2W |
| Home Aggies | W-L 8-1 | (28-17/season) GB | Home | Road | Streak |

	R	H	E	LOB
Purdue Fort Wayne	2	5	2	3
NM State	4	8	0	9

WP Roach (2-0)
LP Boyd (1-3)
SV Allen (1)

The Men in Blue

Trey Plummer 3   Doug Watt 1
John Casado H

Doug Schreiber

Diamond positions: Tish-back 8, Harrington 9, Himenez 4, Peterson 3, Roach 1, Duffy 5, Sigma 7, (name) 6, Bush 2

		1	2	3	4	5	6	7	8	9	10	11	AB 12	R 13	H 14	RBI 15
1) #13 Aaron Chapman Soph. Waterford, WI 2B	.333/0/2	K		5-3			5-3	5-3								
2) #10 Jack Lang JR Fishers, IN .448 OBP SS	.385/0/5	2-9		5-3			F-8	K								
3) #16 Garrett Lake JR / Ryan Mo-let / Pierce CF	.244/0/4	4-3			BB		Inf. 1B	K								
4) #28 Alex Eve-in-sin JR Minnetonka, MN	.333/0/5		4-3	4-4-3 DP			4-3	F-9								
5) #24 Robert Young III Ph-SS Indianapolis CF	.4/in 20 0/5		Inf. 1B	K			K	3u								
6) #5 Garrett Mahler Ph-SS New Haven, IN DH	.300/0/3		1B		4-3		BB									
7) #22 Lucas Koh-ich-vitz Fenwick Oak Park, IL	.4/in 15 0/0		1B RBI		1-3		1B RBI									
8) #8 Trenton Stoner JR Granger, IN 3B	.312/0/4		5-4-3 DP		K		5-3									
9) #2 Dylan Stewart Soph. Milford, Ohio C	.4/in 15 1/5			5-3		K	K									
Runs			1		0		1									
Hits			3		0		2									
Errors			0		0		0									
LOB			1		0		2									

4-3 W5 Pitchers for PFW	IP	R	ER	H	W	K
Chance Roach	7	2	2	5	2	5
Mitchell Allen	2	0	0	0	0	3

Team ERA 4.3

Senior
Temecula, CA

Adam Young agrees that the requirement for a baseball broadcaster to keep score and master the art of talking while writing sets it apart from broadcasting other sports.

"I think so. Over time it's gotten better. I remember whenever I started it was a nightmare. I would look down and I had forgotten to write down what the previous batter did. But, yeah, I think that's probably the toughest. I know a lot of basketball broadcasters who still keep a point total on their spotting boards. They will keep the points, even the rebounds, themselves. I'm a little 'new school' I guess, so I rely on the stat monitor, which I probably shouldn't do, but I just find it's too much for me to call the play-by-play of a basketball game and write down the points scored. For baseball, it's obviously essential. You just can't concentrate on a stat monitor if you're trying to keep score that way. That's not gonna help. I think that fine line between not missing anything on the field and keeping a good scorebook is big. I do more than most but less than some. I know a lot of broadcasters that will count pitches on their scorebook, to where if it's a long at-bat they can say it's a 13-pitch A-B. I would love to have that information. I wish I could. But I think for me and what I can process during the at-bat, it's a little too much. For some people, they somehow pull it off."

Tailor Made

Adam's baseball scorebook: "When I got into the business, this guy named Herb Smith in St. Louis was making scorebooks. He didn't do many, but he made them for the number one guy with the Grizzlies and a few other people around the country. The first scorebook I ever used calling games was his.

"He told me, 'Each year I'll continue to make your scorebooks. Just let me know if you want any changes.' I tweaked it over time.

"It got to the point that he had about 15 of us broadcasters from around the country from college to the big leagues. We were all using the same scorebook and then we'd make changes to it.

"A couple of years ago he decided not to do it anymore. He just sent us our pages.

"I just take it now to FedEx or Kinko's and I just have them bind a scorebook with the pages. My pages for baseball are specifically designed for how I want them. I have to add exactly how I want it. As far as keeping score and what I write and the different doodles during the game, I've changed that over time. I'll highlight strikeouts in orange so it's easier to count, easier to identify. I'll highlight walks in green. I'll highlight where a pitching change was made so I know where the break was from pitcher to pitcher. I'll highlight that in yellow. I use highlighters a lot. I write a lot of information in my scorebook: trends, stuff I just want to hit on during the game, a lot of pitcher information for the starters. That's my template for baseball."

New Dance Partners

Changing analysts can be an issue for some play-by-play broadcasters. "I've been fortunate here," said Adam Young. "On all the games I do on TV

I've had pretty much the same analyst for each sport, but obviously from sport to sport I'm working with different people. I feel for the ones who are doing this at a network level, where they fly into a city and they meet the analyst for the first time and they go on the air and do a game with them for two hours, because it's really hard. You have to develop a rapport, a relationship with them so they can trust you, you trust them.

"A lot of times it's body language so they know when to talk, you know when to talk, that kind of stuff," said Adam Young. "Then you have analysts who don't really have a lot of experience. I had a baseball analyst this year – the baseball analyst who worked the last couple of years couldn't do it any more – so we had one of our former players do it and he had basically no experience on the air, no experience doing a game. So that kind of opened my eyes to the need to pull him in at all costs. Whenever I got a chance to pull him in or set him up, I did.

"And I think that made me better because that's one of the biggest things I still work on to this day: on TV, try to listen to your partner, engage your partner, set up your partner well."

Go for the Assist

"I think that helped me kind of get back to that and reach a higher level of doing that," said Young. "You're making it easier on your partner. On TV, your partner's the star of the show. You're just a traffic cop. You're trying to set them up, listen in your ear to your producer, who's getting directions from the director, that kind of stuff. I think especially on television, trying to make sure your partner is comfortable and knows when they can talk and maybe when it's not a good time to talk….especially on radio. When I do a game on radio, I think that's the biggest thing for a radio analyst. They don't know when to talk sometimes."

After keeping a scorecard for years, I added balls and strikes on each hitter at the time the at-bat ended by putting a dot on the bottom of each square and a dot just above that bottom for a strike. If there were three dots on the bottom and two on the

top, the count was 3-2 when the at-bat ended. If a hitter was batting for the fourth time and he had a 3-2 count every time he batted in the game, that rated a mention. The hits are in red ink, so it is easier to tally the hits and give totals at the end of the inning. Whatever works for you is fine, but you'll probably change your system a little over a period of years because somebody else does it a little better in your opinion.

Adam prepared the following list of go-to baseball phrases to vary his language.

Baseball Play-by-Play Phrases

To Hit: the basics: ground, line, fly; drive, knock, stroke;

to pull, as in when a right-handed batter hits to left field: jerk, yank

to hit to the opposite field: poke, punch, shoot, slice

to hit to the outfield when jammed: muscle

to hit with great force: bash, belt, club, cork, crank, cream, crush, drill, hammer, lace, lash, pound, power, rocket, smack, smash, swat, tattoo, turn on it

to hit with very little force: dribble, nub, roll, squib, tap,

to hit a hopping ground ball: bounce, chop (or Baltimore chop if very high), tomahawk;

to hit a fly ball: elevate, fly, lift, pop, sky;

to softly hit a fly ball into the shallow outfield: bloop, flare, loop.

Pitching: Winds and fires, comes home, downhill, on the way, fires home, sends home the 1-1, brings home the 1-1, deals, winds and deals, turns and fires, delivers ------ plunges, drops, dips, grabs, dots, settles, moves, paints ------ knees, belt, waist, letters, chin high ------ inner-third, inner-half, corner, black, over-but-low, outer half, inner black, outer-third, outside half

To Run the Bases: Bolt, cruise, dart, flash, gallop, gun, hightail, hurry, jog, race, rumble, sail, scamper, scoot, speed, sprint, stampede, stumble, trot, zip, zoom.

To lead off a base: creep, inches off the bag, walking, wander, strayed too far off.

To Field: backhand, fetch, glove, gobble, grab, handle, pick, receive, spear, squeeze, vacuum; to misplay in the field: boot, botch, drop, fumble, kick, mishandle, muff.

When a ball just drops in front of an outfielder, it "gets down" in front of him.
When an infielder or catcher moves left/right, they "shuffle"
Turning a double play (4-6-3, 6-4-3), to "spin it"
A hitter can "launch" the ball or "rollover" on a ball creating a groundball
A fielder can "shuffle" the ball, especially when turning a double play

Dotted Squares

You'll see the little dots on a scorecard for Game 5 of the 2019 World Series. By looking at the card, you can tell that Springer walked on a 3-2 pitch in the first inning, Altuve hit the first pitch as you can tell because there are no dots, and Brantley grounded out on a 2-2 count. When Altuve grounded into a double play, 6-4-3, the line connecting his square with Springer's square tells you that. In the second inning, Gurriel got an infield hit from 1-6, meaning the ball caromed off the pitcher and went to the shortstop. Gurriel's run has a "7" at home plate, indicating that he scored on the left fielder, Alvarez's hit.

2019 World Series Game 5 (Brown)

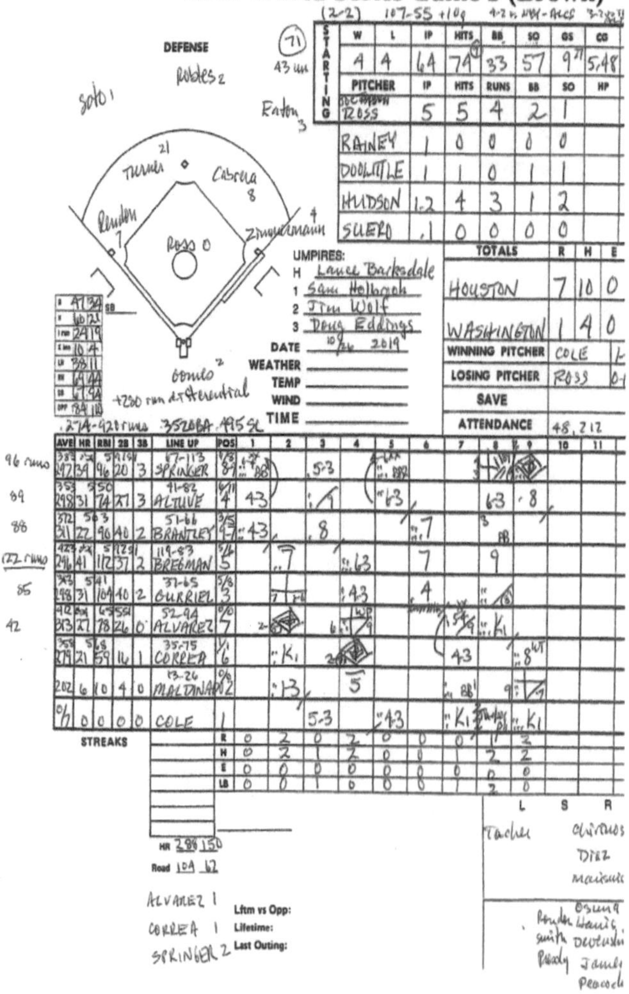

At the major league level, statistics run wild. Some fans love numbers; others don't. Developing some feel for what you should do takes some time. Statistics are best used to support a point. If the game is tied, 4-4 in the eighth inning you may choose to call on a number written in your scorebook: last at-bat wins. It would not be meaningful too often generally. But if your team is 11-3 in games decided in the final at-bat, you keep a stat like this in your back pocket until it becomes relevant. This could be the time for it, especially if you can add something, like perhaps in the last week your team has won three times in their final at-bat.

At that point, your analyst may make that number significant by recalling something like the leadoff man has reached base in all of those innings when they've won in the final at-bat. Or, you may choose to save this statistic until the ninth. That is your call.

Different Courses for Different Horses

You can see a couple of differences in this scorebook from the pages in Adam Young's book. Since this book is used in major league games, it has many statistics that are not used much in independent baseball, let's say. Just in case you need it, you have both team's records at home and on the road, in one-run games, in extra-inning games, against lefthanded and righthanded pitchers. You need to have stolen bases and attempts for both teams in the season at your fingertips. Also steals and caught-stealing by opponents. You may go through an entire game without using some of these statistics. Also on this scoresheet, there are home runs hit by your team and your opponents, including your team's home runs and opponents' home runs at home and on the road. These numbers are not used much, but many of us write them down for every game.

Starting pitchers' statistics are always written in the scorebook. Their lifetime record against the opponent is at the bottom of the page, as well as their career lifetime record. You will be mentioning their last starts and the statistics from them.

You will say that a pitcher has a five-game winning streak, for example, or a five-game losing streak.

You will add that he has beaten his opponent in each of his last three starts against them. All of this will come out at some point in the broadcast, but usually in bits and pieces. If you were to inundate your audience with a string of statistics about this pitcher lasting two minutes straight, there would be snoring noises!

Where's Some White Space?

I started writing a batter's seasonal numbers against his opponent and career numbers against that opponent in the extra inning squares on the scorecard, as the next page displays. What if there are extra innings in this game? Good question. In that case, I write over them! They have served their usefulness by then.

The white space on the right page of the scorebook is for notes. They can be anything you decide is important for that game. One need a play-by-play broadcaster has is to update important hitting streaks. You will see a player's hitting streak circled after his name on this card as a reminder that he has a 13-game streak alive. A team's streak will be circled at the top of the page near its overall record. If it's a five-game winning streak, there will be a +5 circled near the team's win total. A losing streak would be indicated by a circled -5. If a team has won 11 of 13, it will be indicated by +11/13.

Bench players and bullpen pitchers are listed at the bottom right of each page. As they are used in the game, they are crossed off. This keeps you up to date on how many lefthanded pinch hitters are available to the manager, for instance.

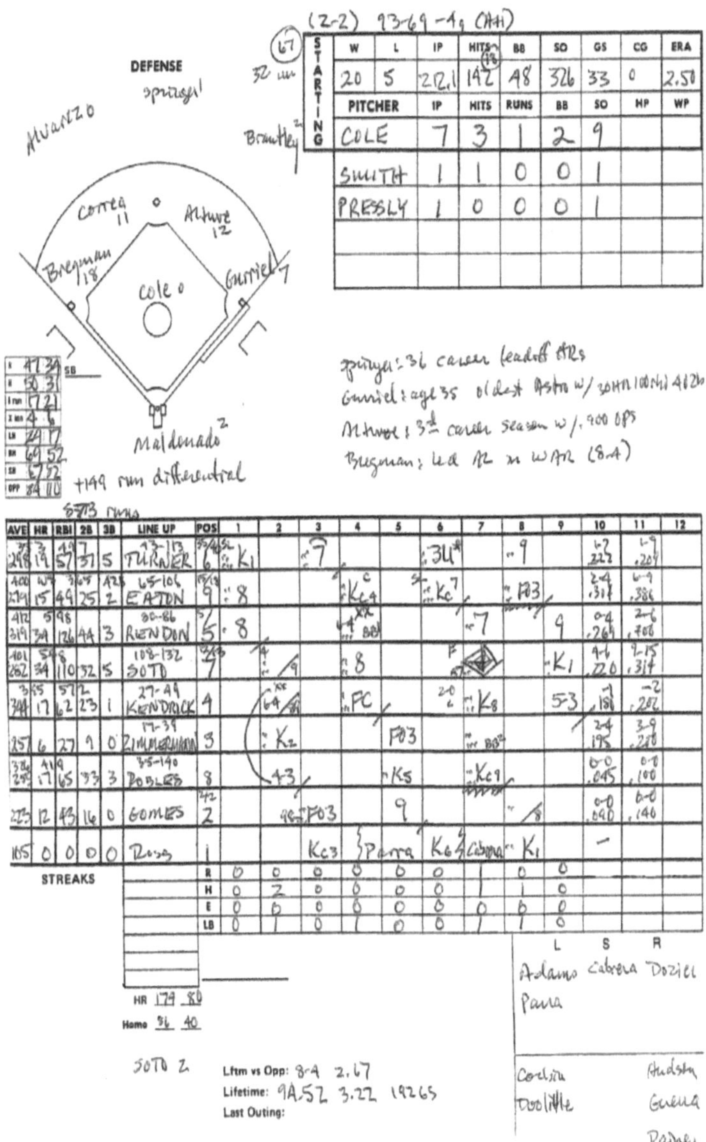

Lanny Frattare of the Pittsburgh Pirates kept index cards on all the players. In the 1990s he explained his system and I copied it. Few broadcasters used it, but it gave me mental relaxation for games to know that I didn't have to memorize everything about the players, because all those little factoids were on the index cards. You'll see what they look like below. When on the air, it's easy to just shuffle through them. Most broadcasters today use tabs on their laptops to have the pages ready on each player in the lineup. That's your call, but if you're not that busy in the winter there's plenty of time to prepare these cards. And we all have our own preferences when it comes to exactly what we want and where we want it!

The Jose Altuve card for 2020 and the back of Justin Verlander's card are next.

ALTUVE, JOSE(30)5/6   .298-31-74 HOU 500ab 27 2b 3 3b
FA 9/06($15,000) 5'6"170   41bb 82k 6sb/11 .353oba .550sl
    6-time All-Star   5 Silver Sluggers
.315-128-538 4985ab 299 2b 28 3b 360bb 623k 254sb/328 (77%) .364oba .463sl 4GS

'11: .276-2-12 HOU 221ab 10 2b1 3b 5bb29k 7sb/10 .361-5-25 CC 144ab 7bb 14k
        .408-5-34 Lanc 213ab 13 2b 7 3b 19bb 26k 19sb/28 .451 .606   200 hits in '11
First ML HR was inside park vs SF leading off – first since Richie Ashburn '48
'12: *.290-7-37 HOU 576ab 34 2b 4 3b 40bb 74k 33sb/44   Club MVP
'13: .283-5-52   626ab 31 2b 2 3b 32bb 85k 35sb/48 .316oba .363sl
'14: *.341-7-59   660ab 47 2b 3 3b 36bb 53k **56sb**/65 .377oba .453sl **225 hits-cr**
'14:most hits by 2bman since '36(Gehringer) Team MVP **.414 vs LHP**
'15: *.313-15-66 638ab **200hits** 33bb 67k **38sb**/51 .353oba **.154-0-2post**
'16:* **.338-24-96** 640ab **216hits** 42 2b 108 runs 60bb 70k 30sb/40 .396oba .531sl
'17:* **.346-24-81**   590ab **204 hits** 39 2b 4 3b 58bb 84k 32sb/38 .410oba .547sl **AL MVP**
'18: *.316-13-61   534ab 149 hit   29 2b 2 3b 55bb 79k 17sb/21 .386   .451
Hits:4 Streak:19 ('17) Hrs:3(ALDS '17) (1 walkoff) RBI:6 SBs:3
Maracay, VZ   Maracay, VZ   5 yrs. minors

Manakin-Sabot, VA   Old Dominion(7-6 3.49 as jr) 1 yr. minors
'05: 0-2 7.15 DET 2GS11-15-5-7 2-0 0.28 Erie 7GS 32-11-7-32 9-2 1.67 Lakeland13GS
'06:17-9 3.63 DET30GS1cg1ShO186-187-60-124**ROY**0-0 **5.06ds**1-0 **6.75alcs**0-2 **5.73ws**
'07:*18-6 3.66   32GS1cg1ShO201-181-67-183 no-hitter vs. Mil
'08:11-17 4.84   33GS 1cg   201-195-87-163
'09:*19-9   3.45   **35GS** 3cg1ShO**240**-219-63-**269**
'10:*18-9   3.37   33GS4cg 224-190-71-219 no-no'11@Tor **1-0 5.00ds 1-1 5.56alcs**'11
'11:*24-5   2.40   34GS4cg2ShO **251**-174-57-**250** CY(unan), MVP 10th **to win both**
'12:*17-8   2.64   33GS **6cg1ShO** 238-192-60-239 **2-0 0.56ds 1-0 1.08alcs 0-1 11.25ws**
'13:*13-12 3.46   **34GS** 218-212-75-217   **1-0 0.00ds 2GS 0-1 1.13alcs 1GS**
'14: 15-12 4.54   32GS 206-223-65-159   **0-0 5.40 1GS**
'15: 5-8   3.38   20GS 1cg 133-113-32-113
'16: 16-9 3.04   34GS2cg 227-171-57-**254**
'17: 15-8 3.36 Det/Hou 33GS0cg 206-170-72-219 27hr **4-1 2.21 postseason**   9sb/10
'18:*16-9 2.52 HOU **34GS** 1cg1ShO214-156-37-**290** **26QS**

For major league baseball, the information flow is an avalanche. You'll see an example of the paperwork you can find in the press box for a major league game. There's much more on the internet, of course, giving the broadcaster a choice of where to go for it and how much time to spend building a file that can be used during the broadcast. For play-by-play, it's really necessary to lock in when a player needs two hits, we'll say, to reach a milestone. The play-by-play broadcaster must be ready when that moment comes. If Justin Verlander needs four strikeouts for 3,000 in his career, the countdown is on when the game starts. If a hitter has a chance to hit for the cycle in a game, there's some drama that goes with the countdown to the final step in that process.

Countdowns

Let's say that Bill Spiers is on fire, as he was in 1997. He's getting on base every time he comes to the plate! The game notes will keep you abreast of the club record. You can do your own research to add to the moment when he breaks the record and reaches base for the 13th consecutive time. The game notes will tell you that he walked nine times, had three singles and was hit by a pitch once. If you research each plate appearance, you might come up with a nugget you can use when he reaches the milestone. Maybe he's walked on 3-2 counts in six of the nine bases on balls. You might be the only one with that information, so it makes sense to use it if you think it's interesting. Then maybe your analyst adds that Bill has been walking more often because he's laying off the curve ball out of the strike zone, and that's been a big improvement in that area of his game.

Here's a look at a Game Notes package for the 2019 playoffs. The information in those pages is about the size of a large lake, but we comb through it and highlight what we like for the broadcast.

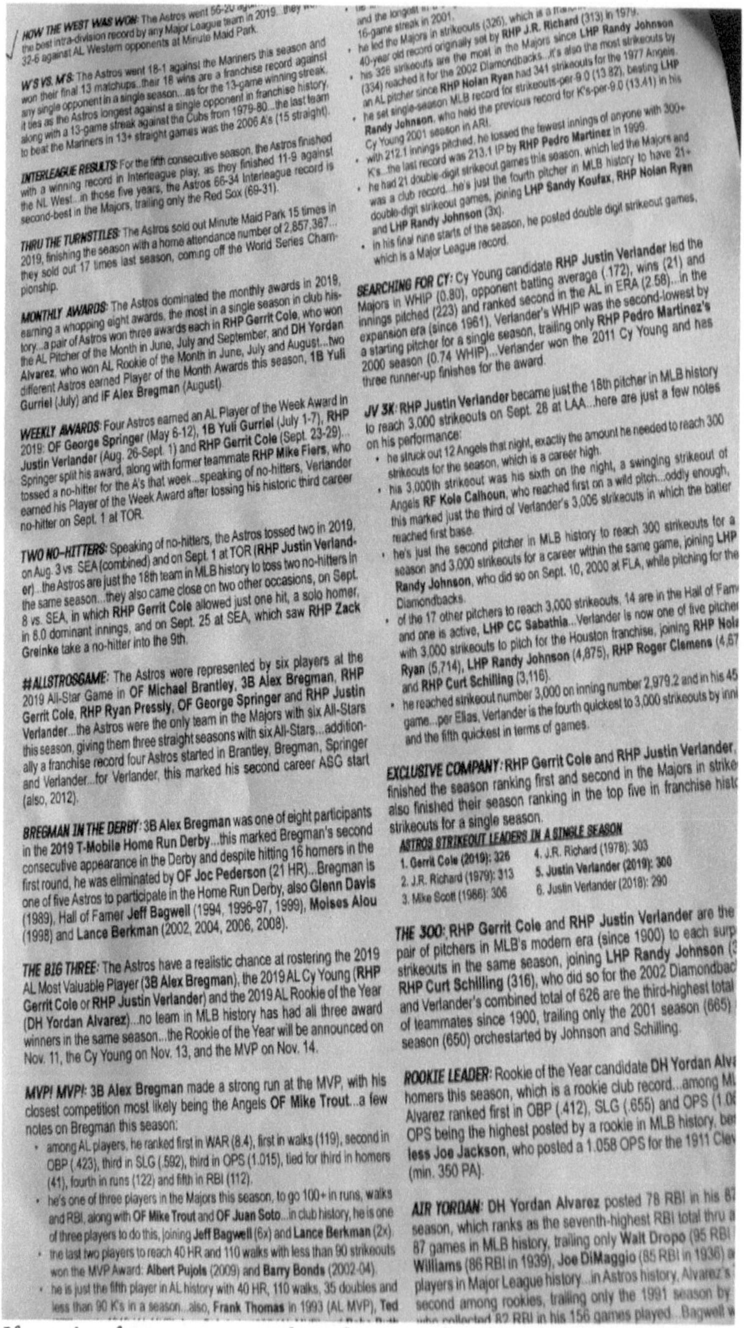

HOW THE WEST WAS WON: The Astros went 56-20 against... Major League team in 2019...they wo... the best intra-division record by any Major League team in 2019...they won... 32-6 against AL Western opponents at Minute Maid Park.

W'S VS. M'S: The Astros went 18-1 against the Mariners this season and won their final 13 matchups...their 18 wins are a franchise record against any single opponent in a single season...as for the 13-game winning streak, it ties as the Astros longest against a single opponent in franchise history, along with a 13-game streak against the Cubs from 1979-80...the last team to beat the Mariners in 13+ straight games was the 2006 A's (15 straight).

INTERLEAGUE RESULTS: For the fifth consecutive season, the Astros finished with a winning record in Interleague play, as they finished 11-9 against the NL West...in those five years, the Astros 66-34 Interleague record is second-best in the Majors, trailing only the Red Sox (69-31).

THRU THE TURNSTILES: The Astros sold out Minute Maid Park 15 times in 2019, finishing the season with a home attendance number of 2,857,367... they sold out 17 times last season, coming off the World Series Championship.

MONTHLY AWARDS: The Astros dominated the monthly awards in 2019, earning a whopping eight awards, the most in a single season in club history...a pair of Astros won three awards each in RHP Gerrit Cole, who won the AL Pitcher of the Month in June, July and September, and DH Yordan Alvarez, who won AL Rookie of the Month in June, July and August...two different Astros earned Player of the Month Awards this season, 1B Yuli Gurriel (July) and IF Alex Bregman (August).

WEEKLY AWARDS: Four Astros earned an AL Player of the Week Award in 2019: OF George Springer (May 6-12), 1B Yuli Gurriel (July 1-7), RHP Justin Verlander (Aug. 26-Sept. 1) and RHP Gerrit Cole (Sept. 23-29)... Springer split his award, along with former teammate RHP Mike Fiers, who tossed a no-hitter for the A's that week...speaking of no-hitters, Verlander earned his Player of the Week Award after tossing his historic third career no-hitter on Sept. 1 at TOR.

TWO NO-HITTERS: Speaking of no-hitters, the Astros tossed two in 2019, on Aug. 3 vs. SEA (combined) and on Sept. 1 at TOR (RHP Justin Verlander)...the Astros are just the 18th team in MLB history to toss two no-hitters in the same season...they also came close on two other occasions, on Sept. 8 vs. SEA, in which RHP Gerrit Cole allowed just one hit, a solo homer, in 8.0 dominant innings, and on Sept. 25 at SEA, which saw RHP Zack Greinke take a no-hitter into the 9th.

#ALLSTROSGAME: The Astros were represented by six players at the 2019 All-Star Game in OF Michael Brantley, 3B Alex Bregman, RHP Gerrit Cole, RHP Ryan Pressly, OF George Springer and RHP Justin Verlander...the Astros were the only team in the Majors with six All-Stars...additionally a franchise record four Astros started in Brantley, Bregman, Springer and Verlander...for Verlander, this marked his second career ASG start (also, 2012).

BREGMAN IN THE DERBY: 3B Alex Bregman was one of eight participants in the 2019 T-Mobile Home Run Derby...this marked Bregman's second consecutive appearance in the Derby and despite hitting 16 homers in the first round, he was eliminated by OF Joc Pederson (21 HR)...Bregman is one of five Astros to participate in the Home Run Derby, also Glenn Davis (1989), Hall of Famer Jeff Bagwell (1994, 1996-97, 1999), Moises Alou (1998) and Lance Berkman (2002, 2004, 2006, 2008).

THE BIG THREE: The Astros have a realistic chance at rostering the 2019 AL Most Valuable Player (3B Alex Bregman), the 2019 AL Cy Young (RHP Gerrit Cole or RHP Justin Verlander) and the 2019 AL Rookie of the Year (DH Yordan Alvarez)...no team in MLB history has had all three award winners in the same season...the Rookie of the Year will be announced on Nov. 11, the Cy Young on Nov. 13, and the MVP on Nov. 14.

MVP! MVP!: 3B Alex Bregman made a strong run at the MVP, with his closest competition most likely being the Angels OF Mike Trout...a few notes on Bregman this season:
- among AL players, he ranked first in WAR (8.4), first in walks (119), second in OBP (.423), third in SLG (.592), third in OPS (1.015), tied for third in homers (41), fourth in runs (122) and fifth in RBI (112).
- he's one of three players in the Majors this season, to go 100+ in runs, walks and RBI, along with OF Mike Trout and OF Juan Soto...in club history, he is one of three players to do this, joining Jeff Bagwell (6x) and Lance Berkman (2x).
- the last two players to reach 40 HR and 110 walks with less than 90 strikeouts won the MVP Award: Albert Pujols (2009) and Barry Bonds (2002-04).
- he is just the fifth player in AL history with 40 HR, 110 walks, 35 doubles and less than 90 K's in a season...also, Frank Thomas in 1993 (AL MVP), Ted ...

and the longest ... 16-game streak in 2001.
- he led the Majors in strikeouts (326), which is a fran...
- 40-year old record originally set by RHP J.R. Richard (313) in 1979.
- he led the Majors ... the most in the Majors since LHP Randy Johnson (334) reached it for the 2002 Diamondbacks...it's also the most strikeouts by an AL pitcher since RHP Nolan Ryan had 341 strikeouts for the 1977 Angels.
- he set single-season MLB record for strikeouts-per-9.0 (13.82), besting LHP Randy Johnson, who held the previous record for K's-per-9.0 (13.41) in his Cy Young 2001 season in ARI.
- with 212.1 innings pitched, he tossed the fewest innings of anyone with 300+ K's...the last record was 213.1 IP by RHP Pedro Martinez in 1999.
- he had 21 double-digit strikeout games this season, which led the Majors and was a club record...he's just the fourth pitcher in MLB history to have 21+ double-digit strikeout games, joining LHP Sandy Koufax, RHP Nolan Ryan and LHP Randy Johnson (3x).
- in his final nine starts of the season, he posted double digit strikeout games, which is a Major League record.

SEARCHING FOR CY: Cy Young candidate RHP Justin Verlander led the Majors in WHIP (0.80), opponent batting average (.172), wins (21) and innings pitched (223) and ranked second in the AL in ERA (2.58)...in the expansion era (since 1961), Verlander's WHIP was the second-lowest by a starting pitcher for a single season, trailing only RHP Pedro Martinez's 2000 season (0.74 WHIP)...Verlander won the 2011 Cy Young and has three runner-up finishes for the award.

JV 3K: RHP Justin Verlander became just the 18th pitcher in MLB history to reach 3,000 strikeouts on Sept. 28 at LAA...here are just a few notes on his performance:
- he struck out 12 Angels that night, exactly the amount he needed to reach 300 strikeouts for the season, which is a career high.
- his 3,000th strikeout was his sixth on the night, a swinging strikeout of Angels RF Kole Calhoun, who reached first on a wild pitch...oddly enough, this marked just the third of Verlander's 3,006 strikeouts in which the batter reached first base.
- he's just the second pitcher in MLB history to reach 300 strikeouts for a season and 3,000 strikeouts for a career within the same game, joining LHP Randy Johnson, who did so on Sept. 10, 2000 at FLA, while pitching for the Diamondbacks.
- of the 17 other pitchers to reach 3,000 strikeouts, 14 are in the Hall of Fame and one is active, LHP CC Sabathia...Verlander is now one of five pitchers with 3,000 strikeouts to pitch for the Houston franchise, joining RHP Nolan Ryan (5,714), LHP Randy Johnson (4,875), RHP Roger Clemens (4,67... and RHP Curt Schilling (3,116).
- he reached strikeout number 3,000 on inning number 2,979.2 and in his 45... game...per Elias, Verlander is the fourth quickest to 3,000 strikeouts by inni... and the fifth quickest in terms of games.

EXCLUSIVE COMPANY: RHP Gerrit Cole and RHP Justin Verlander, ... finished the season ranking first and second in the Majors in strike... also finished their season ranking in the top five in franchise histo... strikeouts for a single season.

<table>
<tr><td colspan="2">ASTROS STRIKEOUT LEADERS IN A SINGLE SEASON</td></tr>
<tr><td>1. Gerrit Cole (2019): 326</td><td>4. J.R. Richard (1978): 303</td></tr>
<tr><td>2. J.R. Richard (1979): 313</td><td>5. Justin Verlander (2019): 300</td></tr>
<tr><td>3. Mike Scott (1986): 306</td><td>6. Justin Verlander (2018): 290</td></tr>
</table>

THE 300: RHP Gerrit Cole and RHP Justin Verlander are the ... pair of pitchers in MLB's modern era (since 1900) to each surp... strikeouts in the same season, joining LHP Randy Johnson (3... RHP Curt Schilling (316), who did so for the 2002 Diamondbac... and Verlander's combined total of 626 are the third-highest total of teammates since 1900, trailing only the 2001 season (665) ... season (650) orchestarted by Johnson and Schilling.

ROOKIE LEADER: Rookie of the Year candidate DH Yordan Alva... homers this season, which is a rookie club record...among ML... Alvarez ranked first in OBP (.412), SLG (.655) and OPS (1.0... OPS being the highest posted by a rookie in MLB history, be... less Joe Jackson, who posted a 1.058 OPS for the 1911 Clev... (min. 350 PA).

AIR YORDAN: DH Yordan Alvarez posted 78 RBI in his 87... season, which ranks as the seventh-highest RBI total thru a... 87 games in MLB history, trailing only Walt Dropo (95 RBI... Williams (86 RBI in 1939), Joe DiMaggio (85 RBI in 1936) a... players in Major League history...in Astros history, Alvarez's ... second among rookies, trailing only the 1991 season by ... who collected 82 RBI in his 156 games played...Bagwell w...

If you're fortunate enough to have a play-by-play job for many years, you'll probably go through some great years and some awful ones. After three straight 100-loss seasons, somebody asked me how we stay so positive on the air. Sometimes I had the attitude that nobody was going to spoil the good mood I was in that day. The negatives are swirling everywhere around a bad team. Fans are bailing out, the media is circling around ready to report people being fired and there might not be much help on the horizon. In 2013 when the Astros lost 111 games, it seemed to us that we spent as much time on the air talking about minor league prospects as on that night's major league game. Our producer would run video of a top prospect who had a big night at Class A and it would be grainy footage from the Internet, but we'd rather discuss that than talk about a high definition shot of a major leaguer hitting .124. Nonetheless, the drive in to work would provide opportunities to see road construction workers and men on the roof of a house on a construction project in 95-degree heat. How could we not feel blessed to have a job talking about a ball game?

CHAPTER 8

MLB RADIO PLAY-BY-PLAY

Robert Ford

Houston Astros

"Next stop, Kingsbridge Road!" The New York City subway conductor opens the doors and the riders pour out. That voice could have been Robert Ford's. **"The first thing I wanted to be when I grew up was a subway conductor on the New York City subway, because they got to announce all of the stops on the train and I knew all the stops on the subway, so it was a chance for me to speak and express my subway knowledge. Speaking was never an issue for me."**

How did Ford go from subway conductor to sportscaster? "It really started in high school. My sophomore year of high school we had to take global studies. The way it went in New York City public schools you did two years of global studies. My teacher in tenth grade was Mrs. Goodman. She was assigning us a paper about every other week. The papers weren't that long – maybe 3-5 pages, but still, as a high school student at a pretty rigorous academic high school, that just seemed like a lot."

Sportswriter

"She got to see a lot of my writing," recalled Ford. "She was the first person to tell me that I was a good writer. She said that I should write for the high school newspaper because, the way she put it, 'Most kids who write for the high school newspaper can't really write, but you can.' I thought to myself, 'I like sports, and they do have a sports section, where they cover the school teams, so maybe I could write about sports for the high school newspaper. I think the first thing I wrote was about the boys' and girls' volleyball teams. That kind of got me interested in journalism.

"As I started looking at colleges, I realized I wanted to do something with journalism, but I felt that broadcast journalism was more interesting than print journalism. It seemed like that was kind of the way to go at that point.

"I graduated high school in 1997, and at that point newspapers were starting to see their numbers shrink and things like that, so I thought broadcasting might be right up my alley. I always did like to talk."

How many African-American major league play-by-play voices are there in 2020 who did not make their names as players? Two. Dave Sims of Seattle is the other. Against steep odds, Robert Ford measured his chances to compete with talented young broadcasters-to-be such as Andrew Catalan and Carter Blackburn, who are both in the CBS stable now. He did it by taking the road less traveled. "I got into Syracuse, broadcast journalism major. It was about the latter part of my sophomore year that play-by-play was what I wanted to do. Before that I thought maybe I'd like to be a sports anchor on television or something like that, or a sports reporter. Syracuse is a great place to get a lot of play-by-play reps.

"WAER is a well-known campus radio station that broadcasts basketball, football and lacrosse. The list of alums who have worked for WAER and gone on to bigger things is pretty lengthy," said Robert Ford.

Late to the Party

"But the thing is, because it's Syracuse and it's so competitive, you basically have to walk in your freshman year, the first day of your freshman year, to WAER and say, 'I want to do play-by-play.' Because there's a whole track, there's a whole progression. You start off doing sports shows and producing. Then by the time you're an upperclassman, maybe you get to do a handful of games. So, I knew by the latter part of my sophomore year WAER wasn't an option for me.

Although Ford was getting important experience calling games, he wasn't calling them on the air. Only the people who listened to his tapes could give him feedback. He found a way to rectify that. "I got a job my senior year – well, I really can't call it a job because that implies that I was getting paid and I was not – calling Fulton High School football for WZZZ Radio. Hopefully I didn't put the listeners to sleep like the call letters! The Fulton High School Red Raiders. Fulton is a little town right outside of Syracuse.

"They wound up making it pretty deep into the playoffs and in New York state they play a lot of the high school football playoff games at the Carrier Dome. I got to do some of those games, getting some experience."

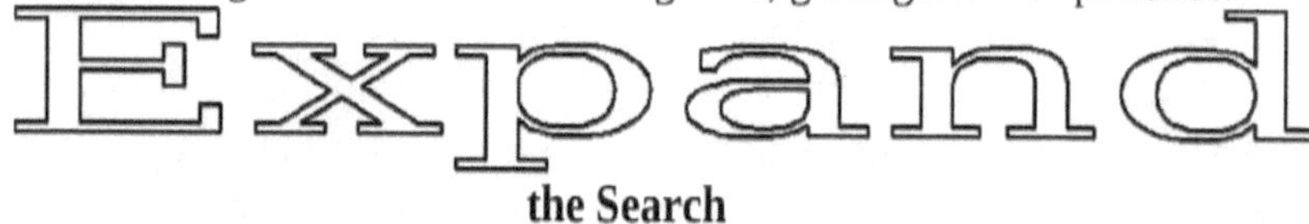

the Search

Ford counsels students to find their own way. "You can't just go to any school, let alone a Syracuse or a Missouri or a Northwestern and just think that opportunities are going to fall into your lap. Or that, 'OK, I'm working for the student station and that's all I need to do.' One of the nice things about being in the Syracuse market is that it's big enough so that there are other opportunities, but it's small enough where those opportunities aren't swallowed up by those people with experience, like being in Boston or Chicago or even Houston. So, you can get on the air on commercial radio as an undergrad. I did that with the station in Fulton, New York but I also did that in my senior year. A good buddy of mine and I did games for the Syracuse Crunch.

"Bob McElligot, who now does play-by-play for the Columbus Blue Jackets, did games the previous year and my buddy Joe Babic and I were the rink-side reporters for the radio broadcasts of the Syracuse Crunch our senior year on the sports station in Syracuse. We would trade off.

"I would do the first and third period and Joe would be the rink- side reporter for the second period. Then the next game we would flipflop that. Joe and I would do the postgame show on radio. There were a handful of times when they had games on TV and Bob moved over to television. For those games, Joe would be the play-by-play guy and I would be the analyst, which was very interesting because the play-by-play guy knew a lot more about hockey than the analyst did!

"Bob could not have been more helpful, could not have been nicer. Bob was an inspiration for me, a mentor to me early in my career and has gone on to do really good things in the National Hockey League. I took it as a learning experience. I remember I bought a copy of *Hockey for Dummies* before the season started so I could learn some of the basics. That's how bare bones it was for me."

Top universities offer some attractive internships from major media companies who interview on their campus. ESPN has long been a connection for Syracuse students, as we learned earlier. Did Robert get a broadcast internship? No, he got a different job.

"I was a tour guide at the American Museum of Natural History in New York City in the summers my first two years. I did get a job the summer before my senior year with a minor league baseball team, the Queens Kings, playing on the campus of St. John's University at Queens, New York. It was the year before they became the Brooklyn Cyclones.

"They didn't broadcast their games. I did get to do on-field emceeing and some PA announcing."

As a fan, Robert appreciated the radio work of Gary Cohen on the Mets games and Mike Breen on the Knicks. He also enjoyed the TV work of Marv Albert on the NBA. "Mike Breen did radio for the Knicks with Walt Frazier when the Knicks had those really good teams in the early to mid '90s. I listened to a lot of Knicks playoff games on the radio with Mike Breen.

"I told him this when I met him a few years ago: I learned how to call basketball on the radio listening to Mike Breen, because he was so descriptive – always knew where the ball was. He was the first person I ever heard do basketball on the radio, and then when I listened to other guys I was like – wow! – how come these other guys aren't as good?

"I was fortunate to listen to somebody who was so unbelievable. He's obviously moved on to television with ESPN and ABC. I always tell people as good as Mike Breen is on television, he was a million times better on radio as a play-by-play guy."

As young broadcasters, we get a chance to try to add our favorite qualities of the established names to our wish list. Such as Marv Albert. "The things I always liked about Marv was his dry sense of humor. And he worked with a lot of different partners, whether it was the Knicks or NBC, and it always seemed like he was best friends with his partner.

"He always seemed to be able to find a way to make his partner feel comfortable and he also seemed to have a good rapport with whomever he worked with. And that's something that I took away from listening to Marv."

Ford did not have any broadcasting offers after graduating from Syracuse, but he landed a job as a sports reporter for the Japanese newspaper *Yomiuri Shimbun* in New York City.

He covered the World Series, Super Bowl and the U.S. Open Tennis Championships.

But he still had his eye on play-by-play, to the extent that he took his tape recorder to Yankee Stadium and Shea Stadium to continue his preparation in the stands. He called a game-winning walk-off single in a Yankee game and also described Mike Piazza's home run at Shea Stadium in the return of baseball to New York City after 9/11.

As so many aspiring baseball broadcasters have done, Robert attended the Winter Baseball Meetings in December of 2001 and shopped his demo tapes to anyone who would listen, seeking to begin his climb to the major leagues up a boulder-strewn mountain. His demo tape included clips of the big games involving the Yankees and Mets from a few months earlier.

Ford missed out on a job with a whopping $200 a month salary, but he landed something better. Thanks to his major league work from the stands, the Yakima Bears signed him for his first play-by-play job in radio. He bought his first car and made the drive from New York to Yakima, Washington for his first trip to the West Coast.

Job-winning Calls

As he drove across the country, Ford was sure that his resume tape got him the job including these calls from the seats amongst the fans: "Karsay sets at the belt. Here's the one strike pitch. This is hit DEEEEP to center field! Andrew Jones is back...FORRR-GET IT! Two-run home run, Mike Piazza! And the Mets take a 3-2 lead!!!" And, "Jeter comes up now with two outs and two men in scoring position."

Moments later, "4-3, Boston leads the Yankees. 1-1 pitch by Arrojo – this one is hit down the right field line, will it stay fair? Fair ball down the right field line! Brosius will score. Justice will score! Two-run single for

Derek Jeter, and the Yankees have taken a 5-4 lead!"

The general manager of the Bears, former sportscaster Bob Romero, critiqued Ford and became a mentor. When Ford moved up to the AA Binghamton Mets, he sent his play-by-play CD to every major league broadcast director for critiques. He got a lot of "failures to respond", but Rob Brooks of the Phillies advised him to be more descriptive, letting the listener know when the pitch is coming and the importance of addressing the pitch.

Deliver the Pitch

"Brooks used the analogy that baseball is a rocking chair sport. The listener is leaning forward in that rocking chair when he hears, 'Here's the 2-1'…Then you say 'Ball outside' and they're leaning back," says Ford.

"If you say, 'Here's the 2-1' and the batter hits a double, they're already leaning forward because you've already kind of set them up that something may be happening right now. That's something that Rob really helped me to understand. It's easier now to find people's email addresses and reach out to them on social media. That's why I have my Astros email address listed in my social media accounts, so that any kid who wants me to listen to something or wants some advice can email me and I'll get back to them."

There are just 30 "radio primary play-by-play voices" of major league baseball teams. Before television became prominent, radio was the premier broadcast medium for enjoying baseball when not attending a game in person.

With the advent of regional television networks and the proliferation of telecasts, TV broadcasters have become more prolific than they were a few decades ago. Nonetheless, the radio voices still have reached the top of their profession. Robert Ford was chosen in a competition with some veteran, well-known contenders for the job. How did he win the job?

"I was in Kansas City at that point, doing pregame and postgame shows for the Royals' flagship station. I would do the postgame call-in show. I was at all the Royals home games. It was well reported that Milo Hamilton had retired and the Astros were not bringing back Brett Dolan and Dave Raymond and there would be a search for a new broadcast team. I put together a demo.

"Every year for a handful of games I would sit in an empty broadcast booth and bring my recorder and do play-by-play into my recorder so I would have clips to send to other teams. That's the other thing that I tell people. You only want current material. You don't want to send something out from two, three, four years ago.

"This was not on the air – just me calling games into a recorder. I put together a demo on CD, sent it to the Astros. That was probably in October."

The Big Opportunity

"In early December, I got a phone call and the Astros wanted me to fly in for an interview. I was at the radio station and I was in the sound booth preparing for a talk show. Of course, during the hour-long talk show all I could think about was that phone call! At first, I couldn't believe this was really happening until I got an email with the airline ticket. I went to Houston December 10.

"I'm generally not someone who gets too nervous, but I was a bundle of nerves that day because I had never interviewed with a major league baseball team before. This was my dream job.

"And you don't want to screw this up. You don't know how many chances you'll get to interview for something like this. All this has made me a bundle of nerves. I interviewed with several groups, maybe 13 different people. Flying back to KC I had no idea how it went. Did I present myself well? It was just a blur."

See Ya Later! Or Not!

"Early January, I get an email from the Astros, basically saying, 'Thank you for interviewing. We're going to go in a different direction now.' I thought, 'I guess I'm out of the running.' And I was disappointed, but I got pretty far. A friend of mine said, 'Hey, you made it farther than most. You made it to an interview and to the last handful of people, so there's something to be said for that.' OK, great. A little disappointed, but at least next time I have an idea of what to expect. On Martin Luther King Day I'm home. I get a phone call that Monday from George Postolos, who says, 'Just wanted to let you know you're still under consideration.'

"I told him I got an email telling me I'm out of the running. He said, 'Really? That was a mistake.' (Owner) Jim Crane called me and asked, 'Why should I hire you?' I said, 'You listened to my demo tape, right?'

"He said, 'Yes, you were broadcasting from a booth at Kaufmann Stadium, right?' I said yes. And I said, 'What you heard on that CD is just the tip of the iceberg. I'm much better than that. If I get a chance to do games every day, I will sound much better than on any of the demos that I sent you guys.' And I believe that, because that's how confident I am in my abilities."

Robert Ford ascended to the Houston Astros radio play-by-play position for the 2013 season after seven years of minor league play-by-play training and four years as host of the pregame and postgame shows on Kansas City Royals broadcasts.

His favorite calls are Alex Bregman's game-winning hit in Game 5 of the 2017 World Series (below), Jose Altuve's walk-off home run to end the 2019 ALCS (below) and no-hitters by Mike Fiers and Justin Verlander.

"First pitch...and Alex lines this to left center field – that's a base hit!

Fisher around third and coming home…Ethier up with the baseball…the throw to the plate…NOT IN TIME! ASTROS WIN! ASTROS WIN! Alex Bregman comes through with a walk-off RBI single and the Astros win 13-12 in 10!!! They lead the World Series three games to two!!!"

"Jose readjusts the batting helmet…settles back in with that two-toned bat, windmills it around. Now ready to hit. Here's the 2-1…That's driven to left center field…Gardner is going back, looking up…SEE YA LATER! SEE YA LATER! SEE YA LATER! Astros headed back to the World Series! Jose Altuve a walk-off two-run homer! And the Astros beat the Yankees, 6-4, win the ALCS four games to two!…….. Altuve mobbed at home plate!"

On Twitter @raford3: "I tell novice broadcasters that you want to work to get better every day. It could mean listening back to your game the next day, like @Joe_Davis did, tweaking your prep, getting critiques from others, etc. Regardless, you should literally be trying to improve every single day."

Robert Ford (L) and Steve Sparks broadcast road game from home booth in 2020

Eric Nadel
Texas Rangers

- **Inducted into National Baseball Hall of Fame in 2014**
- **42nd year as Voice of Texas Rangers in 2020**
- **8-time Texas Sportscaster of Year**
- **Texas Baseball Hall of Fame inductee**

On his way to all the accolades he has achieved, Eric Nadel decided to learn Spanish. Part of his acceptance speech at Cooperstown, New York for the Ford C. Frick Award honoring the best broadcasters in the sport was delivered in Spanish. He routinely did one inning per game in Spanish on the Texas Rangers' Spanish language radio broadcasts. He explains why.

"I did that when the Rangers started Spanish language broadcasting. They didn't travel a second guy. The play-by-play guy actually worked alone, and he asked me if I would come in and take an inning so he could take a break. Luis Mayoral was the guy. I had to learn how to do it. At the time, I had only been learning Spanish for a few years. I said, 'I'll make a list of the words that I need,' just like I made a list of phrases when I was learning how to do it. 'Here they are. How do you say this? How do you say this?' He translated this long list of hundreds of things and I memorized those words. I could kind of do a play-by-play pretty quickly in present tense. Once something complicated happened, I was in trouble – where you all of a sudden had to use subjunctive and past participles, I wasn't accomplished enough in Spanish to do that correctly and I probably sounded terrible.

"But usually Luis would go to the bathroom and then have a smoke and then come back and stay with me for the rest of that inning. Every now and then, something crazy would happen when he was out.

"I remember once in Cleveland there was a huge argument over whether a home run was fair or foul and both managers were out there screaming at the home plate umpire at the same time and all of a sudden now I'm not doing play-by-play in the present tense anymore, and it was a complete and utter grammatical disaster. He was more conscious after that when he heard the crowd go crazy that he came rushing back to the booth to help me out."

Attracted to the Ice

When Nadel grew up in Brooklyn, New York he listened to many New York Yankee and New York Met games on radio, but his favorite sport was hockey and he embarked upon his broadcast career near the ice.

He cut his teeth in broadcasting at Brown University. That's not known as a broadcasting factory. In fact, Brown had no journalism classes when Nadel was there.

"The advice that I got when I was in high school, which was really good advice, is if you're interested in broadcasting you don't necessarily have to go to a school with a broadcast department. You just need to go to a school where you can get on the air. And it doesn't matter whether it's an online station or if anybody's listening, as long as you get mic time. I went to Brown University and we had a really good college station, and we had no classes in broadcasting or journalism. Everything you learned, you learned at the radio station from the students above you in the upper classes. They taught me how to do play-by-play and they taught me how to do a newscast. All of that stuff came from them.

"There's a lot less competition usually at schools like that, as opposed to going to a Syracuse, where there are a hundred guys who want to be play-by-play announcers.

"Go to a place that isn't a broadcast factory, and you're more likely to get more reps I think as an announcer.

"But if you're absolutely certain that you want to be in   broadcasting and you're not sure that you want to be on the air – like, maybe you want to be in production or something behind the scenes like directing, then you're definitely better off going to a school with a broadcast department, where you can learn all those other skills. In my case, the only thing I was interested in was being a play-by-play announcer."

Turn a Phrase

"The other thing I tell people about that is to be very aware of the phraseology that announcers use in whatever sport it is.

"Because that's basically what play-by-play is, it's just having the phrases on the tip of your tongue and plugging them in. I tell people that's what I was told when I was learning at Brown, to make lists of phrases that describe things. How many ways can you describe a ground ball to short? 'Here's a ground ball to short.' 'Here's a slow roller to short.' 'Here's a high hopper to short,' etc, etc. The more ways you have of describing something, the better your play-by-play is going to be. I would practice doing that in front of the TV or at hockey scrimmages. Guys weren't even wearing jerseys. They were wearing sweatshirts. But I would still be saying, 'Yellow, flips on the right wing for green. Green rifles it back to yellow.' Stuff like that. You can do it and get a lot of practice doing it without actually being on the air. Or at least you can get the vocabulary down pat. But actually going to school and choosing a college – that's a difficult one as to whether or not to go to a place with a big broadcast department."

Now that it's time for Nadel to pass along advice to Generation Z about college,
here it is:

> "Even when I tell people to make sure you take a lot of English - because writing is usually an important part of these jobs, too. A lot of these jobs - minor league jobs or college jobs - you're also a PR guy or a sports information assistant, and you've got to write program stories and press releases and things like that, so it's really important the more command you have of the English language, the easier everything's

Nadel left the East Coast for his first experience in professional sports. "I was from New York City and I went to Muskegon, Michigan to do hockey. I didn't realize until I went out there that the entire state of Michigan is crazy about the Tigers. I got out there and it was July when I moved there, and our little two-bit station was on the Tigers radio network, so I got to hear Ernie Harwell every night."

Converted to Baseball

"I became more interested in baseball than I had been in the previous years in college when I had kind of lost interest in it. That's when I got back into it. I remained interested in it when I went to Dallas to do minor league hockey with the Dallas Black Hawks. I went to a lot of baseball games. With the hockey offseason being the baseball season, it was really easy to be a baseball fan without having to take away from any of the work that I was doing with hockey."

Nadel met some Texas Rangers executives at charity affairs, including general manager Dan O'Brien. O'Brien had heard Nadel speak and recommended him for an opening on the Rangers' broadcasts, even though he had never done baseball. "Since I had never broadcast baseball, they let me do a four-game audition into a cassette recorder and they hired me based on the tape."

Nadel was a raw broadcaster, but that was not all of his job.

The other part was selling commercials on radio and television. He thinks the sales component of his job was perhaps even more critical to his longevity with the team   than his broadcasting.

"I was making the transition from a hockey announcer to a baseball announcer, which is probably the biggest transition you can make within the world of play-by-play. You're basically going from the fastest sport with the least time to fill to the slowest sport with the most time to fill. I had never broadcast baseball, and I was a lifelong baseball fan and I had listened to thousands of games as a kid growing up – Mets games and Yankees games – and after listening to Ernie Harwell, I knew what a baseball broadcast was supposed to sound like. But until I actually had to do it, I had no conception at all with how you develop the proper rhythm, pacing, and conversational style that a baseball broadcast requires. *I was clueless and I sucked!* I was really lucky that the people I was working for were patient enough to let me learn on the job. At that time, I don't imagine the Rangers had huge audiences anyway."

Dinosaur Tracks

"So that sort of thing where they hire a kid to do baseball who had never done baseball, which probably couldn't happen now, could happen then. I was allowed to learn on the job and I honestly believe one of the reasons I could learn on the job was that I was selling air time and I was doing pretty well and bringing in money. And if they fired me, all of a sudden they lose a few accounts.

"It seemed like every year I would bring in a few new accounts. That's how I earned the right to keep doing it for a few years," said Nadel.

"Jon Miller was my first partner in '79, and he was really helpful to me in starting to get a feel for the conversational style and using your personality, which you really didn't do very much in hockey.

"But it really wasn't until 1982, until Mark Holtz came and became the primary play-by-play guy and my partner on radio that we both worked every game on radio, that I was able to work every day with somebody who was for me the ideal baseball announcer – the perfect combination of a relaxed, conversational, very warm, likeable style, with the ability in the dramatic moments to be truly dramatic and capture the feel of what was going on at the ballpark. I was on one-year contracts for probably the first 20 years. Each year I thought, 'Well, they might change general managers, they might change owners, they might change radio stations, I'm not that good at this yet. I could be the one to go.'"

Because of his own experience, Nadel is convinced that versatility and value to an organization should be considered by young sportscasters.

> "Learn how to sell, because in these minor league jobs that's how you make your money - not the couple of hundred dollars a week they actually give you to do the games. If you're going to make any money in those jobs, and you're going to get better jobs, you do it by making THEM money!" Eric Nadel

"I had no background in sales. I had a liberal arts education. I didn't even take a business course. I wish I had. I tell kids to take business classes. Take sales classes. Learn how to sell, because you're going to be selling yourself for one thing, in trying to get jobs.

Even though Nadel has worked on television, he is grateful that radio is his medium. "Television is no fun for me. You don't get to describe things, and that's the part of the job I love the most. I also love my freedom on radio, which I never had on TV because of the need to talk about what the viewers are seeing. I refuse to wear a sport jacket at a baseball game and that's an issue too. And I would hate to miss broadcasting the post-season when the team I am working for makes it. On TV, when the regular season ends, you are done for the year as the national guys take over."

Eric Nadel has been known to wear shorts at the ballpark. With his stature in the game, that's fine with the Texas Rangers.

Broadcasters of Rangers' opponents appreciate the friendship and helpfulness Eric has provided. He emails pages of detailed notes about the Rangers to his cohorts. The notes make his fellow broadcasters much more knowledgeable about the Rangers. They contain anecdotes and analytical information that is not available elsewhere.

The Cincinnati Reds were broadcasting a game on radio in the 1970s and popular former Reds pitcher Joe Nuxhall was their analyst. He did a pregame interview on his tape recorder in the clubhouse. One of the players decided to prank him and dropped a bat on his foot just as the interview was beginning. It went something like this, "Hi everybody, this is the Old Lefthander, Joe Nuxhall, with Junior Kennedy on the pregame show. Junior, how are you........OUCH!!!!....you XYZ&%$!!!!!.....you xx#$*&!!!!. Interview cut 2 in three, two, one….. Hi everybody, this is the Old Lefthander, Joe Nuxhall, with Junior Kennedy"………. Joe had committed one of the unpardonable sins of broadcasting. He had left what we call a "false take" on his tape recorder, followed it on the tape with the "real" interview, and failed to notify the engineer that when he cued up the tape he needed to cue it past the mistake with all the cussing.

As a result of the profanity that got on the air, he apologized before the next night's game in order to keep his job. That uncomfortable moment could have been avoided.

Chapter 9

Interviewing

If you're the play-by-play voice of a team or a sportscaster or talk show host, interviewing will be important. The best interviewers are the ones who are prepared. Sometimes your guest will save you if you aren't knowledgeable enough to ask the right questions, but that's never a good plan. The top interviewers in the business often know what answers they'll get before asking the question, because they researched their subject.

You may be doing a daily or weekly coaches' show or manager's show. Those are potentially difficult interviews if the team is not playing well, because leaders of teams have many worries and they often see the pregame interview as an obligation they want to dispose of quickly. Being friends with the manager or coach certainly helps!

A safe approach is to ask short, straightforward questions. Let the guest have plenty of time to answer and feel free to follow up if his answer raises another question. Many of us are nervous when we are inexperienced and we don't listen to the answer. We feel a need to move on to our next prepared question because we're afraid we'll ask the wrong question.

Here is a partial transcript of a radio interview on the Colorado Rockies pregame show. Rockies play-by-play broadcaster Wayne Hagin interviewed Hall of Fame broadcaster Vin Scully. Scully is considered by many to be the best broadcaster in baseball history. You may be able to see why from his comments. Also, notice the questions in the interview. Hagin's questions are in bold type.

My guest today is the man I admire most in this business and in this game of major league baseball – Vin Scully, 51 years the Hall of Fame voice of the Dodgers. 51 years! My goodness, Vinnie, You have to love this game to do this for 51 long seasons.

"Well, I think you're right. And thank you for the kind words. I still put out the garbage at home.

As far as the game is concerned, I think part of the love affair really is the crowd. When I was very little I fell in love with the noise of the crowd when I crawled under my parents' radio to listen to football games. That was the only thing on the air. I would get so excited listening to the crowd, and to this day if anything happens – if the Rockies do something wonderful and the ballpark just goes bananas, I just exult in emotion. I really still do. As long as I have that feeling, I think it's a great privilege to be here and be allowed to do the games, and I guess I'll continue, but it's the old story – if you want to make God smile, tell him your plans."

You're talking about emotions. You nearly wept in 1955.

"Well, '55 was rather remarkable, having grown up in New York and having understood really the depth of the frustration of the Dodgers. And then to join this group of men – men I was in total awe of – Gil Hodges, Jackie Robinson, Pee Wee Reese, Duke Snider, Carl Furillo and on and on. Roy Campanella. So just to travel with them was really scary the first couple of years. And all I wanted to do was do my little bit, try not to make a mistake and shut up. Finally, by 1955, which was my sixth year, as things happened, I was doing television. I was on the last half of that fateful game, so that I was privileged to say, 'Ladies and gentlemen, the Brooklyn Dodgers are the champions of the world.'

"People asked me later, all that winter, 'How could you have been so calm?' The answer was, I wasn't calm at all.

"Had I had to say one more word, I would have broken down. Because I really felt for them, and the feelings that they had of relief and joy that they finally did it."

You will never remember this, but I was a college student at San Diego State. I don't know how many times you had been approached prior to this day. I was 19. I walked up to you and I said what so many kids had said before, 'Mr. Scully, so nice to meet you. Can I ask you some advice about broadcasting baseball?'

I'll never forget you said, 'Always come in the door and realize that that's the only thing you bring in that's different, is yourself. I'm 19, don't have a clue about what you said. I always remembered it. Then, about the fifth year of doing major league baseball it dawned on me. I walked through that door and I said, 'You know what he wanted me to do is to be me.' And it takes time. I've talked to Ron Fairly, a man you know very well. It took him a number of years to figure out how be Ron Fairly on the microphone. I've just got to tell you, that was great wisdom. It just took me till I was about 25 or 26 to figure it all out.

"Well, anybody who knows me knows that it is wisdom that I passed on having received it from somebody else. Red Barber was the one who said it to me, and when Red said that to me (You bring something into the booth that nobody else can bring in), I had no idea what he was talking about. And then he said, 'Yourself.' It says it in the Bible: Be thyself, Learn thyself. And it's hard. Especially because when you begin, you don't have the confidence of being yourself, and it takes a few years to know what yourself means. Then finally it falls into place. You're relaxed. And the true Wayne, the true Vin, the true Ron finally comes to the surface."

Great moments for you. I'd have to imagine that you were caught by surprise when Kirk Gibson hit that home run. You're doing the game on NBC, national television. You had talked about him being down in the trainer's room. He had heard it. He got inspired by your words. Were

you surprised that night?

"Oh, sure. I remember asking the director when we came out of commercial to go into the dugout (with the camera) and follow me, and I was looking as if anybody in the ballpark would look to see him and then he wasn't there. And then when he came up and he was obviously limping, he was using the bat somewhat as a cane. My only thought was he had such a great year, I just don't want him to strike out. If you remember, he hit a bunch of little dribblers foul that would have been outs if they could have been fielded. So then, when he hit the home run I'm like everybody else. I was totally and completely in shock....The line that came out of me, under the circumstances, I had no idea where it came from. I said, 'In the year of the improbable, the impossible has happened.' But where that came from – it must have been divine intervention, from the crowd, something."

You know what's fun? As I talk to people who are my friends in Los Angeles, they say Vin Scully in the year 2000 sounds every bit as he ever did in 1959, '60, '61, all the way up. Preparation. That's everything to you, isn't it?

"Oh, of course. God has been good. I've kept my health. And if you're healthy you can do a lot of things."(Interview continues for several more questions)

How would you like to be remembered by baseball audiences in Brooklyn and Los Angeles?

"I think first of all that I was a good man. I think that's most important. A family man. And that I was accurate and fair. Probably one of the greatest compliments I ever received – there was a big magazine article in Los Angeles written about me. The title was "The Most Trusted Man in Los Angeles." That's pretty heavy. So, when that came out, I went around telling people, no, it was a misprint. It should be the most trustING man in Los Angeles, and I have contractors and electricians who can vouch for that."

That was a long-form radio pregame show interview. Generally the interviews you do may run in the 2-3 minute length. For the short interviews, the short questions are necessary. In a basic approach, you might ask a coach, "Your team is 12-2 to start the season. Do you think you can continue at this pace?"

If you get a short answer, you should listen to it and then decide whether to follow up with something to go deeper into the area of the answer or move to a different question. You should have 5-7 questions generally in your mind in case all the answers are short. If you're nervous, it's fine to write them on a note card.

Most listeners would say that the interviews they enjoy the most sound like conversations. That can be your goal as you develop your interviewing skills. If you interview the same person often, it makes sense to explore different areas if that is acceptable. When Sparky Anderson managed Cincinnati, he wanted to be asked tough questions about his game strategy, because he wanted to explain his thinking to the fans. That is rare!

Chapter 10

On Camera

Todd Kalas
TV Play-by-Play

The little guy in the Houston Astros uniform sits in the lap of his father, who became a Hall of Fame baseball broadcaster and the famous voice of NFL Films. Why wouldn't a kid want to follow in the footsteps of a father like Harry Kalas? Harry joined the Astros in 1965, moving from Hawaii to become a major league broadcaster for the first time in his career. His son Todd was born December 31, 1965. In some businesses, a son is born and immediately is in line to take over for his father and inherit the family business.

That's not the way it works in sports. Joining father-son major league baseball broadcasters Harry, Skip and Chip Caray (three generations), Jack and Joe Buck and Thom and Marty Brennaman, Todd eventually made it into the group of contemporary sons whose fathers all reached the Hall of Fame. But when Todd found his way back to Houston as the TV voice of the Astros, it was only after a long and winding road created by his own achievements and skills.

As a youngster, Todd was always keeping his own scorecard at baseball games and compiling his own statistics. They were statistics only of the games he scored, enabling him to develop the mathematical mind that led him to higher achievement scores on SAT and ACT tests than on verbal skills. When Todd chose the University of Maryland, math had more prominence in his plans than broadcasting. His thinking changed, as did his major in college.

Todd Kalas with his father Harry

Todd transferred to Syracuse University as a sophomore and decided to pursue dual degrees in marketing and sports journalism. He wanted to have a backup plan in case broadcasting didn't develop. He also planned to compete with other sportscasters to see if he fared well enough to continue down that road.

The competition was stiff: Sean McDonough (network), Dan Hoard (University of Cincinnati), Jim Jackson (Philadelphia Flyers and Phillies),

Mike Tirico (ESPN/ABC), Charlie Palillo (Houston radio sportstalk) and others like Dave Ryan and Dave O'Brien, among others. That prepared Kalas for the competition in a broadcasting career after college.

"Everything at Syracuse was based on meritocracy."

Webster: Definition of

Meritocracy

: 1. A system in which the talented are chosen and moved ahead on the basis of their achievement.

"We started out writing sportscasts for the guys that were already cleared to go on the air. It's a tiered process from there. You write for a while, showing up at 4:30 or 5 in the morning to write for the morning sportscasts. Usually you don't get an afternoon shift until you've been writing for more than a semester. At that point, you can practice and tape your own sportscast on a recorder to see if you can get cleared to do sportscasts, and that's the first step in the process. After that, all the sports are individual: basketball, football, lacrosse. They have only a club baseball team, nothing for broadcast. You have to sit in the stands and gather your notes and do the best you can and get cleared for those individual sports."

Kalas fared very well in the midst of that stable of talent. He did football and basketball play-by-play at Syracuse. "I was lucky enough in my last year to be able to call both a Syracuse-Auburn Sugar Bowl in New Orleans and a regional basketball game when they wound up going to the Final Four. Quite a dream year in 1987 – my last full year there.

"If you would have asked me when I left Syracuse what sport I enjoyed calling the most, I would have said football. But baseball always had a special place in my heart."

Kalas got into baseball after college. His father wanted him to be his own person and didn't push him into it, but Todd did AA Reading Phillies games after college on cable TV and recalls describing some Ken Griffey, Jr. at-bats for the Vermont Mariners. He later worked his way into football and basketball play-by-play and color for the University of Delaware. How much did the Syracuse pedigree have to do with his early success? "A lot of the most talented kids in the country just automatically flocked to Syracuse. I think they're getting the best talent based on the reputation. I'm not sure that definitively Syracuse and their curriculum would put you in a better position than any other school.

"But for many years Syracuse, going back to Marty Glickman, Marv Albert, Bob Costas – those guys have always been the forefathers of what everybody knows to be the cradle of sports broadcasters."

Loving warm weather cities, Todd landed a position as sports director of Vision Cable in Clearwater, Florida. He flourished there with a job that allowed him to branch out as a producer, writer and play-by-play broadcaster of many different sports.

He was well versed in live sports, including talk shows. He focused on baseball and went to the winter meetings, where the Louisville Cardinals hired him to replace Joe Buck. After one year there, he joined the New York Mets in 1992 as a pregame and postgame radio host. After two years, he was reunited with his father in Philadelphia, handling some TV duties with Prism Cable.

But Prism disappeared from the Phillies' association and jobs went with it, leaving Kalas on the move again. Florida was calling again, and Todd moved to St. Petersburg without a job. He focused on a job with the expansion Tampa Bay Rays and was selected to be a part of the inaugural season. He stayed for 19 seasons until the Astros hired him. With the Rays, Todd was the pregame and postgame host and field reporter with some games as play-by-play voice.

When Todd joined the Astros, he discussed with AT&T SportsNet Southwest how much he enjoyed the way Julia Morales was a big part of the telecast. The fans voted the Astros' telecast the fifth best in the majors. Analyst Geoff Blum will be featured in another chapter.

Team of its Own

How has the transition to Houston gone for Todd Kalas? "Every broadcast is different, so there's a rhythm and a style to each broadcast. I kind of let the natural flow of what Julia and Geoff Blum did prior and watching telecasts of previous years. Winning baseball makes you sound so much better as a telecaster, and to win 101 games in my first year and a walk-off home run in extra innings by George Springer in the first series – to have all the star power – 101, 103, 107 wins the first three years in an organization.

"I appreciate all the accolades the fans gave us in *The Athletic*, but I've been very blessed to have this team play as well as they have during my first three years in Houston."

"Any repetition you can get, the more experience you
can get - I tell people all the time, Syracuse is a great
school. If you take every class possible and you graduate
with a 4.0 grade point average and you don't participate
in anything outside the curriculum, you're still not really
getting the most out of that college. You need to work at
the campus radio station or the campus TV station. You
need to intern at either the local cable TV station or one
of the local affiliates. You need to do more than what's
offered at that school, because the more you can
diversify yourself, the better off you are."

Kalas's first memorable call came in his third game with the Astros April 5, 2017. The Astros trailed the Seattle Mariners, 3-2 in the 13th inning with two outs and George Springer at the plate: "High fly ball to left field......all the way back...and GONE! WALK IT OFF GEORGE SPRINGER! Astros down to their final strike twice in the bottom of the 13th! They're 3-0!

"Baseball broadcasting was always in my blood. I never really wanted to be Harry Kalas, Jr. and, you know, be with the Phillies for 20 or 30 years. It would have been great if it would have worked out that way, but I was more hoping to establish myself in another market and just be Todd Kalas, let Dad have his legacy and not tarnish that. If you had asked me in college what I would have foreseen as my goal 20 years down the road, I probably at that point might have mentioned doing some college basketball or pro football work."

Julia Morales
Sideline Reporter

Victor Morales was the television personality in the family in 1996 when he was the Democratic candidate for U.S. Senate in Texas. Victor, a Vietnam veteran who was a teacher, was dared by his students at Poteet High School to run for a Senate seat. He defeated three career politicians in the primary with no staff and $15,000 in campaign funds. His young daughter Julia was captivated.

"The first time that I kind of fell in love with the idea of being a news reporter at the age of 10 was all because of my dad and his dream that he had," says Julia. "With that, he was an ordinary man and he was doing the unthinkable. People loved that story, and it ended up gaining a lot of media attention. He ended up winning the primary and people wanted to know who this guy is from a small town, taking on the incumbent. He was a schoolteacher, and that was part of the story. He was driving around in a little white pickup truck, and he was trying to get people to register to vote, and that was really his campaign. The media just loved it, and it became a national story. With that, there were reporters at my house. They were sitting at my kitchen table – magazines, they wanted photo shoots. A ten-year-old girl growing up in Crandall, Texas where there were no stoplights - all of a sudden, my world was opened up to the world of journalism and my eyes were open to this really cool career that I hadn't really thought much about. I loved the idea of it, and I loved the idea of the live interviews because I watched the reporters be counted down by their photographers and the red light would go on. I have vivid memories of that as a kid. I wanted to do it any way possible. I started to pay a little more attention to the people on the news at night - the local news."

Her parents both played sports in college. Watching games on television was part of the family entertainment. Julia enjoyed sports, but she was focused on news then. That's how it started for her. She attended Kilgore Junior College, where she was a Rangerette, and then moved to the University of Texas.

"Broadcast journalism was something that I studied at UT-Austin, and that's where I started taking things extremely seriously by taking the internships, and that's where I met a female weekend sports reporter," said Morales.

"My whole outlook on the career changed that day. I asked her a lot of questions, and it blew my mind that day. I thought, 'Wait a minute, I don't have to cover car accidents and homicides and city council meetings. I can cover football games and NBA Finals and all of these things and still have the journalism side of it and still ask questions and tell that story on TV.'"

Sixth Street is That Way?

Julia was headed in a different direction than many of the students in Austin. "When you're 21 years old and you're living in Austin, Texas, everyone that age is likely headed toward Sixth Street (bars downtown). But that was not the case for me, because I realized that I could be at a high school football game every Friday night." She loved watching the sports reporters do live reports. Her friends outside sports did not understand. She learned how reporters shot video footage, took it to the production truck, edited footage and prepared their reports.

In her journalism classes, Julia learned more about the reporting and tape editing process. She delved into writing within her broadcast journalism group and teamed with other students on delivering newscasts. And friends helped.

"It was the internship that really helped me put my first tape together," said Julia. "Going to a TV station where they have great cameras, they're going to make you look good. They've got a reporter with you. They put good lighting on you.

"I even had a reporter who let me borrow her fancy white coat one time, and it looked like I had money, but I didn't. I was a college kid, but all of a sudden I looked like I was a reporter with a real job. I thought, 'This has to make the tape, because this is the most special I've looked in my entire life.'"

The journalism degree in 2007 led to her first job in Sherman-Denison, Texas. It took her four or five months, many mailings of "all those little DVDs" and a couple of rejections before she grabbed a weekend sports anchor job.

No Retirement Plan

She made $15,000 a year in the 161st ranked television market of 210 markets. She was doing live shots every day, and the tension created by inexperience melted away. She lifted the heavy camera and shot video on her assignments, breaking a few pieces off the camera in the process. Two years later, she was ready to move to a larger market in Tyler, Texas. She covered Dallas Cowboys games.

Two more years later, she returned to Austin when a job opened up. "There was a Triple-A baseball team nearby, which would change the direction of my career once again." It was her first daily exposure to covering baseball. "Minor league baseball is a whole different world than the major leagues, and I would tell anyone that you don't know baseball until you know minor league baseball. Because it is so much of what baseball is. I was almost a beat reporter for our station." Julia hosted a 30-minute weekly show on the Round Rock Express.

She benefited from the time she had for in-depth conversations with players, coaches, managers and front office executives.

"I can't say that enough. That was so huge in my career. Falling in love with the game the way that I did, learning the ins and outs of the game, put me in the perfect spot to be ready for a job like the one that came up with the Houston Astros."

CSN Houston wanted a field reporter to work every game "and be able to share stories a little more elaborately and have access that we'd never had before. That was a big job."

Julia had just signed with an agent. She was ready for a new challenge.

"The industry had just changed. Men and women were getting sideline jobs, digital host jobs - there were more things popping up that were being created. We were watching the industry just kind of blow up in front of our eyes. So many jobs that were not even a thing a few years ago were now very prominent, and everyone was getting them in all these different cities. So, it was like, 'This train is moving fast, and I need to get on it.'"

When she was told she had the job with CSN covering the Astros, "I burst into tears. It didn't feel like real life. When I tell people I'm gonna be the Astros sideline reporter and I'm gonna travel with the team to all these road games, to all these different cities, and this is my job? This is real life? I was all in."

Following Julia through the Minute Maid Park crowds proves her popularity. She's the darling of Astros fans. Her talent and personality have endeared her to them. She described how important it is to get to know the players as individuals.

"That was something I had to learn," said Julia. "Coming in, you weren't going to get anything anyone else couldn't get unless you had some kind of relationship and built some credibility. The relationship part of it was everything and is everything still. I tell people to this day when they ask what is the key to being a good sideline reporter, 'Well, it's all about how you develop that relationship and how you use it during the time you're working with that player or that coach.'

"There's a lot of trust that goes in it as well," explained Morales. "At the end of the day, working for the team's broadcast network, I'm not out to break news or dig up something on these guys, and they have to learn that."

"When I started, they didn't know me from another reporter and they didn't understand the difference between a network and a local news station or a beat writer."

Walk-off Interviews

If a player wins the game with a walk-off hit, Julia is there with a microphone for a quick live interview. There's not much time for her to have her questions ready. "Every game is so different, and that's the reason why I love my job so much," said Julia. "Anything can happen. It could be the most historic night at the ballpark, or it could be just a 2-1 game that happened to run two hours and 30 minutes and we all went home. But it is your job, no matter what the game is, to get reaction from a player of the game or some key moment of the game. I keep notes constantly and I'm also keeping score of the game. You just have to pay attention. I have to watch everything, because you have no idea when that huge double play is gonna come that has to be asked about after the game. That is the sideline reporter's job. There is the walk-off, there is always the fun walk-off, that you really can't prepare yourself for, other than being in the moment.

"When you get really good at this, a lot of it has to do with the years that you put in, the relationships that you have with the players, all of that makes a really good walk-off interview. I know that George Springer is gonna respond differently to a question than Michael Brantley. That's because I've had experiences with both of those guys. That's such a big key to having a good walk-off interview. Was it just the big hit? Was it the big walk that set up the big hit? You are totally in the moment with them. That's how you get the best questions, I believe. You need to let them do the talking. Give them the floor. I am not the story, it's always them."

Julia Morales was voted the best sideline reporter in baseball in a poll of fans of each team by *The Athletic* in 2020.

ADVICE FROM JULIA

"Always look at it in the most positive way possible, because it can only help you later in the experience that you gain. My first thing is to always say 'yes' to things that you're maybe not real comfortable with right out of the gate, because you don't know how many opportunities will be there for you. It's so competitive. If you're in a situation to do things maybe for free or for little pay, just for the extra experience or to see what it's like, then you will put yourself in a better position to keep moving. Networking is so big in this industry. It feels really large in the beginning and it feels like you'll never ever run into the person that you see on TV every night. Not the case. This is the smallest industry at the end of the day. I try to tell people that. Shake hands. If there's somebody you want to meet, meet them. We're generally a

"She has a lot to say. She brings great content to the broadcast," says Todd Kalas. "I always would look around at other telecasts and I remember saying I loved the fact that you guys made Julia almost like a third person in the booth, and she could interject anything during the course of the game. Julia was kind of the new kid when she came in there and started that role. Julia was kind of the most tenured person on the crew when I came in, so I assumed that role would be expanded. I knew how good she was and how sweet of a person she was, so I was really looking forward to working with her."

"Julia's willing to do whatever it takes to make a good
show. She cares so much about the show and the team. She's
all about doing things the right way, having fun and being
passionate about the sport."
producer Carl Patterson

Chapter 11

The Analysts

Steve Sparks
Radio Analyst/Play-by-Play
"You are the light of the world. A city on a hill cannot be hidden. Neither do people light a lamp and put it under a bowl."
Matthew 5:14-15.

Detroit Tigers Hall of Fame broadcaster Ernie Harwell read the Bible passages in Bible study meetings on the road. Steve Sparks, who won 14 games in 2001 for Detroit, said, "When Ernie would come to Bible studies, I couldn't wait for his turn to read a passage from the Bible, because it literally felt like the voice of God was speaking." Although he had a great friendship with Harwell, Sparky was not pumping him with questions about broadcasting. Steve had no thought of being a broadcaster.

After pitching for 19 years in professional baseball, nine in the major leagues, Sparks retired. He was at a charity golf tournament when Dianne Brown noticed what a great voice he had and told him that he should go into broadcasting baseball. Sparks followed her advice and spent seven years doing pregame and postgame shows on Houston Astros telecasts.

He remembers that host Kevin Eschenfelder would watch games with him and make comments about the game at almost exactly the same time the play-by-play broadcaster (yours truly) made them, and Steve would say something almost identical to Jim Deshaies' remarks. In effect, he and Kevin were doing the play-by-play and color as they were watching.

In his eighth year of working Houston Astros radio games, Sparky now knows the routine thoroughly. "Sometimes it can take you two hours to go get an interview, sometimes three hours, and really put you behind. Other times you walk in the clubhouse and grab somebody within five minutes, and it really makes your day a lot smoother."

Making the Rounds

Sparks could sit down and do his analyst's job without much preparation. But he has truly dived into his responsibilities with the energy of a rookie. He makes sure he is prepared for his three innings of play-by-play per game. "It's funny how, behind the scenes, people don't realize how your preparations can get kicked off just by luck, depending on whether or not you get a pregame interview." Sparks spends time in both teams' clubhouses during a series doing interviews. "I would spend literally the entire time during my 45-minute drive to the ballpark thinking of questions and preparing myself for four different people who I might be able to run across when I got into the clubhouse.

"To be able to prepare for somebody who might give short answers - during a four-minute interview it might take ten questions. Sometimes it might take three. But you have to be ready for either scenario."

OK to Lag

"One thing I've learned about play-by-play more than anything else is that it's OK to lag when you're describing, especially on the radio" said Sparks. "Be on time for the crack of the bat, because they can hear the crack. After that, lag for about a second. That way you can just describe what you've already seen, and things come out of your mouth much more smoothly, I believe, when you do it like that. You just get comfortable with that pace. I would say in my seven years, as far as my play-by-play goes I'm not in as big a rush. The science and mechanics of a broadcast have become easier because I'm taking my time and describing things maybe a second or two after I've seen them."

Steve Sparks

Postgraduate Work

As a player who always studied the game, his knowledge of it is extensive. Play-by-play was completely new to him, and when he accepted the job he didn't know he would have that responsibility. "I didn't go to school for that. I wasn't prepared for that. I found out three days before I started my fulltime job as a radio broadcaster that I was going to be doing play-by-play work. I didn't listen to a game the way that someone who wants to do play-by-play listens, because I wasn't thinking about this as a profession. I was listening just for the action. I was picturing what was going on.

"For me, once I started that I think it helped to have a thick skin because it would have been an embarrassment. I really fell on my face quite a bit. I tried to get ahead of myself."

Emotion

"The hardest thing for me, and I think it's because I'm an ex-player doing play-by-play, is to show emotion. Because as a player you were trying to stay as even keel as you could. You didn't want your heart rate to really get going because you wouldn't be ready for your next pitch or what's gonna happen next. You tried to stay as even as possible. Milo Hamilton would hammer that home to me quite a bit on my rides home from the ballpark, about pushing myself to try to get more emotion out on a triple or a home run call, or something like that.

"You know, for whatever reason, two or three years into the gig it finally clicked where I almost turned into not an ex-player but a fan calling these games. A lot of people have told me probably the best broadcasts they listen to are when it sounds like a couple of guys just sitting in a bar and you're just having a conversation with them.

"I also got some advice from somebody in his last year, and I loved this piece of advice to try to make it seem more intimate and make it seem like you're talking only to them. I love these little phrases, and I think Jack Buck used to do this, say little things like, 'just between you and me.' Whatever's going to be able to draw somebody a little closer to the speaker to hear what you have to say."

On the Fly

Thrown to the wolves with his play-by-play, Sparks learned on the fly at the highest level. That's not the way the old-timers were schooled. "It is a tough way to learn it, but I thought it was also a very challenging and fun way to learn it," explained Sparks. "I was very fortunate that the Astros were very bad my first two years, so I don't think there were a ton of listeners.

"I'm sure there were a lot of people feeling like they were listening to fingernails on a chalkboard when it was my turn to do the play-by-play after Robert (Ford) was so eloquent in his six or seven innings, but I do feel I've gotten better. There's plenty of space in my scorebook for preparation, depending on the game. I've learned from a lot of people that if the game is good, you just call the game, and that's when things are easy. But it's really up to the analyst more than anybody to be prepared for the games that aren't really entertaining."

This Game's Headed for the Toilet!

"To keep people listening, I think you've got to tell stories and you have to have a lot of preparation – to talk to people in the clubhouses and the dugouts and the coaches' offices. You've really got to draw on your stories from your playing career and keep things entertaining. As the game is going on, you get a feeling that the game's gonna go sideways, I start writing notes down that I can come back to at a later time when we need them. It might be only three words, but it can last an inning."

"As a radio broadcaster, I'm cognizant number one of the time it's being aired back in Texas," explained Sparks. "When it's day games, I know a lot of people are listening on their way home from work. By the end of that game, it's drive time. So, we've got a pretty good audience for an hour, which is some of our best ratings.

"I don't think I'm ever gonna run out of stories, because in the back of my mind I know a lot of people listen to every inning of every game. I know there are some out there. But most of our listeners are 15-20-minute shots. That's how long we've got. So even in the course of a long day, you're gonna repeat yourself. If you really look at the data of who's listening and when, it's usually when somebody's going from the grocery store to the house to watch it on TV."

Concentration

"There's a big comparison between the concentration a player needs and the concentration a broadcaster needs. For the player, it's paying attention to detail. It's something I learned in the minor leagues. It was something that was gonna serve me very well, and I think it came from the way I was raised. My dad and my brother, who was five years older, had a tremendous work ethic.

"I always felt like I was very disciplined as a player and I was very disciplined growing up, but I always paid attention to detail.

"When I see somebody's pitching delivery and I watch the entire delivery and somebody lets go of the pitch, I really think I'm taking mental snapshots along the way. I think I see 30 or 40 snapshots. When I see something a little bit off on the next one, I can spot it right away. It's just a part of paying attention to really minute detail.

"So, when you think of broadcasting and how much concentration it takes and you start thinking of ways to work, you're way less nervous when you're prepared. It shows up on TV and radio."

7:07

"You can always tell when broadcasters are in a good mood and when they like each other. You learn things along the way. How am I gonna be at my best at 7:07? To be prepared and to do it in a leisurely way where I'm not hurried.

"And to put in the work. When I was pitching, somebody told me, 'Treat practice like the game, and treat the game like practice.' That's a good way to look at the broadcast too.

"It's more about learning the other person's cadence and when there's an opening to describe things. For radio, it's learning to be concise enough to be able to stop before the next pitch so the action can be described, because that's very important on radio. So, it's just learning each other. You're kind of looking at each other or making a little gesture.

"Every once in a while, I'll just put a finger up, and Robert will know I want to come back and get into something a little later and he'll ask that question. We spend a whole lot of time together, so you almost know what the other person's gonna say.

"We've had some good action and we're coming out of our seats and high fiving, but you can't hear that on the radio, hopefully. We're enjoying our jobs."

Minor League Pitcher to Major League Broadcaster

"To be able to do this at the major league level after I spent almost ten years as a minor leaguer is almost unfathomable," analyzed Sparks.

ADVICE FROM STEVE SPARKS

"My advice to anybody getting into this business is not to be afraid to be embarrassed. I think that was the thing for me right away. When I found out I was going to do play-by-play innings, my first instinct was really trying to push back. But I didn't. I didn't say anything. That's the biggest thing. Don't be afraid to be embarrassed. You can ask questions. You can try to learn. But you're going to make mistakes. But that's OK. One of the greatest things I learned as a player, playing for 19 years, was not to worry so much about myself, because nobody cared so much about me. Take the focus off yourself and not to be embarrassed, I think, is the big thing."

"What makes this even more unique is that I didn't play for the Astros, so to be able to do this at home where I live for the Houston Astros – man, I couldn't ask for anything better."

Geoff Blum

TV Analyst

"Blum hits it into right, down the line…it is gone! Geoff Blum, the former Astro, goes deep….and here in the 14th inning the White Sox take a 6-5 lead." Joe Buck, Fox TV

Game 3 of World Series October 25, 2005 at Minute Maid Park

In his 14 major league seasons, Geoff Blum was a dependable player who could play any infield position. That night in 2005, he was not in the game until it was five hours old. Selected by Manager Ozzie Guillen to pinch hit, Blum hit his only career World Series home run. It was such a big moment in Chicago White Sox history that it has been immortalized as a part of a bronze statue outside of U.S. Cellular Park.

Growing up in Southern California in the 1980s, Geoff was a big fan of the Los Angeles Dodgers and the Los Angeles Lakers. He was watching Hall of Fame broadcasters Vin Scully and Chick Hearn broadcast for those teams.

As he played baseball for the University of California-Berkeley, he enjoyed the work of Jon Miller, Duane Kuiper and Mike Krukow on the San Francisco Giants games. When he made it to the major leagues, Hall of Famer Dave Van Horne was there to welcome him to Montreal.

When he was traded to Houston, he became an admirer of the work of Jim Deshaies on Astros TV games. But Geoff did not try to fit into Deshaies' style when he joined the Houston television broadcast in 2013. "No. I know that might be a surprise. I thought about that quite a bit when I got the job, because Jim has such a unique style, I feel, for color analysts in baseball that he was so successful at it, and I knew I wasn't going to be able to replicate that."

Jim Deshaies

"If I took anything from him, it might have been that casualness or authenticity that he had, because when I was playing with the Astros I had the fortune of being able to play golf with Jim Deshaies and some of the other TV crew guys that worked in the truck, so I started to develop a little bit of a knowledge. But what I noticed was that he didn't really have that super 'on camera persona.' You guys were who you were, but when you were calling a game you were the same guys. You were just calling a game. It was just a different atmosphere you were in, so the authenticity of Jim Deshaies is as pure on camera as it is off camera, and that's what I kind of appreciated about him. And that's what everybody loves about him. The one-liners that he has and the distinct humor he has in the game – that's as pure as it gets.

"And that's something I really wanted to have for my own and needed to make my own, because there's no way I was gonna try to repeat or duplicate what Jim Deshaies did. He was too good!"

When asked when he started to think of himself as a broadcaster, Blum joked, "Probably about 2015." He actually did a few games in 2012, so he was making fun of himself. "I did two games the year I got released from the Arizona Diamondbacks, and I don't think they went well at all. You're always gonna be your toughest critic, but I remember the first two games didn't go well, and I had a conversation with Tom Candiotti (former pitcher who became a broadcaster) after the second game. He gave me the best piece of advice that I've ever gotten."

Is it fair to assume that a veteran player can make the transition from player to broadcaster at the major league level? It is not, although major league front offices make that assumption routinely.

"The question that I get all the time is, 'Did you study for this? Did you go to school for this? Did they have a program after you retired and taught you how to do this?' They didn't. There's no training whatsoever. Literally they put you down in this booth and they say, 'Here is your headset. There's the cough button. There's the talkback button if you need anything. Go get 'em and have a great show!' That's where I stumbled a little bit. Hanging around other broadcasters helps a lot. It was kind of like riding a bike without training wheels out of the chute at about a hundred miles an hour," analyzed Blum. "When you're doing a big league game, there are a lot of eyes and ears on these teams. I felt a lot of pressure early on. You've got to give these guys a little bit of slack and a little understanding that they are not trained in this profession and they're doing the best they can."

Part of History

"The Astros broadcast history is phenomenal, and I'm not sure a lot of people realize that, but through the years the Astros have done a very good job of bringing in incredible talent to call the games. Just to be mentioned with Larry Dierker and Jim Deshaies and to be in that line – I'm greatly appreciative of that, too."

Joining Todd Kalas

"It was a unique circumstance for me because I had gone from doing 81 to 100 games to 150 or more. As they were going through the audition process, one name that kind of jumped out at me was Todd Kalas, because I was playing when his dad was announcing for the Philadelphia Phillies, so he already had the name equity in broadcasting.

"But at the same time, I knew Todd when I played for the Tampa Bay Rays in 2004, so I was comfortable with him. I was comfortable with who he was, too, and that's a big deal because it's not just an on-air relationship. You're gonna be traveling with each other extensively, so you have to be compatible off the air too. Julia is a phenomenal talent in her own right."

Style Changes Since 2015

Geoff has settled into the job and feels a comfort zone now. "I do. I think it's gotten a little more comfortable and a little bit better, because early on you have an idea of what you think your show should be or what you think your play-by-play guy should be or how the interaction should be. Then as an analyst – Julia and I are kind of co-pilots on this broadcast and the play-by-play guy is the pilot. Your full concern as the color analyst is 'How am I going to be brought in? How am I gonna find my way into this telecast? Is it gonna be a situation where the play-by-play guy asks a question, or is it going to be a situation where I butt into the conversation – and that's usually uncomfortable when you have to do that. But TK had great awareness of when to bring me in, and I think a lot of it is because we have conversations before our broadcast. Now that we're 3-4 years into our relationship, I think we're getting to the point where we can almost anticipate what each other is going to do or what each other is going to say or when we might have that opportunity to be able to get our opinion out there."

Analysts More Prominent

The television analyst has grown in prominence through the decades. Todd Kalas is committed to involving Geoff Blum more extensively. Their broadcast has trended more in the direction of a conversation.

"Yes, absolutely," agrees Blum. "That's a credit to the people who are around us. I feel comfortable enough with TK to be able to say, 'Hey, I've noticed this about a player. I want to talk about it a little bit.' Or, 'I went down and talked to the player. I have some background on this, so if you can give me an opening at some point, that would be great.' Because I feel like I've got some good information to bring into it. And luckily, Todd trusts me enough to be able to do that.

"If he didn't trust me or if I was a whack job he wouldn't welcome me into the conversation. There's a certain amount of trust involved between the play-by-play guy and the analyst."

Teamwork

"As far as talking about the support and being able to get those color analyst conversations in there, Julia does a great job of laying out to give me the opportunity and give Todd the opportunity. But it's also that a lot of the guys in the truck have to know what we're talking about too. So, we really have to get together as a team outside of just Todd and I. I feel like the more information I give Todd about what my thoughts are, he does an equally great job of trying to find statistical information to support what I'm bringing up, and that's where I think we separate ourselves."

Working in Stats

"I think early on I was trying to put too much information behind what I was seeing on the field, so what I'm trying to do better is pick one. We need to remember that we are moving toward an analytical world in baseball, and the Astros are the tip of the spear as far as really forcing the idea of using statistical information to evaluate a player or explain something. A lot of times I'm trying to explain why Altuve's on a tear or why Carlos Correa is doing a better job of driving the ball the other way.

"So, I'll try to delve into the numbers a little bit and pick 'A' number –

not numbers. I'll try to really break it down to one number that I can use to put into the conversation. If a guy's slugging percentage is spiking, I'll try to find out if he's taking more pitches. Is his strikeout percentage down also? That'll tell me that he's in the zone and trying to make the pitcher throw more pitches to him and therefore he's able to go out and drive the ball a little bit better.

"Or if a guy like Gerrit Cole is striking out hitters at an incredible rate, what pitch is he doing it with? And I'll try to find out if he's elevating his fastball."

On the Couch

"One of the biggest compliments I think any broadcaster can get, and I got this before – one of the biggest compliments is that people kind of get lost in the game a little bit and they feel like we're sitting in their living room on the couch having a conversation. We are fans at heart, and that's why we're in baseball. I really feel like TK and I absolutely love the game of baseball and that's why we can have a conversation. There are plenty of times we've been leaning back in our chairs between pitches and just kind of turned to each other and literally had a conversation about the event that just happened on the field."

> "This is the greatest job I've had. I want to encourage everybody to do it. But do your homework. Never lose your sense of self. The biggest thing is don't be afraid to be yourself on air. Show the enthusiasm, show the disappointment. Show that passion." Geoff Blum

TV PRODUCTION

Houston Astros

The Houston Astros televise their games on AT&T SportsNet Southwest in Houston. Their telecasts involve many different employees. Some of them are employees of the Astros, some are employees of AT&T and some are freelancers.

The camera operators are freelancers, many of whom work other sports events in Houston or occasionally for other networks. The gigantic production truck is parked outside the stadium and has millions of dollars of state-of-the-art equipment, including a mind-boggling bank of monitors on the front wall showing each camera's view as well as screens for replay machines, graphics and other sources. There are many skilled technicians, roughly 12-15, who work in the air-conditioned truck. Typically, they are at work early in the afternoon for a night game. Statistics are prepared for use on the telecast, and highlights are edited for use as well.

The producer of most of the games on AT&T SportsNet Southwest is Carl Patterson. Unusually, he is also skilled as a director.

Carl Patterson
Producer

Somewhere over Arizona early in the morning of July 15, 2019 on the Houston Astros charter flight to Anaheim, Carl Patterson was bending over his laptop and examining an Excel program to make his plans for the next night's game against the Angels. He checked the list of sponsored items from the TV format and put together a list of the content he wanted to include.

He thought that a listing of the top home run hitters in the American League would be a timely item, since Alex Bregman and George Springer would be in the lineup and both were having banner seasons.

He formatted that graphic for the top of the second inning with the sponsor's logo on it. The game would be starting at 9 p.m. CDT and he needed to run that item early in the game when viewership was higher.

Daily Planner

Carl Patterson is always preparing for the next telecast. Producers are, by their nature, people who live by details. Their organization is one of their best qualities. Another is their ability to work with many different types of people. The producer is the catalyst of a telecast. He or she initiates the planning, has conversations with everybody involved, and sees that the plan is executed. Since he began producing Astros games in 2013, three of his favorite telecasts were the Memorial Day game in 2017 and no-hitters by Mike Fiers and Justin Verlander in 2015 and 2019 respectively.

On the Fiers no-hitter, "I don't know if you remember, but we actually ran the last out of quite a few of the Astros no-hitters. We stayed on the air between the bottom of the eighth and the top of the ninth.

"The end of the game – the way we let it breathe – I remember walking away from that thinking we did a really nice job on that."

Doug Johnson, Patterson's coordinating producer at Fox Sports Ohio, paid him a great compliment. He told him, "You know, one of the things I like about you is that no matter what you're doing, you treat it like the Super Bowl."

That worked in Carl's favor when he did 2013 Houston Astros baseball for a team with 111 losses. "Every day I was going in like this is the best team in baseball. The main thing that first year was just kind of figuring everybody out and the speed at which everybody wanted to work." He was working with the Houston crew for the first time that year, and it took some adjustment.

"It's really about personalities, figuring each other out and learning to work with one another's strengths and weaknesses. It probably took more than a year, but by 2014 we were in a pretty good groove."

Storytellers

"Everybody is telling the story of the baseball team in different ways. You can't just tell a story from only your point of view if everybody else isn't buying into what you're doing. It's going to be obvious to the viewer. My job is just finding the stories that every person wants to tell and putting the best ones together in a cohesive way. You can't put so much in a show that the announcers don't have time to talk about baseball. It's hard because we have so much sponsored stuff in the show now."

The chaotic atmosphere inside the truck presents challenges because several people can be talking at the same time. That makes it hard for a producer to concentrate on what the broadcasters are saying. "As a producer, I learned how to listen and what gave the announcers joy to talk about."

Patterson stepped off the University of Cincinnati campus and into the studio at WCPO-TV in Cincinnati, running the teleprompter. Then he became a camera operator.

In Portland, Oregon he moved up to producer and director of high school and college sports, making $55,000 for televising games out of a little van with four cameras attached to it.

He was the director for Cleveland Indians and Cavaliers telecasts at Fox

Sports Ohio on some Emmy Award-winning productions. His experience as a director makes him a better producer.

As you'll see on the next page, the director is the person who actually calls the camera shots. The producer generally decides where the telecast is going and the director gets it there. One very important facet of directing is giving the camera operators warning a second or two ahead so they can be in focus when the director calls for their camera to be used on the air.

His advice to those headed into broadcasting?

"Never stop looking to learn the next thing that's going to make you more versatile and less dispensable, and always be looking for that next chance to advance."

This is the portable office of the producer, director and video crew for sports telecasts. The production trucks move from one sports venue to another. Owners of these facilities spend millions to put together these rolling control rooms. They are connected by miles of cable to cameras inside the venues. In order to make the financial investment in such trucks worthwhile, they must be scheduled frequently for telecasts. Typically they move from one baseball stadium to another venue after a homestand during the summer.

Paul Byckowski
Director

A triple is considered to be the most exciting play in baseball. Here's how veteran director Paul Byckowski would call a triple on his headset to the camera operators:

"Ready two-TWO. (He just hit the ball). Ready four – FOUR. (Four's got the runner rounding first base so I can see his face. That's one of my things. I'd rather see his face than his back. I just don't like that.

"The ball may be in the corner, so I want a tighter shot. Ready three – THREE. Now I want to pick up the runner. He's digging around second base. Ready four – FOUR. He rounds second base. Now I know camera three's tight. I don't want to go to camera three because I want to see a wider perspective, so I go back to two: Ready two - TWO. Now he's digging past the shortstop. Ready one – ONE. He's coming toward third base and he's gonna dive in. He dives in headfirst and I stay there. I may cut to camera two again, if it's a close play, or I may stay. Now his face is turned toward first base. I go 'Ready five – FIVE.' Now we see his face. He looks at the dugout.

"He gives them the thumbs up like they do now. I may go to the pitcher now. Ready one – ONE. I go to five for his face again. Ready five-FIVE. Ready Effect A."

Whew! Most play-by-play broadcasters will agree that the director's job on that play is tougher than theirs. Byckowski explains his thinking.

"Whenever there are runners on base, that's obviously the most difficult. Baseball's the hardest game to direct, especially when you're talking about the timing and the pacing of the game. And that's the key. Baseball is the only sport that the ball doesn't score the points.

"When that happens, you have to go to the home plate camera to show the runner scoring. You can't just assume he scores. You have to show he scores.

"That's why baseball is so difficult, because there's a timing, and you want to cut it fast enough where you're showing exactly what's happening, but you don't want to cut too soon."

Paulie, It's You Now

Byckowski has called about 7,000 live events in his 35-year career as a director. He chose his profession when he was a teenager, watching Chicago Cubs telecasts with announcers Jack Brickhouse and Harry Caray. He remembers them saying on the air, "Arne, can you get me a shot of Billy Williams?" Arne was the director, Arne Harris.

"I kept saying to myself, 'Wow, that is really cool. They keep saying Arne's name. They're talking to the guy who's giving them those shots.'"

Now Byckowski is giving the shots to Houston broadcasters, supervising a large crew including up to 20 cameras. Many of the cameras are robotic cameras.

Regardless of the technological explosion during his lifetime, Byckowski credits the early trailblazers like Arne Harris. "Baseball's been cut the same way for 60 years. They had it down."

As a broadcasting student at Northern Illinois University, Paul found himself without much competition when it came to volunteering for duties in the television studio. "One thing that I would say to students is that I found that even in my class the teacher would say, 'Who wants to be the director?' You'd look around the class and no one would put up their hand. And I'd say, 'I'll do it.' No one raised their hand to be the talent for a studio show either.

"A lot of the students really didn't have the passion, at least that I did, to become a broadcaster. I really wanted to be a director and have the Arne Harris recognition."

Singled Out

"At the end of my college career the teacher told me, 'Paul, there's really one person that's going to make it out of all these people. It's going to be you.' I'll never forget that. I think he was a news director from Detroit who became a teacher and he told me, 'You're the one with the enthusiasm and desire to do something. The rest of these people will have other careers.' I can't even tell you how many people told me, 'Don't go into broadcasting. You're never gonna make it. You don't know anybody. It's a tough business.' I didn't listen to them. My dad gave me a great piece of advice. He said, 'Paul, if you don't get a job in broadcasting, you'll just do something else.'"

But he certainly didn't start with an Arne Harris salary. After being an ESPN stringer in the early days of that network, Paul left a job paying $5.50 per hour at a production house to work for $2.20 per hour to work as a floor director at a TV station. He was sleeping on the floor of his friend's house trying not to notice the mice running along the baseboards at night. His father asked him, "Did you go to college?" when Paul told him of his huge pay cut.

He explained to his father that he needed to learn the TV business from the bottom up. The natural progression was from floor director to camera operator to graphics operator to audio specialist to TV news director. He wanted to say, "I've done every one of those positions," and he now advises students to follow that same path.

Byckowski moved to Houston to take a job at KTXH-TV (Channel 20) when that station carried Astros, Rockets, Comets, Rice University, University of Houston and Texas Terror arena football games.

He was hired for $12,500 per year as the lead photographer. Then he was promoted to director for $19,000, which was the low salary range for that job. He told the general manager that he would be working hard and he would be earning nearer to the higher range of the job - $31,000 – soon. Two weeks later, the GM agreed and elevated him to that level. Paul started a run of 15 years at Channel 20, seven years as executive producer.

Ready for Advancement

Fox Sports Southwest hired him to take over the Astros road telecasts. He eventually became the Astros fulltime director.

What are the biggest challenges to directing baseball? "The slower the game, the harder it is because you have to fill that void. If the announcers are talking about a player, I don't want to take their attention away from that. At times I lead the announcers and at times the announcers lead me. But I like to leave shots up so people can absorb them and appreciate them.

"If you show the runner while the outfielder bobbles the hit and you miss the bobble, replay can fill it in later. When you're directing you're making the decisions live, instantaneously. There's no delay. Is it a mistake? In my mind, yes. In the public's eye, maybe not. We got the point, the runner advanced.

"The same thing has to happen with the producer and director. If they're not in harmony, because we're with each other for six months…we're on the road together, flying together, eating together…you're talking 10-12 hours being together with the same person.

"If you don't have that cohesiveness, it makes it tough. Sometimes it happens really quick. Other times it comes apart. The producer is in charge of how the show is going to go – how the flow is going to go, what his main goals are for the telecast. "The features that we run, the players that we talk about, what elements we have to use.

"My job is to document the game – do all the things that I think are important in the game and then incorporate all the things that he thinks are important in the game. Sometimes it gets tense, because I'm trying to show one thing and the producer wants to go somewhere else. But the producer's basically in charge. The bottom line is when the producer and director are on the same page and they have the same goal – providing great television, providing the viewers great coverage, that's when the telecast is best."

Ralph Kiner, former Hall of Fame player and New York Mets broadcaster:

"On this special Fathers Day, we'd like to wish all of you a very happy birthday."

"If Casey Stengel were alive today, he'd be spinning in his grave."

"The Hall of Fame ceremonies are on the 31st and 32nd of July."

"Jose DeLeon on his career has 73 wins and 105 RBI.
"Daryl Strawberry has been voted to the Hall of Fame five years in a row."

Network Cameraman Rick Stogsdill

At Sam Houston State, Rick Stogsdill butted heads on the football field with teams featuring future NFL stars Wade Wilson and Darrell Green. He faces physical challenges to this day as a freelance cameraman at many major league baseball games, NFL games on NBC, the Olympics, The Open and other golf tournaments. Rick can average more than **200** nights on the road in a hotel during an Olympic year.

When Stogsdill was in high school, he never doubted that he would be involved in sports after being an avid viewer of Howard Cosell narrating football highlights on Monday Night Football. "Like everybody else, upon graduation I wanted to work in a big market like Houston, Dallas or San Antonio. I didn't understand why nobody wanted to hire somebody fresh out of school with no experience or internships on my resume.

"Looking back, that was one of the things I should have done during the summer months," said Stogsdill. His first staff job was at KCEN in Temple, Texas.

Stogsdill moved to something more suitable to his dream, contacting many of the production companies he had only heard of through the commercials they had supplied the station.

The search landed him at Texas Video & Post, a production company within KTXH-TV located in Houston, Texas and just across the freeway from the Astrodome. Within a year he began working Houston Astros games as a freelancer. "After six plus years of basically working a staff job during the week and freelancing at night and weekends, I had crafted a foundation of live sports as well as a better than average list of contacts.

"I didn't just jump off the deep end, making sure I had secured enough work to make at least what I was making annually at a staff job. Deciding to freelance full time in 1991, I ended up giving myself approximately a 35 percent raise. I would not have done it without having some of these contacts beforehand," Stogsdill explained.

As a cameraman, Stogsdill relishes the physical challenge in his job, often covering multiple miles with 30 plus pounds of camera on his shoulder canvassing the stadium looking for meaningful shots to add to the telecast. "Sadly, the digital world of high definition hasn't made the equipment any lighter," said Rick of new cameras.

"Although the amount of information that can be processed fiber optically without signal loss throughout the television compound is more concentrated, that same mentality has made the high def lenses and much of the equipment heavier actually than in the analog days of the past. The difference is night and day."

When the starting pitcher takes the mound for the Astros, the cameraman trailing him is often Rick Stogsdill. That has become the norm the past few years. "I didn't really care for it, actually," he said. "I'm beginning to get a little more comfortable with it upon accepting it's not going away. A couple of years ago, then Astros pitcher Gerrit Cole looked over and said to me, 'Hey, that's enough,' feeling I had overstayed my invitation, as it were. The next day during batting practice I apologized to him.

"His response was, 'It's OK, I get it, but at that point, you're between the lines,' said Stogsdill. "I thought that was a very prudent answer because at that point it's no longer pregame, and I'm in the guy's office." Thousands of people are watching Stogsdill on the field just before the first pitch.

Advice to Students

"In the beginning of your career, find a suitable situation where you're not going to be pigeonholed. You're gonna make mistakes when you're starting out, so make them on a smaller scale that matches the potential costs and consequences. Those things really allowed me to specialize.

"You have to know the rules of whatever it is you're covering, because on any given day whether you're the only camera or one of many, never forget the best shot is the one that nobody else has. Know the situation and know where all the other people are. I guarantee you if I'm running the camera at field level, I know exactly what the guy up in the stands is shooting and I know what the person in the outfield or endzone is shooting."

"Opportunities will appear when you least expect them. Always be ready so when someone calls in sick or any other last-minute emergency situation arises, it's really important for you to become that person that they can plug in wherever they need somebody," advises Stogsdill.

Rick has been to 48 states on assignment, missing only Idaho and Alaska. Not surprisingly, his favorite events are the iconic, recognizable ones. Augusta National, Lambeau Field in Green Bay, the various Olympic venues and the Astrodome stand out for him. He also has special memories of the Triple Crown horse races. He worked the night that Brett Favre had an incredible game against the Raiders the day after his father passed away.

Of NBC Sunday Night Football, he says, "In our NFL show, any of our cameras that are RF or Wireless are allowed to go on the field during timeouts. That's one of the things broadcasting has committed to in an attempt to enhance the telecasts. That show has 27 manned cameras and 40 cameras total so when someone comes up to me and says, 'Hey can you get tickets?' I'll respond by saying, 'You really don't want tickets. For a prime time telecast, you want to be sitting at home in front of your cozy 4K TV set, because you're gonna see every angle that you just don't get on your standard 12 noon or 3 pm telecast. The coverage is three times what you normally get.'"

During the 2020 pandemic summer, baseball telecasts could be controlled from the studio, such as this one from ATT Sports Southwest. Production trucks could be bypassed in order to run the telecast more economically.

Chapter 13

Pre and Post

Kevin Eschenfelder
Pregame and Postgame Host
Play-by-Play

In the 1960s when the Houston Oilers were followed closely, Vernon Eschenfelder was a spotter and statistician for the radio broadcast team. Dan Lovett, Ron Franklin and Jerry Trupiano were among the play-by-play voices who kept their audiences entertained. Eschenfelder, an athletic trainer at the Houston School District, was earning some extra money and enjoying the games from one of the best seats at the Astrodome. Jeppesen Stadium, the Oilers' first home, was where Eschenfelder worked often as a trainer. By the time they moved into the Astrodome, Vernon's eight-year-old son Kevin was sitting on the back step of the broadcast booth.

And at the end of each quarter, Kevin passed out statistics sheets to the reporters in the press box. He got an extra thrill when he handed one of the sheets to NFL owners like George Halas of the Chicago Bears. Owners watched from the press box in those days.

Spotter for the Stars

Kevin was taking it all in as he trained himself for the future, when he would be spotting for some of the NFL's best broadcasters. He worked with Jack Buck, Marv Albert, Dick Enberg and Verne Lundquist.

"They all had different styles, and it was the style that they were all comfortable with. No one knew how prepared the announcer was more than me, because I was their spotter," said Kevin.

When Kevin graduated from high school, he was bitten by the play-by-play bug. And he was ready to seize a quick opportunity.

"I went to Alvin Community College. They had an outstanding radio station. The guys who had been doing Alvin high school football left. I had gotten into the sports department, doing the sports reports on the station.

"I was thrilled to get an opportunity to go do those games. I did the play-by-play on those games. Then a couple of years later when I was still in college, I got the opportunity to do Houston Baptist University basketball. They were Division I at the time in the Trans American Conference. That was my first opportunity to travel – get on an airplane and go game to game. Those were the first play-by-plays that I really did. I took it really seriously. I saw people that didn't. I would drive to the next city and get the starting lineups from the coaches. That's how you did it back then.

"You didn't have a guy email you the starting lineup. You would literally go take a pen and paper and write down the starting lineup. The quarterback is number 12, backup is number 10 and so on."

Kevin had a college internship at KTRH. He screened calls for a talk show and got some tape after Astros and Rockets games for the sports shows. "I loved the job and didn't want it to end, even though I was never paid," said Eschenfelder. When the semester ended, he got three credit hours, but he kept coming in to the station and working. Nobody questioned why he was continuing to work because they assumed he was getting paid. He stayed on for two more years with no paycheck!

Background in the Business

The native Houstonian also got a behind-the-scenes background working in the production truck at Houston Astros games. "I think what always helped me was being a person who started as that stats guy – that guy that worked in the truck. Not everybody can do that, but I had such a better idea of what was going on in the truck from a technical standpoint.

"You knew when to ask questions, and when their hair was on fire you would leave them alone and let them figure it out and do your game.

"I always thought that was a huge key – to get that sense of what it was like from the other side of that IFB (interruptible foldback, communication through headsets on a broadcast) coming from the director to the producer."

With credentials to roam inside the Astrodome, Kevin found his way to the broadcast booths and quietly observed the broadcasters.

"For the most part I was more of a 'keep my ears open and my mouth closed' kind of guy, and watch what people did. I had a great appreciation, sitting next to Gene Elston. But it changed so much.

"What guys would compile would take hours to come up with for that day's game – now you can get on the computer and it would take 15 seconds. But back then Gene Elston had his file cards. What I saw with that was just how much work went into that - the organization, staying on it every single day. It's a seven-day-a-week job. That's what I learned from that. I always had a good basis – I knew that no matter what you did, you always did better at it when you were prepared."

Armed with Information

That's what has served Eschenfelder for his 32 years in broadcasting. He has been hosting Astros and Rockets shows since 1997 as well as many other assignments. He also does some Astros TV play-by-play. "I've always felt like I was better when I was more prepared. The more prepared I am, the less I think and the more I react. It's not unlike when you hear about a quarterback that he knows the offense so well. He's not back there thinking about where he's got to go with the football.

"I can't put enough value into that because: A. You present everything you do with so much more confidence. B. You don't seem as though you're thinking but you're reacting to what's in front of you because you don't think: 'Do I remember this?' Or 'Do I remember that?'"

With his extensive play-by-play experience before the studio assignments came along, Kevin made the transition seamlessly and without training. "It was simple compared to play-by-play, because on play-by-play there are so many aspects that you have to be ready for. When you're in a formatted show, you pretty much lay those aspects out.

"There's not going to be a whole lot – things could change on the fly late – but for the most part you're gonna have a rundown and we're gonna talk about what's on the rundown.

"Play-by-play – a guy could run on the field out of the stands, you never know. There's always the unexpected. The thing about the studio shows is that for the most part they're unscripted, but they're well-planned.

"I know we're gonna talk about that night's pitching matchup. I've always been a firm believer that I'm driving the ship, but my analyst has probably had 15 years in the big leagues or in the NBA. The viewers are here to hear what he has to say. To be a good host, you understand that you're there to bring the knowledge out of the analyst."

Day in the Life

The emails fly in the morning of a night game between the producer and the broadcasters. Each broadcaster has a chance to request any content he may want in the show. By the time all of the staff meets in mid-afternoon, the format is handed out and they all continue their preparation.

The broadcasters write notes they will use in the studio, in addition to the graphics and videotape they examine before going on the air. They hit the air at 6:30 for a 7:00 game.

They grab a quick bite to eat while watching the game telecast, writing notes about what game highlights they want on the postgame show. They wait for the game to end and are ready to go on the air immediately after the final out.

Sometimes they have waited four hours or more for long games, including rain delays. It can be a lengthy day, and there aren't many days off.

> Kevin Eschenfelder's advice: "To know the game, first. Know what you're talking about. And you have to have that passion. We all had that vision of always wanting to do it. We were not the best players on the sandlot, but we knew how we would call that play. It's work. It's not easy. It's bad hours and bad pay early in your career when you're getting established.
>
> "It's a tough job to get into, but somebody's got to get into it. That's what I always tell people. Don't ever let anybody tell you to do something more stable. Somebody has to get this job, and why can't it be you?"

Mike Stanton
Analyst

As a major league pitcher, lefthanded reliever Mike Stanton made 1,178 appearances over a 19-year career. That's second on the all-time list to Jesse Orosco. He says he really would have preferred being a position player, because he loves the game so much that he wants to play every day. The native Houstonian who grew up in Midland, Texas and attended Alvin Community College is an analyst on AT&T SportsNet pregame and postgame shows and also does commentary on some telecasts.

Stanton's first major league team was Atlanta. He enjoyed talking about pitching with Hall of Fame pitcher and broadcaster Don Sutton, but Mike had no ambition to be a broadcaster while he was playing. About two years after he retired, Patti Smith of Fox Sports Houston asked him if he wanted to be an analyst.

Two-man Team

Mike teams with Kevin Eschenfelder on many pregame and postgame shows, and their show takes place in the open center field studio before games at Minute Maid Park. "I really had no idea how to do it," remembered Stanton of his first season as a broadcaster. "I had no idea what to say, so I did a whole lot of research, and it wasn't until I got into the office that they said, 'Listen, just talk baseball. We've got other people that can deal with ERAs and stuff like that. We want your experience. Tell some stories. Give us your views on sports through your eyes.' That's what I still try to do on my pregame and postgame. I still do my numbers research to make sure I've got all the numbers correct. But it's really more about my experiences through the years that I played and how I view the sport. So far so good."

How has he been able to learn from feedback about his work? "I've gotten a little bit here and there, but that's one of the problems that I think we have in the industry, is that everybody is doing a job, to start off with. Nobody's just sitting and watching my broadcast or watching the production. Any little feedback I've gotten has been tidbits here and there. I've watched myself. I don't do it a whole lot. And then I have friends who have been in the industry that have watched the broadcast and they'll give me little pointers here and there. But I think that's one of the problems of the industry – that there's not a lot of critiquing about the right way to do it.

"When you're playing the sport, there's always somebody critiquing you," said Stanton. "But in broadcasting, it's such a broad stroke – and everyone has their different approaches, everyone has their different personalities. You have your opinions of how things should work. And it's worked for you, but that doesn't necessarily mean it'll work for me.

"A lot of it is taking tidbits from where you can get them and shooting from the hip a little bit, coming up with your own style."

Comments from Family or Friends

How does he decide which comments about his work are worth his attention? "It depends on who it is. If I get something from my wife, she can be kind of blunt. She tells me her view of it and it carries a lot of weight because she is my wife and I know she's not sugarcoating it. If it's from my mother, I know she's biased, so I have to take that with a grain of salt."

Looking Through a Different Lens

"When I was a player, it was all about the game. Now that I've been doing the broadcasting thing for a while and know how things are behind the scenes, I can actually critique the production. Do I know it all? Of course not.

"Just like every broadcaster has a different personality, every producer has a different personality and you can tell if you watch it enough which producer is producing a game or a show by the content and by how the show is run. There really is no right or wrong way. There are some things that you need to do, some things that you don't need to do.

"I can tell you before our pregame and postgame shows we have a preshow meeting. We go over the rundown, go over the subject matters, if there are any special things we're gonna do. Maybe we're going to do a standup session to explain something. The postgame is a little bit different because you just kind of shoot from the hip after the game just ended. You don't have time to set the show up like you do the pregame show."

Differences Between Game Telecasts and Studio Shows

"There is a lot more prep for the game telecast. Obviously, you're on air a lot longer. You need to know the individual players. It's not as formatted as a 30-minute show. There is a lot of discussion beforehand with the producer. You're on the headset between innings talking about what's coming up. You need to know the players, the stats, the young guys. My job as the analyst is predicting the game. Is there a move to be made? Is this a good time for a hit-and-run? There's a lot more that goes into broadcasting a game."

Radio vs. Television

"In radio, dead air is the enemy. You have to remember that the listeners are not getting anything. They're not getting any analytical work. You need to have that ongoing conversation for the most part. When you go over to television, the picture tells the story. One of the things I always struggle with is trying to overanalyze. On television a lot of times you need to sit back and let the picture tell the story."

"Because of my experience, I look at a baseball game in a bit different manner than the average fan. That's why you have a color analyst and that's where the experience comes in. Maybe the pitcher is doing something a little different than the inning before. Or the hitter has a different setup, something like that. Where would I attack the hitter? Defensively, if the player made a really nice play, why did he make the play? Or why did he boot the ball? Whatever it might be. That's why you have a color analyst, because of the experience and the view that he has of the game is gonna be different than an average fan's."

The Everyday Sport

"The proverbial day game after a night game, you still have to get up, you have to be sharp, you have to be articulate and mentally be on top of the game. That's what I love about the game. When I was in high school I told my parents there's no way I wanted to pitch. I wanted to be a position player, to play every day. I think that's one of the reasons I wanted to be a reliever. I was coming to the ballpark every day thinking that I could play. I might not, but at least I had the opportunity to play. So, I always considered myself a baseball player that pitched."

Phil Rizzuto, New York Yankees former shortstop and TV broadcaster, was working a game on TV. Phil arrived late from a golf game and barely made it to the booth when the red light went on the camera and he was on the air with his partner Bill White. White said something like, "Hello everybody from Yankee Stadium, where tonight the Yankees play the Chicago White Sox. Scooter, the Yankees are facing lefty Tommy John and he's been tough on them."

RIZZUTO, "Yeah, the last time they saw him he was a guy who.....AH, let's start this XY&*M%$ over again."

WHITE: "Scooter, we can't do that, because we're on live!!!"

Chuck Wepner, boxer

"I was six foot one inch when I started fighting, but with all the uppercuts I'm up to six foot five inches."

Glenn Healy, hockey player

"I was three-quarters down the list of guys I would be facing in my first game when I realized I was looking at guys on our own roster."

Chapter 14

Depth in the Booth

L-R Texas League Pres. Tim Purpura, Dan O'Neil, Michael Coffin, Reid Ryan

Class AA
Michael Coffin
Voice of the Corpus Christi Hooks

"Welcome to Astrolaunch from The Ballpark of the Palm Beaches. This is Michael Coffin alongside Steve Sparks…" The 2020 spring training broadcast of the Houston Astros featured one man doing two jobs. The voice of the Corpus Christi Hooks was filling in for play-by-play broadcaster Robert Ford when Ford had a day off. He was also performing the duties of producer/engineer Matt Boltz, who also had the day off.

It was a rare occasion on a major league broadcast when one man was charged with doing both jobs, and he did it four times in 2020.

It wasn't rare at Corpus Christi, though. Coffin serves as both the director of broadcasting and media relations director with the Hooks. On a normal home game, he is in the office in the morning after a night game, attending staff meetings.

He interfaces with the marketing department and coordinates how certain promotions and events are handled in the media and on the broadcast. He's in charge of printing the statistics sheets and assembling them in packets for the media.

He writes the game notes for the media, usually consuming about two hours of work. But that work is a part of his game preparation for the broadcasts, and it's especially enjoyable for him. He orders the food for the media in the press box for every home game. He makes sure the press box is cleaned properly and kept orderly. He hires some personnel for those jobs.

He arranges for the official scorer for each game, the scoreboard operator and the statistician. He estimates that broadcasting the games is about 20 per cent of his overall duties for the team.

"We're scrambling to get all those things done, and it becomes a little overwhelming at times," says Coffin of the small staff's duties.

Broadcast Prep on the Back Burner

"We're trying to get people to the ballpark. If your broadcasts are not getting people to the ballpark, you're not much of an asset." His goal every game is to finish his other duties so he can attend batting practice and talk to the players. He makes it about half the time.

Coffin grew up following the Astros and dreamed of working for them. He did his own play-by-play when he was in grade school, turning down the TV volume and providing his own description. At his side was *Baseball Almanac* and other reference books as well as his Gene Elston scorebook. "I just knew I had to do it," said Coffin of play-by-play.

"I felt like I was part of the team because it was every day. I can't imagine not doing this." The Corpus Christi Hooks are owned by the Astros, and that has brought some perks. Coffin went from Sam Houston State University to an internship with the Astros to the Hooks in 2006.

He's worked 12 major league games with the Astros during the regular season the last few years. And he identifies closely with the major league club through his lifetime association as a fan and as a broadcaster when George Springer, Jose Altuve, Carlos Correa and Alex Bregman wore Hooks' uniforms.

When Coffin attended Sam Houston State, he learned as a student the value of building associations with those who could help his career. He introduced himself to the Sports Information Director (SID) upon arriving in Huntsville.

That introduction led to doing the play-by-play for about 20 baseball games as a freshman simply because other candidates were in class during the afternoons when the games were played, and Coffin had been wise enough to schedule classes that did not meet Tuesday or Thursday afternoons.

Mixing the Sounds

The Astros use Comrex broadcast equipment. The Hooks use Tieline. He was taught how to troubleshoot and solve problems when they arise, and he takes pride in knowing the technical side because he wants to make sure the broadcast mix sounds good on the air. Boltz has helped him learn the Comrex, but Coffin credits Boltz with being "an artist" when it comes to creating a vibrant sound on the air.

"The way that he can mix the sounds and the way that he really brings the game to the listener is something that I cannot duplicate, at least when I'm calling the game and engineering at the same time. Boltzie anticipates when things are going to happen on the field, so that he has different mics at his disposal and he can utilize those mics, whether it's the crowd mic, the plate mic, the bat crack. There's a lot of technique to it.

"My first game doing play-by-play with the Hooks was July 5, 2007. We had a rainout on the fourth and I was supposed to work that game because Matt Hicks was sick. Hicks was still sick the next day and I got to call a doubleheader. In 2011, I was doing fill-in work with Hicksie. Reid Ryan gave me (Hicks') job at the All-Star break that year when he was hired by the Rangers. I felt like I really had to perform that last part of 2012 because I knew that Ryan-Sanders Baseball are old school. They value radio."

Rolling Bunkbed

Travel in the Texas League is grueling. "Our longest bus ride is to Springfield, Missouri – 14 hours. Our shortest is seven hours to Frisco. We have 140 games in 150 days. We'll play a night game in Corpus Christi and get on the road at midnight and arrive at noon the next day sometimes, and these guys will play at 7 that night."

Working a radio game at Frisco, he had to do a game from the writers' area with the press box windows closed one time. "I'm talking to myself. They had Seinfeld on the television blaring loud, and the Hooks lost 10-0. I'll never forget, taking off my headsets, I was upset at my performance, I was exhausted, I was upset with the game." But afterwards, his mood improved when he hung out with Hicks and Larry Dierker after the game. Dierker was one of his heroes. "That's when I first got the idea that 'This is not amateur hour here.' It's easy when you're excited and you have all kinds of energy. But when you're tired, when you're frustrated, you have to flip the switch. People are counting on you to have a smile as well when you're doing these games. That takes a lot of work."

Coffin reflects on the jump start he got in college. "To this day I'm a firm believer if Paul Ridings (SID) hadn't given me an unpaid job, I don't think I'd have had the access to the athletic department that I did."

> How would he advise students to approach their college years? "I use my example of internships, and calling people and building up your network and reaching out to people. Simply working at it. It's a craft. Today's students have something I never had when I was growing up, and that's the MLB at-bat app. I can listen to every single broadcast of every team, every announcer, and you pick up things. My advice to people who ask me is to listen as much as you can, read as much as you can and practice, whether that's into a tape recorder, at a Little League game or wherever it may be. And when you get to college, go find the SID." Michael Coffin

Matt Boltz
Astros Radio Producer-Engineer

Sitting behind Robert Ford and Steve Sparks at a console one step higher than the floor of the radio booth, producer-engineer Matt Boltz surveys his broadcasters and microphones as well as his Comrex sound board as the game moves along. He's happy to have two even-tempered compadres in the booth. When he worked with the Chicago Cubs in the WGN booth at Wrigley Field, he had to be ready to kill a mic quickly. "Ron Santo really kept me on my toes," said Boltz. "He treated his headsets like his third base glove. He would throw his headsets on the counter if something bad happened." Fortunately for Boltz, most of the days have been good in his six seasons with Houston.

After high school in Chicago, Boltz started college at Missouri State (then Southwest Missouri State). He transferred to the University of Missouri and started working at KFRU. He operated the control board during St. Louis Cardinals games and talk shows. He did remote setups for broadcasts, with his goal "to create a remote studio" away from the station.

At Your Service

When Boltz was unpaid and not an intern, he helped every way he could. He cleaned restrooms, shoveled snow in the parking lot and stacked shelves. His mantra was what he tells students today: "Do everything you possibly can if you want to get into that business."

An associate approached him one day. "I'm doing a Jefferson City Jays football game. Would you like to set up the equipment?" Boltz jumped at the chance. Eventually Mike Kelly, the voice of the Missouri Tigers, asked him if he wanted to travel and be the engineer for the radio broadcasts.

"I've never done any live sports," said Boltz. Nonetheless, that was the start of his career in sports. He was no longer interested in his original goal of producing and writing movie productions.

With the Astros, Boltz packs all the audio gear for road trips and arrives early before a night game to set up the booth. For every game, home and road, he sets up headsets for Ford, Sparks and any potential guest who might be on the air. At home he connects to two mics behind home plate. They will pick up umpires' verbal calls and the crunch of a player's spikes walking across the cinder warning track near home plate. He uses other common microphones with the television broadcast. "In my mind, you've got three mics at all times," says Boltz. "Play-by-play, color and sounds of the ballpark."

If the persona of the producer-engineer is an even keel, sounding board type of companion, the broadcasters are always appreciative. After all, they all spend more time with each other during the long six-month season than they do with their families! A good disposition always plays well over the long haul.

Chapter 15

FOOTBALL PLAY-BY-PLAY

Brad Sham

Dallas Cowboys

Nine of the 50 highest-rated sports events in 2018 were Dallas Cowboys telecasts. They were the world's most valuable sports franchise for the fourth straight year at $5 billion. Their play-by-play broadcaster for 42 years, Brad Sham, thinks about his good fortune. Because his dad was transferred from Chicago to Dallas, he's spent his entire professional career living in the Metroplex. "Everything that's happened to me professionally is a result of my dad's work bringing him from Chicago to Dallas." About that time, Sham enlisted in the National Guard because he was about to be drafted during the Vietnam era.

After basic training, he was looking for a broadcasting job with no results after answering ads in *Broadcasting* magazine.

It did open up for him, but not as a sportscaster as he hoped. Radio station WRR had a news job opening. Sham responded to a newspaper ad and was hired. The reasons? 1. He had a journalism degree from Missouri. 2. He was willing to work for $600 a month. "In 1970, $600 a month paid my apartment rent and the upkeep on my car." He was a news reporter for almost five years but he kept badgering his bosses for some sports assignments. On his own time, he went to Dallas Chaparrals practices and did some play-by-play for them.

He covered Dallas Black Hawk games, Dallas Tornado soccer games (where he did play-by-play) and finally his station gave him a chance to do more sports. He recalls making about $10,000 a year.

The station said he would not be paid any more to do sports events, but Sham said he didn't care about the money; he wanted to do sports. ***That's one of the messages I give kids all the time. You can't be chasing money.***

Sham was rewarded with the host position of the first call-in sports show, on a Sunday night. He continued to do play-by-play. But he treasures the news experience he got.

Most Iconic Brand in Sports

Sham has done four Super Bowl games and 27 Cotton Bowls. He's a member of the Texas Radio Hall of Fame and has been voted Texas Sportscaster of the Year 12 times. He admits to feeling more responsibility because of the popularity of the Cowboys.

"Yeah, a little bit. My dad could just as easily have been moved to Indianapolis and maybe I'd have been doing the Colts and it wouldn't have had the same impact. So, it's got nothing to do with me. The brand was what it was and it's only grown and none of that has anything to do with me.

"One thing that's different in the NFL is that there's no local television voice, which is obviously unique. Even though more people are watching television than radio, a lot of them are listening with the sound turned off.

"So the radio announcers in the NFL are the only ones who are constantly identified with the team.

"When the team has the visibility that this one does, yeah, you'd be nuts to say there's not a little more responsibility that goes with that. I view it as a great privilege. I embrace it. I understand that it all has to do with good fortune, depending on your point of view. I happen to be a man of faith.

"I don't think there are accidents, and especially after leaving the broadcast for three years in the '90s and coming back and being welcomed back, I feel like I am doing what I'm supposed to be doing and where I'm supposed to be doing it. And that had better carry a sense of responsibility and gratitude. That is something not to be treated lightly, in my opinion."

Years of Experience Serve Well

Sham agrees that he's changed as a broadcaster after all the years with the Cowboys. "I hope it's better. When I started on the broadcasts, I was number two with Verne Lundquist and I was with him for eight years. I didn't have any football background. It was actually that part of the job. I was hired at KRLD in the middle of the '76 season. The main part of the job was the talk show, because there were only two shows. We had different audiences. The second part of the job was doing afternoon sports and getting tape for the late great Frank Glieber, God rest his soul, for morning drive. Color on the Cowboys with Verne was the third part of the job. Verne was the big dog.

"It took me about two weeks, because even then I listened to my own work for self-scouting (which I still do), to realize that role I was filling – how I was doing it – I wouldn't want to listen to it," said Brad Sham.

"I was really trying to do color because I didn't really feel qualified as an analyst. I was coming in in the middle of the season and I didn't know anybody. The first decision I made was to keep my mouth shut and ask some intelligent questions and learn. I learned a lot from sitting next to Verne.

"The few chances I had to do play-by-play when I worked with him were very much informed by trying to see the game the way he sees the game. Trying to moderate my tone a little bit and be a little bit more under control. We're talking about a Hall of Famer, and I'm not him. But I learned a lot from him."

"We?"

"Whenever anybody said 'we,' the other would say, 'Is there a mouse in your pocket?' Because we never blocked or tackled anyone. There wasn't any question, and there isn't now, about who we were for and I make no bones about it. I've done enough network stuff to know the difference in approach between doing a game – I've done Mizzou in the Cotton Bowl on network radio twice, and that was a challenge because I clearly had a dog in the hunt. But I just had to remember and I always told myself (same thing with Texas. I did Texas football and basketball for two years) I'm talking to people in Bangor, Maine or Portland, Oregon. They don't know who the players are necessarily. They're turning it on to hear the game. If I'm doing a Cowboy game, people are turning it on to hear the Cowboys. They're not turning it on to hear me. It's OK to be for the Cowboys. If you're doing a network game, it's really not OK to be for anything but a good game."

Fairness Doctrine

"I think one of the things I've learned that's certainly different than when I started is that you can say almost anything if it's fair, including critical. Be careful not to make it personal. But if you are fair and striving always for accuracy, my experience is most players and coaches will understand that, even when they don't like what they find out you said."

Brad Sham's Thoughts for Students

"The first thing I tell them is: Know what you want to do, and then have a completely open mind. I knew when I went to Missouri that I went there so that I would have a chance to become a baseball announcer. Not that I would learn how - that I would have a chance because I got the degree. When I got there, I fell in love with reporting, with journalism. That was a great lesson that I try to pass on to kids: Keep the open mind, because you're probably going to discover something that you didn't know existed that is going to ignite your pilot light, trigger your passion wire. That's the most important thing, is to find what you're passionate about. Then I found out once I got out into the world that you could combine journalism and sports and you didn't have to do it in a heavy-handed Howard Cosell-like way. That's informed the way I've always approached play-by-play. Accuracy and truth and fairness in storytelling are the hallmarks of basic journalism."

Marc Vandermeer

Houston Texans

He was in his twenties, selling commercials on radio and television in the Boston area after graduating from Boston University. Marc Vandermeer decided to purchase an hour of time on a small suburban Boston station to host one of the early weekend sportstalk shows at that time, "AM Sports." "It was my show. It was terrible. Maybe nobody listened to it, but I was on the air!" The station called him to do play-by-play of a high school football game on a Friday night. At halftime at that game, "I was hit by a lightning bolt and I said, 'This is what I'm gonna do. This is it. I'm gonna broadcast games. I'm gonna do whatever it takes to do it."

Miami Nice

It took an impulsive decision to purchase a ticket to Miami, Florida and sit in the offices of the decision makers for the University of Miami broadcasting job waiting for an interview that he had never called to request. He got the job. That led to the call, "The Hurricanes win the National Championship!" He did football and basketball there, as he did at Central Michigan University earlier in his career. His goal had been to be the voice of a team. "I always say if you go in the general direction of your dreams, eventually something's going to show up that's going to speak to you," said Vandermeer.

In 2002, Vandermeer was chosen to be the first voice of the expansion Houston Texans in a football-mad market. He has never missed calling a snap since they started. With one game a week, football broadcasters can be faced with circumstances that prevent them from working sometimes. Vandermeer has worked despite being ill, but he hasn't ever vacated the seat.

The Texans have offered him TV exposure on preseason games, but he's only interested in his radio job during football season.

He's worked NCAA basketball tournament games on Westwood One when football teams are in their offseason.

Difference between NFL and college broadcasting

"I think that when you look at pro football, a huge difference is NFL Films, and the fact that NFL Films uses the local radio call as the sound track for what they do. If you watch NFL Network or ESPN, you hear the local radio announcer making the calls. We're the sound track of the National Football League. It's not just what's going on during the game that day. It's recording history, and I think it adds to it.

"I did games for the University of Miami, one of the greatest teams ever, in 2001. When I see highlights of that team, it's usually without my calls. It's whoever was calling the game on television that day, because college football isn't the same. The NFL controls its highlights that way. Sometimes they mix up the home and road announcer a little bit. I'll never forget the game when Vince Young ran 39 yards in overtime to beat us for the Tennessee Titans. On ESPN Pump Up the Volume they used my call of that play. I don't lay down and go soft if the opponent does something against the Texans. I have anger in my voice, like. 'Oh, no.' I have passion in a bad way when something bad happens to us. I felt bad for the Titans' radio voice, Mike Keith, but I thought it was pretty interesting.

"I'm watching television with my kid and they played little snippets the other day and used my call and my kid said, 'Dad, that's you!' That's very cool to me. To me it's a big part of being in this league. You live on. Back in the day of every game not being on television in baseball, the local radio guy in a big market – that was a godlike position. People depended on you to bring them the game, and there's nothing better than that.

"I read about Ken Coleman, who did the Red Sox for a long time, and on his Wikipedia page it said he did the job for the Red Sox in '66 for $40,000 a year. That's huge money in 1966, but today young announcers would say, 'Huh, uh.'

"I just think it's an interesting industry that way. That's one thing I like about the NFL: NFL Films. It's once a week, it's such a big event. Every game is on TV. But I have the Nielsen ratings, and I can tell you this. On a typical noon start for us, we get about 250,000 listeners. Now, they're not listening to the whole game. But they're checking in. Maybe they ran into the store to get something, pick up their kid, maybe they are driving around. That doesn't include our digital listenership."

Roster Size Difference

"College is harder. I remember my first NFL game was a playoff game with the Raiders and Dolphins and I was an emergency fill-in and I got a call at 5 in the morning. I did that game and I just thought, 'Oh my gosh.' Not that it was easy, but that when you're dealing with a 46-man roster on game day and it's just so clean. It's such a clean game, compared to college. And what I mean by that is in college the hash marks are wider, with more players, sometimes with double numbers and clunky clock. The clock in college is laborious. It stops all the time and the game lasts forever. That's fine if you have a great game.

"In the NFL, that clock is merciless. It's grinding. It's like the sands coming through the hourglass. One really great thing about college is you have a lot more stories you can tell. I did I-AA football at UMass. We won the national championship in '98. Those levels – everybody you're talking about is a brand-new story to the listener. That's kind of fun.

"There's not much I can say about Andrew Luck that you haven't already heard. But the quarterback from Bowling Green might have an interesting story that you've never heard about. Two things as a broadcaster that you can't stand are: no chance to win and no chance to lose.

"High school is harder than anything. You're calling a game -sometimes you might have the PA speaker right outside your booth. Loud sounds right into your ear. The yard lines are not clearly marked all the time. You sit down, the game starts and you realize, 'The numbers on the rosters that they gave me are all wrong.' These poor guys trying to get good at their craft!

"Even in the NFL, I'll watch them warm up, and lo and behold the guy they just signed off the practice squad, I'll be like, 'I got to get to know that guy.' Then he'll do something in the game. And in college, the rosters are so big – they'll travel 65."

Boardless

"I do it a little differently. I don't use a board. I am not Mr. Board. I started using boards when I was doing high school games in Pennsylvania, and then I realized I was spending a long time on this board, and what's happening is when I'm stuck for a number I'm looking at the board but the numbers are in depth chart fashion. So, I'm, 'Who's number 42?' And I couldn't find 42. Well, I junked that, because it took a long time to make a good board. Give me the numerical roster, 42 is right after 41 and I don't have a problem finding him. And I'll write my notes on the side, next to the player."

Hit the Wall

"Well, I just paste the stats on the wall. If Will Fuller catches a touchdown and I don't have it in my head that it's his fourth of the year, I'll be like, 'Will Fuller with the touchdown'…then at the back end of the call you can find the stat and say it's his fourth of the year. The numerical roster to me is the almighty. I have that right in front of me.

"However, instead of spending my time on the board during the week, I spend my time memorizing the numbers of the opponent," says Vandermeer. "This makes my life so much easier and so much more enjoyable. When you're broadcasting and you know the names of everybody, it's so much more fun not to look down. I'm in this to have fun, so let me have fun. I don't use a spotter either.

"I used one earlier in my career, but then I realized they make mistakes and I thought I can make mistakes all by myself. If somebody else makes mistakes, my amount of forgiveness that I will have is very little. Let me put the onus on me. For the Texans, I have John Harris on the sideline and he's on cue in my ear, so he gives me a lot of stuff. Sometimes too much. I've got the producer also in my ear if he sees something I'm not seeing. If it's really big, like so-and-so's in a fight on the 20, he'll give it to me."

Nice to be Popular, but…

"I've done the NCAA Tournament, too, and I've done four games in a day numerous times. You cannot memorize all those players. You can

familiarize but not memorize them. You'll go crazy. Keep the rosters handy –
keep your eyes on the court and get through it."

Different Types of Prep

"People ask me about prep time. We do a lot of talk shows during the
week, and you're learning about the other team preparing for them. Radio – I
don't have a lot of time to tell stories. I have like five seconds, maybe ten
seconds to get something in. Andre Ware barely has time for anything. We
have sponsor reads. The whole thing moves very quickly. I will never
sacrifice the basic elements of ball location, time and score because those are
the things that the listener needs to hear. You've got to give that score every
minute and a half. You can't say it too much."

Not Too Ill to Work

"At UMass I had food poisoning, and that was a rough one. I had to get
up off the mat and do that one. I once had a migraine so bad that I told the
guys in the booth, 'Just leave the garbage can right here,' because I was about
to lose it. I didn't. I've always said death of a loved one, birth of a child I'll
miss a game, but fortunately that hasn't happened. I really want to do every
game and I'll do whatever it takes to do it. I love being the voice of the team.
I love living and dying with the results. I still think I haven't called my best
game yet."

> "I think the more you can do, the better it is. My whole career
> has been shaped by doing other things besides play-by-play. I'm
> vice president of broadcasting and digital media. Ten years prior
> to 2012 I was doing a drive time show on Sports Radio 610. At
> UMass, I sold advertising. I ran their radio network, At Central
> Michigan, same thing. Not everybody wants to sell advertising,
> but if you want to, you can do other things in this business
> besides play-by-play to increase your chances of getting gigs,
> moving up."
>
> Marc Vandermeer

Adam Young of New Mexico State is our tour guide for football.

Adam Young's Football Prep

"I think football is the hardest to prep for because you have so many
players. These college rosters are huge and of course you don't have to know
who the backup left guard is or the backup left tackle, but if they come in the
game you should have something written down. The process for football for

me typically starts on a Sunday. After doing a game Saturday I'll get some rest, then start Sunday for the next week's game. I'll start my spotting board and the only thing I'll do on the computer is the number, the name, the height, weight, school classification, hometown and home state. I'll hand write everything else. What I do when I hand write is start by putting in the stats. Obviously for an offensive lineman there aren't any stats, but for everybody else you can at least put in something, whether it be tackles, receiving yards, rushing yards, anything like that. Then I'll start to do trends."

What Trends?

"So for example, for a quarterback I'll write that he completed 72 per cent of his passes two games ago and then 74 per cent last week, which is a season best, no interceptions in two straight games, what he did against the team in their last matchup, his numbers in the previous two games. For a running back, maybe he's had three straight 100-yard rushing games. I'll write in what they did in the past. Maybe they're a junior college transfer or maybe they were first team All-State in high school, just things you may reference."

Experience Pays Off

"I think over the years I've prepared a lot smarter. I used to stuff a ton of information on spotting boards – football in particular – and I learned that you can only use so much of that information. In football on TV, your analyst is the star, so you're trying to get in and out as quickly as possible.

"Quick hitters are usually the best way to go about it. Different stories that you can bring up in the course of the game. I color code everything. So my spotting board looks a little jumbled when you look at it, and there's a lot of colors, but I know exactly where everything is. For green, the highlighted stuff in green, it's what they did last season. For example, the quarterback, at UTEP last year was his first career start and I put those numbers and highlighted that in green so I know where to find it right away. Everything I highlight in blue is some sort of a trend, maybe what they've done the previous couple of games. Everything in orange is a career number or if I highlight something in orange they lead the team in that category."

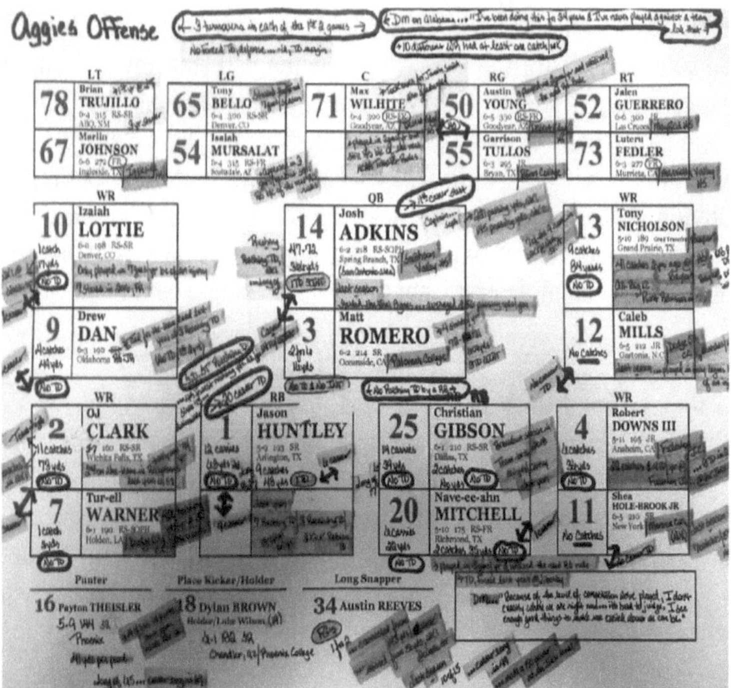

"For a wide receiver, I highlight in orange seven career touchdowns, so if he catches a touchdown pass I know it's his eighth because I have seven career written down," says Adam Young. "If, say, a wide receiver has 55 catches for 610 yards highlighted in orange, I know he leads the team in both categories. Everything in purple is past school or high school stuff. For example, there's an offensive lineman, I put Desert Edge High School and it's in purple so that's where he played last year.

"A wide receiver transferred in from Baylor, so all of his Baylor stats from last year are highlighted in purple. It looks a little crazy I think when you look at it, but it's easy for me to reference stuff right away because I know what every single color means. I've tweaked it over time, but over time I've developed a pretty good reputation as far as knowing what I'm doing every week to get prepared. And honestly, I'm one of those guys that tries to get my spotting board completely finished no later than Thursday for a Saturday game. I know a lot of guys will shoot for Friday or update their boards Saturday before the game starts. On Friday, I'll look over my board just to refresh my mind, but I'll go to practice if I can and do that kind of stuff."

Coach Approach?

"I'll watch film Friday, typically. I watch a lot of film. Obviously, nowadays you can tape pretty much every game or go to ESPN Plus and watch games of the team you're playing. I watch a lot of film, and then I can study the names and the numbers as well. Basically, for the skill players, I'll try to know before the game even starts who #9 is, Allen Ducey, and what he looks like the best I can. Obviously with that helmet guard it's pretty hard to see, but you can kinda tell by body type and where they're aligned on the offensive side of the ball, who they are, what they do and where they're gonna be. That was one of the biggest shocks for me when I started doing football on TV, how hard it can be to see.

"I'll have my binoculars out and I have a pretty good idea going into the game of who #9 is without looking at my spotting board and who the wide receivers are, so there are parts of the game when I don't really even have to use it."

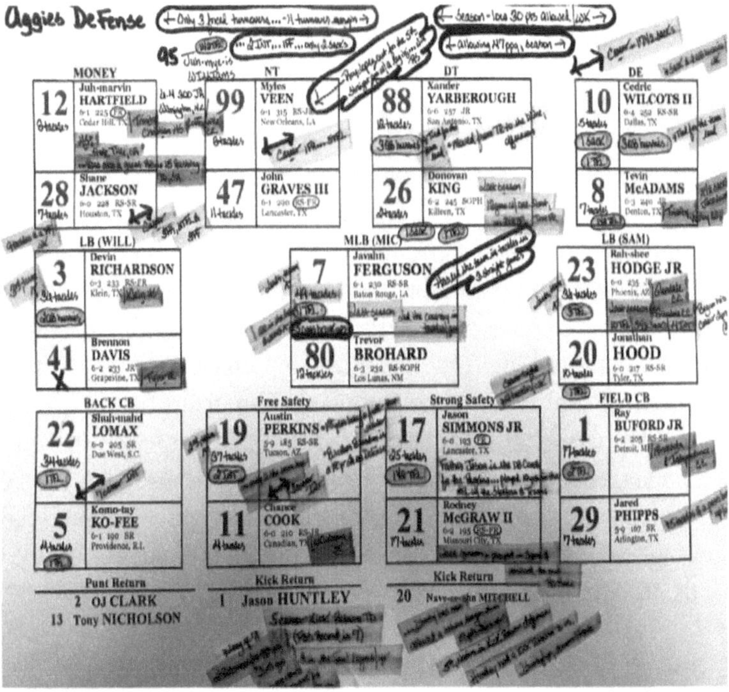

Young said his spotting board is not laminated in case a drink is spilled on it. "Funny you ask. I tape it down to some thick cardboard. I use card stock paper, so it's thick. But I do not laminate it. I use the same poster board every single week and I save all my boards. So, if I want to go back and look at a game a couple of weeks ago because I remember something I wrote down that week and I want to use it again or something like that, I save all my boards.

"So, I tape them down and I put one team's offense at the top and the other team's defense at the bottom. And the same thing on the other side. So, all I have to do is flip it over whenever the possession changes. The tricky part for some people is – where do you put the field goal kicker? Or the punter? Or the punt returner?

"Typically, I'll get a little screwed up sometimes during the course of the game where I'll look down and I'll have the wrong offense at the top and I didn't flip it over because there was a punt or a field goal kick or something like that. I pair up the offense, the punter and the kicker on the same sheet," explained Young. "Therefore, if a team's about to punt I don't have to flip it over. The opposing team's punt returners and kick returners are on the same side along with that team's defense. So, I don't have to flip it during the course of a kick or a punt. It just pairs up easier. And then of course, I need to remind myself to flip it over whenever the new team's on offense. It works really well. It's regular size paper. I've seen bigger boards, but to be honest with you I think if I had it any bigger I'd probably have some trouble with our broadcast location, because we have so many bodies up there already."

Conserve Space

"I only have so much space to use, with the television monitors and our spotter right next to me. And he has a computer out to tell the truck certain stuff. I don't think I have room for a bigger board. But I'm able to jam in all the information I need. And the most important thing is, I know where everything is. I'll also put some stuff at the top of the board. So right above where all the personnel is, both on offense and defense, I'll put in different trends for the team. For example, for the Aggie offense here I have written down, 'No interceptions for two straight games, three fumbles last week, season high 611 total yards last week, three plus turnovers in seven of the previous 10 games, season high 295 rushing yards last week, just stuff like that.

"And then for the opposing team's defense right below that I have written down 'Only 4 interceptions. Allowed 400 plus yards of total offense in 4 straight games. That's stuff I don't need to dig up in a packet or even look down to a different piece of paper. I have it written down on my spotting board because I have room for that above the offensive line and the defensive line.

"For stuff like that, just so I know where it's at and what it is, I'll actually take a sharpie and I'll circle it so it stands out for me. That's something I started a couple of years ago."

Tracking Offensive Drives

"I do keep a drive chart, but it's actually a scoring chart, more so for me. I do not keep a chart for every single drive during the course of the game. All I do is football on TV and I have a really, really good spotter/stats guy who gives me that. So I do rely on him to give me that. It's one of those things where I always thought it was wild whenever I'd hear an announcer go to commercial break right after a punt and say 'The punt was 35 yards, 6-yard return, we're back after this.' I thought, how the heck did he count that in his head as quick as he did? That's one of things I told my college stats partner a couple of years ago. I said, 'Hey, if you could, I really would like punt yardage, punt return yardage...those are two things I really want because when we go to commercial break, I'd really like to use that if possible if it's necessary. Typically, we'll go to commercial break after a punt. He will also give me scoring drives. He'll hand over a little note that says, '10 plays, 77 yards, 3-yard touchdown run by Smith.' I don't need the 3-yard touchdown run because I've already called it. But the play, yard and time of possession I probably will use and he's keeping track of that."

UTEP MINERS			NEW MEXICO STATE AGGIES		
Result	Updated Score	Plays/Yds/Time	Result	Updated Score	Plays/Yds/Time
First Quarter			First Quarter		
Second Quarter			Second Quarter		
Third Quarter			Third Quarter		
Fourth Quarter			Fourth Quarter		

COIN TOSS |

"I'm shocked at how high school football announcers or even college football announcers are able to keep track of everything during a game. So, I try to limit that. I'll use it because I'll typically get that from our college stats person but I utilize him for that. The other thing I utilize him for is…it's really hard…at least for me it is, because I'm trying to look at other stuff too, trying to look at the monitor, get my partner involved…there are big plays or even shorter plays and it's hard to calculate how many yards were picked up on a play. So if there's a pass downfield and it was a 21-yard pickup, the last thing I really want to do is look back and say, okay, they were at the 20 and now they're at the 41…okay, 21-yard pickup.

"Because by the time I do that math in my head, it might take a little while and I might not even have time to use it. If you want to be bang-bang, where the quarterback drops back, he throws it down the middle, Shell catches it, down to the 41, 21-yard pickup..first down for the Aggies…I want to be able to get my partner in there, especially if the offense is moving quickly, so he has time to say something."

Spotter Helps the Flow

"So if I want to get the yardage gained, I probably need a little help. So that's where our spotter comes into play as well. He spots and he also does college stats. So I made this board where it's cardboard…it's just like my spotting board…and I have it in the booth sitting right next to me. I have every number, 1 through 100, and right after the play's done, every single play, and I won't use this all the time, our spotter will point to a number for how many yards were picked up on the play. That takes a lot off the plate for me. Especially on a big play, if he can just point to the number 27, I can say, 'That's a 27-yard connection.' That's been really helpful for me."

What is Young's experience working with good and bad spotters? "I'll never forget this game. We had a game two years ago against Georgia Southern. Our spotter couldn't be there. So we had somebody fill in, and keep in mind too they also do some college stat work for the truck, so they have a headset on and they're communicating with the truck. I kinda knew going into it that this particular person probably wouldn't be able to handle both. It was the first or second play of the game and he looked at me and he said, 'I don't know.' So I kinda knew that I would be on my own. I probably didn't reference yardage as much and I was more focused on that probably than trying to get my partner involved and letting the game breathe.

"Stuff that normally I wouldn't have to focus on I was focusing on. It was a game-changer. I remember after that game I was like, 'I need Anthony!'

"TV is a collaborative effort. There are so many pieces that go into it. There are so many people that play such a big role. If you take out somebody behind the scenes that can really help you, it can hurt. Georgia Southern was a team as well that ran the triple option. So my main focus was the football and…are they gonna pitch it? Run it on a dive? Or they might throw once or twice in a half, but if they do throw, you'd better be ready for it. It was one of those offenses that was tough to pinpoint where the football is. On top of that, you're trying to calculate yardage and identify players and all that kind of stuff."

Coordinating What the Spotter Does

"A lot of announcers will use their spotter to identify who made the tackle or maybe somebody new came into the game, or who's the running back now or just anything like that. They want people identified. I want yardage identified. Because I can see the personnel. I use my binoculars probably the entire game for the most part.

"I find it easier for me to identify personnel and who made the tackle. I typically don't miss who's coming into the game because I'll pay attention to the sidelines and that kind of stuff. So the biggest thing for me is I don't want to have to calculate yardage all the time."

Does the analyst speak right after you give the tackler? "That's the plan. I think it's a little harder to do in football if they have a hurry-up offense. A lot of these schools are now going to a hurry-up offense, where they're trying to rush up to the line and snap the ball as quick as possible. That can make it really tough on the analyst.

"Sometimes in football you only get a couple of big plays in a game. I think that's a little more important than basketball. In basketball, I always tell the analyst 'If somebody goes up and dunks it I don't need to describe the dunk. If you're making a point, feel free to keep on going. That's fine with me.' There'll probably be another dunk in a couple of minutes. In football, in a 10-7 game there would only be a couple of touchdowns in the course of a game. You want to be on top of it. I think it's a lot of body language too. When are you gonna talk, when am I gonna talk, that kind of stuff. I've worked with the same partner the last couple of years. We've developed a pretty good relationship in that regard, where I know when he's kind of winding down. He knows when I'm winding down. We'll look at each other and just a nudge here and sometimes I'll just poke him and he knows 'You got this,' that kind of thing. I think there are also a lot of replays in football and of course you want your analyst to take those and you try to set them up fast to take those.

"The biggest reason I want that yardage so quick and certain things so quick is to get out the way. Information that's big for the viewer is the yardage on the play or that's the longest play from scrimmage all year for the running back, Jason Hundley. That sort of thing. So, if you can give that quickly, and you can relay that information to the viewer, you can get the heck out of the way. By then, the TV truck should have a replay and he can talk about how that play developed and what they were trying to accomplish."

Handling Game Day Emotions

"You try to treat it like any other sport, but in reality in my case I only get a handful of these a year, because I do home games only for TV. I think it's really hard to and here's the thing too – with football, you spend w-a-a-ay more time getting information ready.

"You need to know what kind of information is the most useful for this particular game. What does the viewer need to know? What does the viewer not need to know? You try to control your emotions the best way possible. Here's the thing with football. With baseball, if you're doing game 50 of the season or doing minor league baseball and you're on the back end of a road trip you might need to be digging deep for energy and that kind of stuff.

"I guarantee you for any football game I've ever done, I've not had to dig deep for energy. I've maybe had to pull back more than anything to make sure that I'm not over the top early when it's 0-0 five minutes into the game. You need to save some of that for the end of the game and not be too high early."

Time Flies on Game Week

"I get this question all the time from people: How many hours does it take you to get ready for a football game? My answer is always, 'I don't know. I don't count them. I just keep on going until I feel I'm fully ready for the game. I prepare until I walk into the stadium. I don't have any questions about how ready I am to do this particular game and I'm ready for anything that comes about.

"Football is a game on Saturday, but once you do Monday, Tuesday, Wednesday, Thursday, Friday leading up to that, Saturday is the most important. Because once that mic goes on Saturday night, you'd better be ready. That's the sport where you can really get exposed. There's so much going on. I remember my first football game and I thought, 'Man, this is so overwhelming!' You're worn out after a football game. Because they take 3 ½, 4 hours including commercial breaks and all that stuff. And by the time it's done, with all the information you processed during the week, you're ready to crash when that particular game is over."

A portion of Nate Gatter's Football Board:

WESTERN KENTUCKY HILLTOPPERS DEFENSE (1-2, 1-0 C-USA)

DB

No.	Player
2	Devon KEY — Lexington, Ky
7	Trae MEADOWS — Greensboro, NC
15	Ta'Corian DARDEN — Russellville, Ky
17	Canon JACKSON — L'Ville, Ky
21	Clayton BUSH — Bowling Green, Ky
24	Roger CRAY — Lake City, Fla
26	Dion RUFFIN — Kenner, La
27	Omari ALEXANDER — L'Ville, Ky
29	Beanie BISHOP — L'Ville, Ky
31	Antwon KINCADE — Valdosta, Ga

LB

No.	Player
9	Malik STAPLES — Swainsboro, Ga
11	John HUNTER — Atlanta, Ga
25	Bryson WASHINGTON — L'Ville, Ky
28	Demetrius CAIN — Princeton, Ky
30	Clay DAVIS — L'Ville, Ky
36	Kyle BAILEY — Carrollton, Ga
52	Damon LOWE — L'Ville, Ky

DL

No.	Player
10	DeAngelo MALONE — Atlanta, Ga
34	JuWuan JONES — Sugar Hill, Ga
43	Carson JORDAN — Poplarville, Miss
50	Ricky BARBER — L'Ville, Ky
53	Jeremy DARVIN — Nashville, Tenn
58	DeMon QUINCY — Frankfort, Ky
90	"Jaylin" GEORGE — Atlanta, Ga
99	John MADDEN — [illegible], Ala

PR

No.	Player
21	Clayton BUSH — [illegible] returns for [illegible] yards … L/O

KO

No.	Player
46	Cory MUNSON — Warner Robins, Ga; Seven touchbacks on 12 kickoffs TY

Head Coach: **Tyson Helton** (1st year — 1-2 @ WKU, .333), 42 years old

Defensive Coordinator/CBs: **Clayton White** (3rd season)

UAB BLAZERS DEFENSE (3-0, 0-0 C-USA)

DB

#	Player		#	Player		#	Player		#	Player		#	Player
3	CD DANIELS — B-HAM, Ala. (Homewood)		4	Starling THOMAS V — B-HAM, Ala. (Ramsay)		12	Grayson CASH — Trussville, Ala.		17	Will BOLER — Opelika, Ala.		18	TD MARSHALL — B-HAM, Ala.
20	Devodric BYNUM — Dallas, Texas		21	Will DAWKINS — Vero Beach, Fla.		27	Damien MILLER — Fairfield, Ala.		28	Jaylon KEY — Tallahassee, Fla.		33	Keondre SWOOPES — Hartselle, Ala.

LB/STAR

#	Player		#	Player		#	Player		#	Player
6	Kris "MOLE" — Miami, Fla.		9	A.J. BROOKS — Modesto, Calif.		14	"DIE-thea" TURNER — Florence, Ala.		24	Deshaun OLIVER JR. — B-HAM, Ala. (Ramsay)
31	Kyle HARRELL — Calera, Ala.		32	Luke "BRAY-zhur" — Pell City, Ala.		36	Kobe GRIFFIN — Troy, Ala.		50	Noah WILDER — Beaumont, Ala.

DL/EDGE

#	Player		#	Player		#	Player		#	Player		#	Player
1	Garrett MARINO — Mission Viejo, Calif.		5	Thomas JOHNSTON — Spanish Fort, Ala.		22	Jordan SMITH — LaGrange, Ga.		37	Mike EASON JR. — Beaumont, Ala.		44	Antonio MOULTRIE — Pensacola, Fla.
52	Fitzgerald MOFOR — Brooksville, Md.		90	Tony FAIR — South Bend, Ind.		93	Michael FAIRBANKS II — Powder Springs, Ga.		98	Juante'vius JOHNSON — Lincoln, Ala.		99	Fish McWILLIAMS — Pensacola, Fla.

PR

3	Myron MITCHELL
4	Starling THOMAS V

KO

19	Nick VOGEL — Jacksonville, Fla.

Head Coach: Bill Clark (4th season — 28-14 @ UAB, .667), 51 years old

Defensive Coordinator/LBs: David Reeves (4th year, 3rd as DC)

Here are some football phrases Adam Young uses for variety:

Football Play-by-Play Phrases
LESS IS MORE ON TV / STAY PATIENT

QB Throwing: Fires, 'Rogers throwing on first down', quick slant, quick screen, screen pass, WR screen (screen to a RB as well), going for the home run, swings it out, swing pass, flushed out of the pocket, underneath, across the middle, completes it, incomplete, accurate/inaccurate throw, rifles, tosses, puts it in the air, rocket, lofted, quick strike, in the flat, across the slant, slant, deep ball, lob, dumps it off, fade, deliver, rolls out, steps up, rolls and fires, unloads, airmails, over-shoots

Receiver Catch: Brings it in, hauls it in, snags, snares, receives, makes the catch, makes the grab, reels it in, hookup, catch and run

Running Back handoffs: 'Jones' on the carry, 'Jones' gets the handoff, Inside handoff, the give, pitch, toss, shuffle toss, sticks it into his belly, <'Rose is the lone set back' / 'Rose in the backfield' / Rose is the Tailback'>

Running Back runs: Bolt, cruise, cut back, dart, gallop, gun, hightail, race, rumble, sail, scamper, scoot, speed, sprint, stampede, stumble, zip, zoom, veers, cuts, angles, plunges ahead, cuts back

Tackle terminology: wrapped up, tackle, big hit, sticks him, trips him up, on the stop, makes the play, 'Rose taken down', back side pressure

Defense: Pressure coming, back side pressure, 4 man rush

Kickoffs: Through the endzone for a touchback (start at the 25-yard line/Punt touchbacks start at 20-yard line), angles the punt, 'Hogan back deep', brings it out, 'Hogan brings it out 3/5/7 yards deep, bobbled, muffed, mishandled, downs it at the 7 yard line, 'Jones pins them deep', BALL CAN'T BREAK THE PLANE ON PUNTS/body can, out of the back of the endzone

Other terms/phrases: Trips to the left/Morgan at the top of your screen (bottom of your screen...key players), On tackles it is OK to say the tacklers number, Less is more, back shoulder throw, fade route, toward the pylon, stay patient, AFTER TD...long pause, let crowd reaction take over, Keep it simple (Richards wide open..down to the 1), 1st and goal (Redzone inside 20), OPTION (QB keeps it/here's the option pitch, 'Pistol Back is Rose', 'Rose is the lone set-back'

CHAPTER 16

BASKETBALL PLAY-BY-PLAY

Bill Schoening

Voice of the San Antonio Spurs 2001-present

The young man growing up in Southwest Philadelphia could not have visualized having four World Championship rings some day. Bill Schoening's dad was a bartender and his mother was not employed. When it was time for college, Bill "pretty much had to go where the scholarship money was." For him, that was Temple University in Philadelphia.

"But growing up in the city, you had to take a trolley car to the Broad Street subway and it was an hour commute. When I got there, there were 300 freshmen in my major. I was really anxious to get on the air and write for the newspaper. I wanted to get involved. There were just so many kids who wanted to do that, if you were a freshman you were low man on the totem pole.

"I was told by a few of the upperclassmen that I wasn't going to get a chance to get on the air until I was a junior or senior. I wasn't gonna get a chance to write for the newspaper until I was a junior."

Adjusting to Reality

"So, I really became disheartened at that point, plus I had this long commute and it was in the middle of a tough neighborhood, so staying late after school you were kind of taking your life in your hands when you got the subway. I was not happy there. This small broadcasting school had been recruiting me. They said, 'Hey, look, we'll get you a job, you'll start in a small market somewhere, but if you come, we'll train you.' And it was really an intense six months.

"It was mostly learning board op stuff, writing, sportscasting, newscasting, lighting spots – all the tools that you'll need – running a board – the tools that you'll need in small market radio. And I learned a lot. I never would have learned that stuff at Temple. And I got a job right away. I took a job in Pana, Illinois and it was a news job. They promised me they would get some occasional high school basketball play-by-play there. I was only 20 years old. I thought if there was a chance I could do a little play-by-play there, I would go. My lovely wife, who was my girlfriend at the time, said, 'OK, I'll go out there with you.' She joined me a few months later. That's how I started.

"There was a junior college close by and I was able to do some of their games in basketball…not for any money, just because I was part of a class… but I figured that would look good on the resume."

Kids Have Their Idols

The experience of doing news reporting in the early stages of his career made Bill Schoening a better play-by-play broadcaster. He had developed an early love for sportscasting by listening to Philadelphia Phillies' broadcasters Byrum Saam and Bill Campbell. "By Saam – the odd thing about all this is that By Saam is from Ft. Worth and grew up in Texas and spent 95 percent of his career in Philadelphia, and I grew up in Philadelphia and spent 95 per cent of my career in Texas," said Schoening. "He was very melodic in his play-by-play. He was just wonderful on the radio. He did the Philadelphia A's. He just goes back a long, long way. He worked the old Southwest Conference Radio Network. He was a student at TCU. But when I was a kid growing up in Philly I remember listening to the radio and I just always loved his play-by-play. It was almost like he was singing his play-by-play."

Schoening was still years away from the By Saam phase of his life. He jumped from Pana, Illinois to Lamesa, Texas because of an opportunity to do play-by-play of football, baseball and basketball. But that was only part of his job. "And of course, in small market radio you have to do a lot of stuff, not just sports. I was doing news, I was spinning records, I was producing commercials, turning the station on in the morning. It was a lot of work, but I didn't look at it that way. I thought, 'Hey, man, I'm paying my dues, I'm going to get better.'

"The good news about that station was that for three years I did everything: football, basketball, baseball nonstop basically, even in the summertime. They would do Babe Ruth League. There was a cotton gin that sponsored a Little Dribblers League. I kid you not, I was doing play-by-play of these little 8- and 10-year-old snot-nosed kids running around. Trying to describe their games was fun because there were more turnovers than points! But it was a challenge and I was getting ten bucks a game! I loved that."

Anchored in Texas

Schoening was in Texas to stay, but he moved to Huntsville for his next advancement. He was not attending Sam Houston State there, but he was working for a radio station in Huntsville. Schoening was still involved in news reporting. Although his mission was still to advance in play-by-play, he saw the news coverage as a chance to add to his skills. "I sent a tape before the position was actually open. The guy was looking for somebody who could do news as well. I had been doing news. So, he hired me at the age of 24. That was my first college play-by-play job.

"The news training is great for the job because it makes you write well. I think that because you have to go out and gather and work your b*** off to get the information, then you have to come back to the station and write it – I was writing a lot. I think it really helps your writing skills and communication skills overall. While I was in Huntsville, I covered the prison system.

"During the '80s, that was when they had the uptick in executions. I covered 29 executions for the Associated Press and the local station. And there was overcrowding, there was prison violence, there was a lot of stuff going on in prisons in Texas in the '80s. I was kind of right in the middle of all that. It really was good experience for me. I would definitely recommend that. If you have to start and do some different stuff, covering news *really* helped me in my play-by-play and my sports coverage, mainly because I had to write so much."

Somebody Was Listening

Schoening was doing a basketball game in Huntsville one Saturday when assistant athletic director Allen Jones of Texas A&M was driving through the area on his way to Houston and flipping the radio dials. Jones liked what he heard.

He contacted Schoening a few days later and asked if he could do baseball. Schoening's answer was a quick yes. Jones hired him after an interview to replace a broadcaster who had just left A&M.

While at A&M Schoening met Tom Dore, the sports director of KLBJ in Austin. Dore left Austin to take another job two weeks after Schoening beat out 65 applicants to join him. Schoening moved into the analyst role as well for the University of Texas Longhorns basketball games. After two years, he moved up to play-by-play.

"It was the 'Runnin' Horns' then," recalled Schoening. "Under Tom Penders, they were averaging 95 points per game! They hired me and then Craig Way became my analyst in '92." Now the way was clear for Schoening to thrive doing basketball play-by-play. He had a nine-year run with the Longhorns until he was lured away by the San Antonio Spurs.

He did not apply for the job – they contacted him. They loved Schoening's energy. "Growing up and having quite a bit of passion for sports…you know how passionate the sports fans of Philadelphia are. That was my dream from the time I was ten years old, was to do games on the radio."

No Need for Five-Hour Energy

"And I think early in my career when I had to do all the other stuff just to do my Friday night football game or my Saturday afternoon basketball game, whatever it was, I think that's where that energy came from. I thought, 'This is what I *really* want to do! I don't want to necessarily anchor news five days a week or cover a school board meeting or a city council meeting or watch a guy die in the execution chamber. I want to be here describing a football, basketball or baseball game. Therefore, all my energy went into that. I just really decided this is what I want to do. So, I tried to put as much work into doing a good job of that….and it was really easy for me to be enthusiastic and to be energetic, because this was my passion."

Solo Show

The Voice of the Spurs since 2001, Schoening is one of about eight NBA broadcasters who work without an analyst. Not only does he maintain his energy throughout an 82-game season working solo, he anchors a 40-minute pregame show as well! "I remember in '77 I was a senior in high school when the Sixers lost to Bill Walton and the Portland Trail Blazers in the NBA Finals.

"I turned down Brent Musburger and turned the radio up. I wanted to hear that local energy that the radio, which to me…basketball…you always get that descriptive account of the game that you might not get on television because the picture tells the story.

"But on radio you have to have that audio account. That's where I think Bill Campbell was probably my favorite basketball play-by-play guy growing up. I didn't listen to Chick Hearn. Years later I got to know about Chick Hearn. He's probably in my opinion the best radio play-by-play guy for basketball ever. He had all the catch phrases that caught on. 'Air ball.' 'Dunk.' Things that are part of the regular jargon now Chick Hearn kind of invented. Chick never missed a game. He went from 1965 to 2001 without missing a game. It was, I think 3,388 games without missing a game. I haven't missed a game. I pride myself on that."

Present and Accounted For

"My first year with the Spurs, I was still doing Longhorn football. So, I missed a couple of games because we had conflicts. But my second year I was Spurs only. That was the rookie year for Manu Ginobili. He played 16 years for the Spurs and I never missed one of his games.

"When he goes into the Hall of Fame I told him I want to be there because I was there for every single game he played. He said, 'You'll be there. No problem.'"

Description

"I don't necessarily describe every pass. The main thing for me is, once the ball's in the front court and, in a half court set anyway, to just kind of set up the offense is to try to let people know where the defenders are, if they're in a man to man or a zone, literally try to let the listener know, paint the picture of what's going on on the court."

energy

"I think the energy is important because....I heard Ron Franklin talk one time in 1985. I was at Sam Houston State and I went to an AP convention and he was one of the guest speakers. He said, 'Remember – the game you're doing is the most important game you ever do.' And it always stayed with me because, OK, we'll get to the next game eventually, but the game I'm doing right now – there's someone listening who really cares about this game. So, if I have a slight headache or I'm not feeling 100 percent that day, I've got to put that out of my mind and just really work on this game. And Ron said, 'No matter if you're doing a high school game, or junior college game or a pro game, this is a very important game. Don't think about the next job. Think about doing a great job right now. That next job will come. Don't be too anxious to take that next step. Make sure you concentrate on what you're doing right now.' I've always tried to do that. If I was doing Sam Houston State against Texas-Arlington, I poured everything into that because that's what I was doing at the time."

Bill Schoening

Basketball Vocabulary

"If you do 82 basketball games a year, if you just say someone hits a shot or the shot is good, that would be kind of boring to me.

"When we started bringing in foreign guys, I wanted to have a little fun. For instance, when Manu Ginobili hit a three, and I didn't even plan on saying this, he hit a three-pointer in his first preseason game and I thought, what's the Spanish word for three? *Tres.*

"So, I said, 'That's a Manu tres,' never dreaming he would become the all-time three-point shooter in Spurs' history and have the franchise record for three-pointers made. In fact, a guy came up to me late in Manu's career and said, 'Man, I wish I had a dollar for every time you said, 'That's a Manu tres.' Earlier in the day I looked up how many threes Manu had and I said, 'Well, you'd have 15-hundred dollars, because he's hit 15-hundred threes.' I try to have fun with the international guys and make it a little different. Patty Mills is from Australia. When he hits a three, I say, 'G'Day, Mate.' The listeners know what my little catch phrases are, but I'm saying that so I'm not saying, 'Shot is good,' or whatever. I just want to change it up a little bit. I try to make it a fun broadcast without going overboard."

Tools of the Trade

"I have a basic lineup sheet with all the pertinent information as far as stats are concerned. Points per game, rebounds, assists, all of that. And then on my far-right column I have all of the pertinent information about the players. I have where he went to college, what year he is in the league, as part of…6'6", 205, third year out of Argentina, whatever. But on the right-hand side I have information about his career.

"He played two years at UCLA or he led the league in assists or he was the Pac 10 Player of the Year – whatever information, his bio information, I should say. I have that in my far-right hand column. I use that when the guy goes to the free throw line if there is a break in the action.

'This guy was the 13th pick in the first round out of UNLV and whatever team he played for before he joined the Rockets,' whatever that information is."

Playoff Games

"I don't take things for granted and want to make sure that I appreciate what I have. But there's no question when you get into the playoffs, everything gets amped
up a little bit. You get a little bit more juice, a little bit more excitement, a little bit more energy.

"Now the stakes are higher. But I always look forward to the chance to call a playoff game. Never dreamed that I'd have four NBA Championship rings.

"When you go through a championship season, it makes you hungry for more. You get a little greedy. I'm spoiled, because the Spurs have the best record in the NBA during my now 19 seasons in the league. It's something that you always appreciate when you have a good team to cover. Also, I've had a lot of good guys to cover, too.

"Greg Popovich is the type of guy that when he brings the players in, he makes sure that they're gonna fit in, they're gonna be good guys in the community."

"San Antonio is a one-sport town as far as major professional sports are concerned, so the players really play a big part in the community there. So, he wants guys who are part of the community. I think that's important for him, to make sure he has quality people in the program. That makes it even better for us, because these guys are very cooperative with us, giving us what we need. During the course of a long season, you want to make sure you're with people who are easy to get along with."

Bill Schoening is a four-time winner of the Associated Press Top Texas play-b-play award. He was voted the 2014 Texas Sportscaster of the Year by the National Sportscasters and Sportswriters Association (now National Sports Media Association).

New Mexico State basketball voice Adam Young serves as our tour guide for the basics of play-by-play.

Adam Young's basketball charts

"For basketball, a guy by the name of Barry McKnight who is the Voice of Troy and has been there for a long, long time made basketball and football spotting charts and they were published some years back. He gave me his spotting charts. I tweaked it for basketball and for football. The basketball one is pretty basic. I do it numerically. You can only fit 12 people on there, so it's kind of a smaller spotting board. I will hand write everything except the name, the number, the hometown and the height and weight. I'll personally write in everything else. It's one of those things where I feel that I remember it better by handwriting it in. I have a specific spot where I put in free throw percentage, field goal percentage, three-point percentage. And below that I have a couple of lines for information. I'll put in maybe what they did last season. Are they a two-time All-American? Maybe they were a Top 100 player in high school. So, I have that spotting board with one team on the left side and one team on the right side. It's something I print off on card stock as well, so it's not flimsy and it's pretty hard and it doesn't get beat up too much and I can hold onto it during the game."

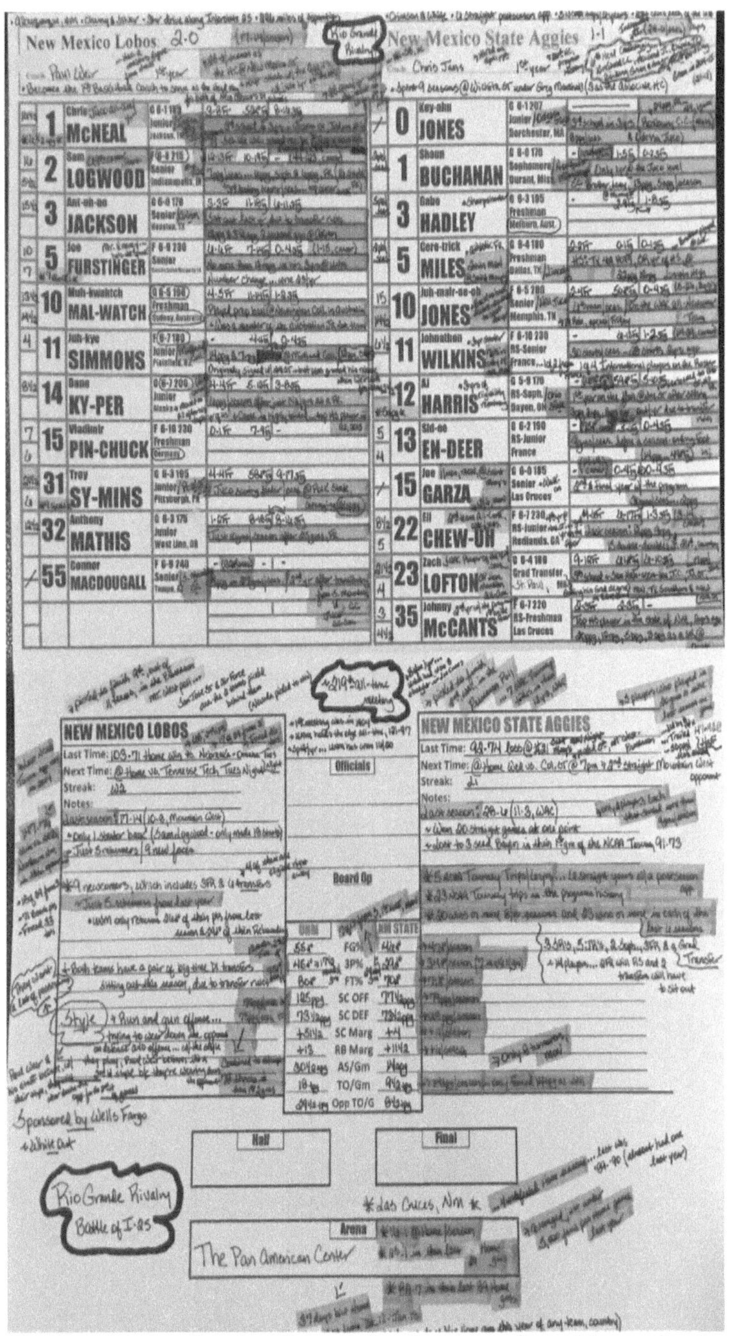

"I tape down what I call an info sheet on the table at the broadcast location. Basically, the info sheet, which I also hand write, has what they did last game, who they play next game, their streaks (have they won three of four, have they won six in a row, that kind of stuff). I have a bunch of room for more notes – I'll write in what they did last season, where they were picked in the preseason as far as their conference, and just anything else. Maybe they're 15th in the mid-major Top 25 poll. Maybe they have 7 international players on their roster, whatever is pertinent information. I have these two sections side by side of team stats. It's field goal percentage, three-point percentage, free throw percentage, points per game, points per game allowed, rebounding margin, turnover margin…all those kinds of statistics.

"Then right above that, I have room to put who the three officials are. I have room for a board op if I'm doing the game on radio. I have room for the TV production personnel. So, I'll write in who our director is, our producer, so I can mention it during the game. Above that I have a little section for series history. And at the bottom I have arena information: the venue, the city, capacity, maybe the team has won 23 straight home games, whatever relevant information. On top of that I'll write in 10-12 story lines on an index card that I would like to hit on during the course of the game. And sometimes I'll cross them off. If I've touched on them, sometimes I'll cross them off during a commercial break. I'll write down the main story lines for each team on an index card. I'll tape it to my TV box or the TV monitor. I do the same process for volleyball."

Working with Different Analysts

"I've been fortunate here. On all the games I do on TV I've had pretty much the same analyst for each sport, but obviously from sport to sport I'm working with different people. I feel for the ones who are doing this at a network level, where they fly into a city and they meet the analyst for the first time and they go on the air and do a game with them for two hours, because it's really hard. You have to develop a rapport, a relationship with them so they can trust you, you trust them. A lot of times it's body language so they know when to talk, you know when to talk, that kind of stuff. Then you have analysts who don't really have a lot of experience.

"You're trying to set them up, listen in your ear to your producer, who's getting directions from the director, that kind of stuff. I think especially on television, trying to make sure your partner is comfortable and knows when they can talk and maybe when it's not a good time to talk....especially on radio. When I do a game on radio, I think that's the biggest thing for a radio analyst. They don't know when to talk. I always tell my basketball radio analyst, especially if it's somebody new, 'Whenever I finish the call, I'll get out of the way. Basically, you have until the ball has crossed midcourt to get your point across. Once the ball is across midcourt, anything can happen.'"

Tracy McGrady, NBA

"My career was sputtering until I did a 360 and got headed in the right direction."

Pat Williams, Orlando Magic GM

"We can't win at home. We can't win on the road. As a general manager, I can't figure out where else to play."

Bob Varsha, Formula One Driver

"The drivers have one foot on the brake, one on the clutch and one on the throttle."

On the next two pages are Nate Gatter's basketball sheets.

WESTERN KENTUCKY HILLTOPPERS (0-0, 0-0 C-USA)

2 — Jared SAVAGE — Bowling Green, Ky. — 6-5 205 R-SR (TR)
Sat. vs. Kentucky State: ST, 30 min.* - 9 pts, 14 reb*
(2-9 / 1-4 / 4-4)

12.2 PPG	4.8 RPG	1.2 APG	36.4% FG	36% 3P	81.8% FT

2nd-year Hilltopper who transferred from Austin Peay ... started all 34 games LY (35.7 mins. per game, 5th C-USA) ... accounted for more than 40 percent of Western's made 3s ... career-high 25 points last November against Valparaiso

Starred at Warren Central HS, only a mile from Diddle Arena ... went to the 2016 NCAA Tournament with Austin Peay ... scored 24 points in the 8th-seeded Governors' OVC championship game victory over UT-Martin, lost to Kansas in first round

3 — Jordan RAWLS — Chattanooga, Tenn. — 6-1 165 FR
Sat. vs. Kentucky State: OB, 17 min. - 6 pts, 1 reb, 3 ast
(4-12 / 0-2 / 0-2)

— PPG	— RPG	— APG	— FG	— 3P	— FT

Averaged 23 points and seven assists per game last season for Hamilton Heights Christian Academy in Chattanooga, Tennessee ... ranked as No. 80 player in the Class of 2020 before he reclassified and officially joined the Hilltoppers in July

Power 5 offers from Kansas State, Ole Miss, and Georgia Tech ... how much pressure could be on him if Kenny Cooper is not granted a waiver? ... Father, Keith, was a standout for Austin Peay in the late 80s when Rick Stansbury was on the Govs' staff

4 — Josh ANDERSON — Baton Rouge, La. — 6-6 195 JR
Sat. vs. Kentucky St.: OB, 19 min. - 14 pts, 4 reb, 1 ast
(6-8 / 0-1 / 2-2)

12.1 PPG	4.1 RPG	1.7 APG	47.2% FG	28.8% 3P	71% FT

Second full season with Western Kentucky; missed first two months of freshman year before he was declared eligible by the NCAA ... one of four Hilltoppers who averaged 12+ points LY, all of whom return this season ... started 28/34 ... 6th man LY?

Broke his nose @ So. Miss on Jan. 24, averaged 17 PPG in ensuing five games with a mask on ... appeared on SC's Top 10 for 3 diff. dunks LY alone ... Career-high 25 points vs. Marshall on Jan. 21 ... consensus top-60 recruit out of Madison Prep Academy

5 — Camron JUSTICE — Hindman, Ky. — 6-3 185 GR TR
Sat. vs. Kentucky State: ST, 28 min. - 11 pts, 9 reb, 3 ast
(4-11 / 2-7 / 1-2)

18.6 PPG	3.2 RPG	2.9 APG	— FG	35.2% 3P	85.4% FT

Grad transfer from IUPUI joined WKU this summer, immediately eligible ... 2nd Team All-Horizon League choice last season, scored in dbl-figures in all but 3 games ... WKU is his third collegiate stop ... began career with a season and a half @ Vanderbilt

Kentucky Mr. Basketball in 2015 out of Knott County Central HS, where he scored 3,588 career points ... the third-highest total in state history

10 — Jeremiah GAMBRELL — Houston, Texas — 6-2 180 R-FR
Sat. vs. Kentucky State: OB, 12 min. - 2 pts, 1 reb
(0-6 / 0-0 / 2-2)

0.8 PPG	0.3 RPG	0.3 APG	1-6 FG	1-6 3P	0-0 FT

Appeared in only four games as a freshman last season because of multiple stress fractures in his leg

Three-star recruit out of Madison HS, where he averaged 23 PPG as a senior

11 — Taveion HOLLINGSWORTH — Lexington, Ky. — 6-2 165 JR
Sat. vs. Kentucky State: ST, 29 min. - 8 pts, 8 reb, 3 ast
(3-7 / 0-1 / 3-6)

14.4 PPG	4.4 RPG	2.2 APG	41.8% FG	31.8% 3P	77.1% FT

Started all 72 games over his first 2 seasons on the Hill and averaged nearly 37 minutes per game LY, the 3rd-highest total in Conf. USA ... 996 CAREER POINTS ... added a point per game LY, but FG + 3 PT % dropped -6 pts ... 3rd Team All-Conf. USA LY

2,563 car. mins., most by a Hilltopper over his first 2 seasons ... Will become only the 3rd Hilltopper ever to reach 1,000 car. pts in 1st game of 3rd season ... most recent? Courtney Lee, 2006 - joint leading scorer in WKU history ... 30th member of 1K pt club

12 — Jackson HARLAN — Albany, Ky. — 6-3 190 FR
Sat. vs. Kentucky State: OB, 3 min. - 0 pts, 1 reb
(0-0 / 0-0 / 0-0)

— PPG	— RPG	— APG	— FG	— 3P	— FT

24 PPG as a senior @ Clinton County HS last season earned him a First Team All-State nod

14 — Matt HORTON — Tuscaloosa, Ala. — 6-11 230 SR (JUCO)
Sat. vs. Kentucky State: DNP

1.1 PPG	1.0 RPG	0.0 APG	3-3 FG	0-0 3PT	5-12 FT

Appeared in 10 games off the bench LY, missed time in December with a bone bruise in his right leg ... came to WKU after two seasons @ Shelton State CC in his hometown of Tuscaloosa, where he went to Paul Bryant HS

15 — Patrick MURPHY — Franklin, Tenn. — 6-5 180 R-JR
Sat. vs. Kentucky State: OB, 2 min. - 0 pts, 0 reb, 0 ast
(0-1 / 0-1 / 0-0)

— PPG	— RPG	— APG	— FG	— 3P	— FT

Sat out LY after transferring from NAIA Martin Methodist College (Tennessee Tech's next opponent), where he spent his first two seasons ... Father, Scott, played @ Austin Peay when Rick Stansbury was an assistant ... Bro, Grayson, is a FR guard @ Belmont

22 — Carson WILLIAMS — Owenton, Ky. — 6-5 230 R-JR
Sat. vs. Kentucky State: ST, 26 min. - 18 pts*, 10 reb
(8-12 / 0-1 / 2-2)

— PPG	— RPG	— APG	— FG	— 3PT	— FT

2nd season with the program, 1st on the court for the transfer from Northern Kentucky ... started 61 games over two seasons with the Norse — averaged 12 points and nearly 6 rebounds per game as a sophomore two years ago for a 22-win club (HL RS champs)

Kentucky Mr. Basketball in 2016 (the year after fellow transfer Camron Justice won it) ... Jared Savage on Williams' exhibition performance: "I go against him every day in practice, and he bullies me all the time. It's nice to see him kick somebody else's butt."

23 — Charles BASSEY — Lagos, Nigeria — 6-11 230 SO
Sat. vs. Kentucky St.: ST, 26 min. - 16 pts, 19 reb, 4 blk
4 fouls in 26 mins.   (6-13 / 0-3 / 4-5)

14.6 PPG*	10 RPG*	0.7 APG	62.7% FG	9-20 3P	76.9% FT

Freshman All-American and First Team All-CUSA LY ... also C-USA Freshman of the Year and Def. POTY ... 2nd player in league history to win both in same season ... as good or better than season stats in matchups against top opponents/big men

Second freshman nationally since 1992 to average at least 14 points, 10 rebounds, and 2 blocks while shooting 60 percent from the floor — the other? Anthony Davis ... Keep in mind, he graduated HS a year early — Bassey just turned 19 y/o last week

50 — Isaiah COZART — Richmond, Ky. — 6-7 225 FR
Sat. vs. Kentucky State: OB, 10 min. - 2 pts, 0 reb
(1-2 / 0-0 / 0-5)

— PPG	— RPG	— APG	— FG	— 3P	— FT

20 PPG/12 RPG/almost 6 blocks per game as a senior @ Madison Central HS in Richmond ... Gatorade Players of the Year in Kentucky ... 2-time First Team All-State choice

Head Coach: Rick Stansbury — 4th season @ WKU (62-42), 18th as D-1 HC (355-208, .631) ... 14-year HC @ Mississippi St. (2 SEC titles, 6 NCAAs, Bulldogs' all-time wins leader) ... Two seasons on staff @ Texas A&M ... Battletown, Ky., native (Northern) ... Since he took over, WKU's attendance has risen 58 percent and LY the Hilltoppers sold out general season tickets for the first time since Diddle Arena opened in 1963 ... 1 of 9 schools w/ back-to-back top-20 rec. classes in '17/'18 (Duke, UK, UCLA, Oregon, KU, UNC, Texas, MSU)

TENNESSEE TECH GOLDEN EAGLES (0-0, 0-0 OVC)

0 — Larry QWIM-ee
Missouri City, Texas — 6-6 215 JR (JUCO)
Exhibition vs. Bryan: OB, 10 mins. - 4 pts, 3 reb, 2 ast (2-4 / 0-0 / 0-0)

— PPG	— RPG	— APG	— FG	— 3P	— FT

Third school in three years — started at NCAA Div. II Oklahoma Christian before spending last season @ Lee College in Texas ... sister, Winnie, is a freshman forward at Jacksonville State, another OVC school

2 — Jared SHERFIELD
Tuscaloosa, Ala. — 6-5 165 SO
Exhibition vs. Bryan: OB, 10 mins. - 2 pts, 2 reb, 1 ast (0-1 / 0-1 / 2-2)

4.9 PPG	2.5 RPG	1.0 APG	43.2% FG	26.3% 3P	75.6% FT

Played in all 31 games for Tech LY — averaged 16 mins. per game ... career-high 20 points (7-9 / 4-5) against Morehead State in Feb. — he joined Jr. Clay and Hunter Vick to form the first freshman trio in school history to all have at least one 20-point game

Out of Paul Bryant HS in Tuscaloosa, the same HS as Western Kentucky senior Matt Horton ... Sherfield was a First Team All-State choice as a junior while leading the Stampede to their first-ever Class 6A state title ... final four mins./OT: 10-13 FT

3 — Keishawn DAVIDSON
Murfreesboro, Tenn. — 6-2 160 FR
Exhibition vs. Bryan: ST, 27 mins. - 26 pts*, 6 reb*, 2 a (9-12 / 6-7 / 2-2)

— PPG	— RPG	— APG	— FG	— 3P	— FT

Three years @ Oakland HS in Murfreesboro and one @ Athens Prep Academy in Athens, Tenn. ... First Team All-State as a junior on 17.5 PPG and 39 percent 3-point shooting ... upped his average to 19 PPG as a senior (still not close to his 26 last Tues.)

Committed to play in Conf. USA @ Middle Tennessee in Nov. 2017, but Kermit Davis departed for Ole Miss following that season and Davidson decommitted in April ... eventually chose Tenn. Tech this past May (offers: UAB, Austin Peay, Morehead State)

4 — Jr. CLAY
Chattanooga, Tenn. — 6-0 160 SO
Exhibition vs. Bryan: ST, 26 mins. - 11 pts, 3 reb, 5 ast (4-8 / 1-2 / 2-2)

14.4 PPG*	3.8 RPG	4.3 APG*	41.1% FG	39.4% 3P	71.9% FT

2019 All-OVC Second Team ... contributor in all areas — led the team in scoring, assists (4th OVC), and steals (5th OVC) last season ... career-high 26 points @ Morehead State in January ... 22 pts/9 reb/8 ast two days later @ Eastern Kentucky

Only 15 freshmen in the country had multiple 20-point games last season — Tennessee Tech has two of them, Jr. Clay and Hunter Vick ... VERY lightly recruited out of HS — TTU was his only Div. I offer ... sister, Chadarryl, played basketball @ Auburn + VCU

5 — Darius ALLEN
Melbourne, Fla. — 6-5 210 SR (TR)
Exhibition vs. Bryan: ST, 27 mins. - 9 pts, 3 reb, 5 ast (4-11 / 1-7 / 0-0)

— PPG	— RPG	— APG	— FG	— 3P	— FT

Third collegiate stop — began his career with two years @ Palm Beach State College before spending last season @ Baylor, where he appeared in only 14 games

Played three of his HS years @ Florida Air Academy, where he once dunked so hard during a game at the City of Palms Classic that he knocked the gym lights out for 45 minutes ... has held offers, either HS or JUCO, from Virginia Tech, Houston, Iowa State

11 — Dane QUEST
Toronto, Ontario — 6-6 185 FR
Exhibition vs. Bryan, 7 mins. - 2 pts, 4 reb (0-1 / 0-0 / 2-2)

— PPG	— RPG	— APG	— FG	— 3P	— FT

Spent last two years of HS in the U.S. — junior season @ South Kent School in Connecticut and senior year @ Lake Forest HS in Illinois

12 — Amadou SEE-lah
Bamako, Mali — 6-6 210 SO (JUCO)
Exhibition vs. Bryan: ST, 20 mins. - 8 pts, 6 reb, 1 ast (4-6 / 0-0 / 0-2)

— PPG	— RPG	— APG	— FG	— 3P	— FT

First season with the Golden Eagles after a year @ Iowa Western CC ... played @ Our Savior Lutheran HS in the Bronx, where he averaged a double-double as a senior to help OSL to a No. 19 national ranking

20 — Hunter VICK
Camden, Tenn. — 6-4 180 R-SO
Exhibition vs. Bryan: ST, 27 mins. - 11 pts, 5 reb, 7 ast* (4-8 / 3-6 / 0-0) 3 blocks*

11.2 PPG	3.8 RPG	2.0 APG	39.7% FG	39.7% 3P	83.1% FT

3rd year — missed what would've been true FR season two years ago due to injury ... started all 31 games LY, averaged 33 mins./game to lead all OVC freshmen ... Tech FR-record 54 made 3s, also blocked 20 shots ... CH 22 pts @ Savannah State last Nov.

Hit 28 straight free throws at one point LY, only two short of the program record (Jud Dillard) ... Two-time All-State honoree @ Camden Central HS

21 — Reece WILKERSON
Miami, Fla. — 6-9 270 R-FR
Exhibition vs. Bryan, 9 mins. - 0 pts, 3 reb (0-3 / 0-0 / 0-0)

— PPG	— RPG	— APG	— FG	— 3PT	— FT

Sat out last season as a redshirt due to injury ... averaged a double-double as a Norland HS senior in Miami

22 — Too-JUAN-tay WILLIAMS
Chicago, Ill. — 6-5 185 FR
Exhibition vs. Bryan, 19 mins. - 11 pts, 7 reb, 2 ast (5-9 / 0-1 / 1-1) 3 steals*

— PPG	— RPG	— APG	— FG	— 3P	— FT

Out of Orr Academy HS in Chicago, where he helped the Spartans become only the fourth program in Illinois history to win three state titles in a row ... averaged 17/7/6 as a senior ... Offers: Texas Tech, Minnesota, DePaul, New Mexico, others

Very active and aggressive during the Golden Eagles' exhibition win over Bryan last week, both off the dribble and on offensive glass

24 — Garrett GOLDAY
Arlington, Tenn. — 6-7 220 SO
Exhibition vs. Bryan: OB, 5 mins. - 0 pts, 0 reb, 0 ast (0-0 / 0-0 / 0-0)

4.2 PPG	2.2 RPG	0.3 APG	42.9% FG	29.7% 3P	12-20 FT

Appeared in all 31 Golden Eagles games LY as a freshman (15 mins. per game)

21 PPG as a senior @ Arlington HS ... father, Clay, played basketball at Union University while former Tech head coach Steve Payne was on the staff (Hunter Vick can say the same about his father)

54 — Cade CROSLAND
Sparta, Tenn. — 6-0 180 SR
Exhibition vs. Bryan: OB, 7 mins. - 0 pts, 0 reb, 0 ast (0-2 / 0-2 / 0-0)

1.5 PPG	0.9 RPG	0.4 APG	11-34 FG	10-30 3P	0-0 FT

3rd-year Golden Eagle who spent his freshman year @ Chattanooga State CC ... Capable shooter from deep who rarely scores inside the arc (30 of his 34 field-goal attempts last season came from long range)

Career highs: 12 points (twice — Nov. 25, 2017, vs. UMES; Feb. 9, 2019, @ UT-Martin) ... 5 rebounds (Nov. 16, 2017, vs. Bryan College) ... LAST YEAR: Season-high 17 minutes against Warren Wilson on Dec. 6, 2018

Head Coach: John Pelphrey — 1st season @ TTU (0-0), 10th as D-I HC (149-126) ... Third stop as a collegiate HC (5 years @ So. Alabama, 4 @ Arkansas) ... 2 trips to the NCAA Tournament as a HC, one @ each school ... Two separate stints as an assistant to Billy Donovan @ Florida (2 Final Fours) ... last 3 as associate HC @ Alabama ... Paintsville, Ky., native (Eastern) who went to the 1992 Elite Eight with UK (Laettner shot) as part of "the unforgettables" who revived UK after the Eddie Sutton sanctions ... His Wildcats' No. 34 is retired

Bill Worrell
Houston Rockets

"Open wide, son," said the team dentist for the Rice University football team in the mid-1950s during an examination of a player. The dentist, William Hamilton "Dub" Worrell, had his 10-year-old son Bill with him. Bill remembers that "Rice football was number one in town" at that time, before the Houston Oilers were established. "He would take me with him, and later on Bud Adams was one of his patients," said Worrell. "As soon as Bud got the franchise, he asked my dad to be the team dentist for the Oilers." Bill remembers that his dad "was having to replace a lot of teeth," leading him to recommend to the Houston Independent School District that mouthguards be mandatory for high school football players. Eventually Rice and the University of Houston followed suit.

Worrell has fond memories of attending Houston Buffs minor league baseball games. He also recalls standing in front of a mirror with a bat imitating the batting stances of St. Louis Cardinals players as he listened to their games on KMOX Radio in St. Louis. Bill's parents hoped he would be a dentist, but after two years at the University of Houston he left that plan and changed his major to broadcasting. KUHF Radio and KUHT-TV gave Worrell and other students a rare platform (at that time) to broadcast baseball and football games on campus, and Worrell could be found on the top row of the bleachers trying to anchor his notes on his lap in a strong wind with no press box in the stadium and no players' names on uniforms. He and Larry Dierker worked some baseball broadcasts. Dierker observed that it would be much easier to broadcast Astros games than college games under those circumstances.

Worrell worked into a relationship with KPRC-TV as a student.

The station recruited him to interview players on camera after games. It was clear that neither he nor his voice would be on the air. "That was my hand that got on television for two years as a student," he described. "But it gave me an in to Channel 2, so that when I graduated, they offered me a job."

Worrell wanted to play major league baseball, but his fastball at the University of Houston was timed at 88 mph. Legendary scout Red Murff had signed Nolan Ryan from Alvin, Texas, but Worrell's fastball was not in the same area code as Ryan's. Spending years in the minor leagues was not attractive to Worrell. He took the broadcasting offer.

Worrell's father put his teeth in braces, but his face and voice were perfect for a television anchor. News director Ray Miller at KPRC-TV was more concerned with Bill's reporting abilities, however. "Ray wanted everybody to come up through radio, so that's what I did for about three or four years," explained Worrell. "I learned how to write a short, concise report. Then he put me on the overnight shift so I could do a lot of repetitive work on a microphone in radio, so I could learn how to develop a style and deliver it. He didn't move me to television until 1974, and I did those little cut-ins in the Today Show. They created midnight news so that I would get a lot of chances to be on television. I had about two viewers, I think. But it was super training, so when I got a better opportunity I was ready to go."

Worrell took over as the sports anchor at KPRC-TV after the tragic death of Bill Enis. Worrell joined a line of top Houston TV sportscasters including Jim Nance, Ron Franklin, Robert Flores and Bob Allen. Dan Lovett was another who moved on to national assignments. Enis was on his way to NBC when he died.

As the dean of the Houston play-by-play voices, Worrell entered his 39th season as the TV voice of the Houston Rockets in 2020. He did Houston Astros games as well for 20 of those seasons!

Questions and answers about his career:

Q. How does a broadcaster handle two different play-by-play sports seasons that overlap each other?

"You have to be young, number one, with a lot of energy. I would stay with the Rockets through the playoffs and then would take one week off before joining baseball. We never had any problems there because the Rockets weren't going to the playoffs for years.

"The Astros' media relations guys, Rob Matwick and Chuck Pool, sent me notes about the team. I looked at box scores and game notes to keep me informed when I was working Rockets games. It was a little different. I wasn't doing play-by-play, so I would complement what you guys were doing."

Q. How did you make the transition from studio work to play-by-play?

"At Channel 2 I was the sports director and I couldn't get out to do enough games," said Worrell. "When I was able to do some games, I just wasn't very good. I did not really become good at my craft until I went to HSE (Home Sports Entertainment, a regional sports cable channel) because there were only two reporters at HSE: Greg Lucas and myself.

"He and I did every sport on demand: baseball, tennis, college golf, even synchronized skating (and I knew absolutely nothing about it), track and field meets. I learned to be pretty good by doing all of those different events. Of course, now there are so many people specializing in every sport, that would not happen today."

Q. How much of an adjustment did you have to make when Clyde Drexler joined you and Matt Bullard in a three-man booth on the Rockets' games?

"It was difficult for about a month. I knew how to adapt, but Clyde had never even done a game. He thought it would be easy because he played the game. I think for Clyde to try to find a rhythm for where he can talk was very difficult, and until he could do that, we were never really able to mesh very well as a team. Bullard and I had already worked together for several years, so we had a pretty good patter down, so to speak. But going into the second and third month working with Clyde, he found where his niche was. We had lots of conversations about it. He was repeating a lot of the stuff that Matt would say. I said, 'You've got to bring something else.' And I had to back off a lot. I had to make way for those two. And if they started talking to each other and they were really on a good topic, I just let them go. If they were just wasting air time, I would pick it up."

In his career, Worrell has covered the Indianapolis 500, the Kentucky Derby and Super Bowls. He did play-by-play of Houston Oilers preseason games. In 2011, he was awarded a Lone Star Emmy. Worrell still speaks to broadcasting classes at the University of Houston. He plans to donate two endowed scholarships, one for broadcasting and one for baseball, when he retires from broadcasting.

Bill Worrell's Advice to Students

"Learn how to write. Learn how to put together short, concise, get-right-to-the-point stories. I'm talking about radio and television. There are two different classes. In the journalism department, that's for writing and newspapers. You can have all these long 27-word sentences when you're writing for the newspaper. You would not talk that way. When you look into a camera, you have to imagine that you're talking to only one person in that lens. You would not talk to that person in a newspaper style. You would talk to them in a short, concise manner. That's what young people can't do. They can't grasp picking what they read when they're taking down notes and turning it into something to convey what you're trying to say.

"How do you do that? If you want to be in sports, you take out the sports page every day and rewrite every story as if you're going to do it on television. Learn how to write so that you make your brain think that way, so that when they send you notes in baseball and football and whatever, you just can almost read off the page and absorb that as you would like to say it on the air. It becomes second nature after a while."

CHAPTER 17

HOCKEY PLAY-BY-PLAY

Josh Bogorad
Dallas Stars

The 16-year-old was lying in bed around midnight, recovering from back surgery. The doctor had ordered him to stay in bed all day. His favorite radio station had a host who said, "We should get into hockey." That was all he needed. He called the station's listener line. Finally, somebody answered the phone and took down his contact information. A few days later, the host called him and asked if he could arrange a Los Angeles Kings player as a guest on the station. The 16-year-old said that he could not, because he was not an employee of the Kings. He was a 16-year-old fan. End of conversation? No, the beginning of a career.

Sweet 16

The 16-year-old, Josh Bogorad, was invited to call the show one night a week and talk about the Kings. That led to more appearances on the air. Josh was on his way toward his goal. "Since I was a kid, a really young kid, I had one specific goal in mind, and it's such a small, narrow goal that I don't know that I ever fully expected it would happen. You work hard and you chase after it and you hope it will, but you don't necessarily believe that it will. And when it does, I think it's more surreal than anything." And it has happened for Josh Bogorad. He's now the TV play-by-play voice of the Dallas Stars.

After high school, Josh selected the University of Arizona. He had grown up in Los Angeles and felt a need to leave California and broaden his horizons. Arizona offered a major sports menu, and he was ready to pursue his dream. He did play-by-play and rink-side reporting for the Arizona club hockey team.

The broadcasters' companion, rejection, came his way after college when Josh made many phone calls for jobs that were not returned, including more than ten to a hockey team in Corpus Christi, Texas.

When Josh was told by the vice president of communications of the Central Hockey League that there would be at least three play-by-play openings and the league meetings were coming up in Phoenix, he jumped in the car and headed for Phoenix. He paid to join the job fair for the league and walked up to the Corpus Christi table, introducing himself to the man who failed to return his calls, the general manager. When Josh mentioned his name, the GM's face froze and took on a startled look.

He concocted a story about not returning the calls because he didn't think it would be fair to talk to anybody before the job fair, giving everybody an equal chance. Josh did not show disappointment, but asked how he could get the job. He got the job after explaining, "Pat, I got in my car yesterday and I drove 400 miles from Los Angeles to Phoenix, and it wasn't to give you a guilt trip. It was to explain to you why I was the right person for this job," said Bogorad. His persistence paid off.

Bogorad went on to become the longest-tenured broadcaster in Corpus Christi hockey history (7 years). "You do wonder, 'Is this gonna lead anywhere?'" It did, when he and his wife headed north to Alaska. But after four straight broadcaster of the year awards, NHL teams were still not impressed. His conversation with himself was, "What do I do now? Clearly, I'm doing something right, but it's not enough."

Big Move to Big D

After moving to the Alaska Aces in 2010, Josh got a shot at joining the Dallas Stars of the National Hockey League in 2013 as a radio host. He moved to TV host in 2014 before reaching his ultimate goal of play-by-play NHL broadcaster in 2018.

"Radulov across to Klingberg. Klingberg shoots, he SCORES! John Klingberg sends the Stars to the second round!!!!" Bogorad called the playoff victory in the first round in overtime.

Ralph Strangis retired after being the longtime voice since the Stars moved to Dallas. Dave Strader got the job, but then tragically he passed away. The doors opened for Bogorad to reach his dream.

"I spent so much of my life peeking over the fence. 'What's coming next? What's coming next?' I was happy with my job when Strader was hired. I wasn't really looking for this to happen, but it did. This dream that I chased literally all over the continent actually arrived once I quit chasing it. I stopped chasing it because it was the first time in my life I was good where I was."

GAME PREP: "It's evolved over the years, but currently what I use is a spotting board. It's a publisher file and it's on a legal- size sheet of paper. It's actually a template I got from a friend. I've gone through so many different templates in my career and if I see somebody doing something interesting, I take a look at it and ask if I can morph it into my own. There's a spot where you'll have 21 players and then two goalies, so 23 is what an active hockey roster would consist of. Usually you've got every guy with potential to play in that game in front of you. It's color coded, with notes. It has their name, their number, their position, height and weight, draft info. The color-coding I use, that's the point of this template, is so you can go back to any game that you do and know what the story lines were at that moment.

"If the Stars are playing the Pittsburgh Penguins in the middle of November, and then they play them again in March, you'll be able to go back to November and note, 'Well, the last time the Stars played Sidney Crosby, fans might remember he was on an 11-game point streak.'"

> **"I basically study for a midterm for every single game, 82 times a year. The way I've explained it to people is you're studying for a test, and you have to know the answer to every single question, but you have no idea which questions are gonna get asked. It is just this mountain of prep work." Josh Bogorad**

Color the Moment Blue

"It's written on my publisher sheet in a light blue color. And light blue is what's happening in the moment that will change game to game. Then in pink is draft information. I've got gold information about milestones and trades. It's long and convoluted, but if you know it, it makes sense. You have other colors with positive trends, what he's on pace for this season, things of that nature. What I've realized over the years is the actual prep of putting this together is more helpful than looking at it during the game. You spend these hours and hours combing through and putting this together, and then you've got these notes, stories and nuggets for when that player gets the puck or something in the game brings that story to life and you can tell it. The preparation leads to a little bit of memorization.

"I've created my own scorebook. It's blank at the start of a season and

I've got about 120 pages in there, and it has both teams. It's a spot where I can keep track of certain things. So, in real time, I'm keeping track of power plays. I'm keeping track of goals, assists, time of goals, shots per period, and then there's a lot of blank space where if something happens during the game I know where I'm writing notes. I also put line combinations and defensive pairings at the start of the game, where you can quickly look down and know if something changed.

"All right, Jamie Benn, Tyler Seguin and Alexander Radulov are starting the game together, and the next thing you know they come out for a shift in the second period and it's Jamie Benn, Tyler Seguin and a different winger. You quickly look down and reference that Radulov is now on a line with these two players, and they moved the third line winger up to play on the right side with Benn and Seguin.

"I've got that in front of me as well as the spotting board and also a copy of the game notes, which are different based on which teams you're playing, but it's pretty uniform in the NHL.

"Hockey is such a fast-moving sport that if you're looking down and reading, you're missing the most important stuff," says Bogorad. "Then you actually have to call the game. The more you know, for me at least, the more comfortable it is. That has nothing to do with actually calling a game. That's just prepping and studying and learning.

"Then you have to call the game, and that is an exercise that cannot be planned. You have to improvise. You have no idea what's going to happen, any shift, any night."

Keeping the Game Fresh

"If you're on the air calling anything for three hours, you have the potential to make it very redundant with how you describe it. Because although every shift is different, they're going up and down the ice in relatively similar fashion for 60 minutes of play. You cannot call everything the same way. I'll go back and critique myself. When I was describing something the same way on back to back shifts, I would almost wince in pain, because I feel like that's one of the worst things you can do, calling it the same way over and over.

"The more variant ways you can describe an activity, the less likely you are to repeat yourself. That's something broadcasters have to learn how to avoid.

"If a player comes across the blue line and cuts and loses an edge on his skate blade and falls down, I can describe it as losing an edge and I will," says Bogorad. "But every once in a while I'll say, 'He blows a tire.' I never went into a broadcast and said, 'OK, I'm gonna try this out. It just sort of came out."

Handling the long European names?

"I was a hockey fan long before I became a broadcaster, and that makes it easier. What I've always attempted to do is to go straight to the source and ask players how they pronounce their names. But a Russian player will use a "w" when we use a "v." So his name is different in Russia than it is in North America."

Chain of Experiences

"If I didn't write for a hockey publication when I was 17, would I have had writing experience to go try to get a job at a school newspaper?" wonders Bogorad. "If I hadn't gotten that FM talk station correspondence gig when I was 16, would I have had the confidence to start my own show on the campus radio station in Tucson at Arizona? All of these things, on the air and off the air, led to this diverse resume. By the time I got to these positions that wound up being key jobs in my life, they needed you to have this experience. The question was, 'Do you have it?' Somehow, the answer was yes. Do as much as you can. That's the number one best piece of advice, because you don't know where your road is gonna take you. You don't know what experience will pay off down the road. But if you do as much as you can when you can, wherever it takes you and whatever is needed, you have increased exponentially your odds of happiness."

"I really do try to respond to anybody who wants some of my time, because I remember how badly I wanted that response and I remember saying to myself countless times, 'If I'm ever in a position where people want my advice, they'll be able to get it.' If you ask every guy how they got to where they are at the major league level, every story will be different. I would tell them to do everything they possibly can. That was a bit of advice I got early in my career that I'm really thankful for. Don't hold out for the best job right away. Just do what you can. If nobody is listening, it doesn't matter if you have an audience of one or zero or a hundred or a thousand. You will never know what bit of experience you needed to get you that next opportunity. I think the first five jobs I had in sports broadcasting didn't pay anything. But they were instrumental in formulating a foundation that I would use the rest of my career. If you can start a podcast, start a podcast. If you can write an article, write an article. If you can host a talk show, host a talk show. You find out what you like more than you don't.

"Nobody gets to start out just being a broadcaster. You're doing a million other things. You're a social media coordinator. You're a salesman. You are a PR guru. You work in team services."

Josh Bogorad

Ralph Strangis

NHL Play-by-play

"Hull scores! Yes! Yes! Yes! The Stars win the Stanley Cup! The Stars win the Stanley Cup!" – Ralph Strangis, 1999

The joy in the voice of Ralph Strangis gave him that little boy feel again, the same joy he felt at certain times when he was 16. That's when he got his first paying job in broadcasting. His play-by-play career began with high school hockey, but he was calling NHL games into a tape recorder at Met Center, the Minnesota North Stars' arena, when he was ten.

During his 20-year career as the play-by-play voice of the Stars (25 years as a broadcaster with the team), Strangis and analyst Daryl "Razor" Reaugh became so popular in Dallas-Ft. Worth that they did a simulcast on both radio and television, allowing their voices to be heard by both audiences.

Now Strangis is teaching a class at College of the Desert in Palm Springs, California. He's brought the same excitement he had in the booth to the classroom. "I'm around a lot of young people who are excited and energized and enthused and who want to know how this business is," says Strangis, who started his training playing rock and roll records on a station in Minnesota. "Nobody had to get me excited about doing this. When I heard about this radio station in high school, it was like, 'You mean I can be on the air? I can go into a station and play with the buttons and stuff?'"

Later, he moved on to do many different sports, including hockey when he was in college. He worked high school sports on local access cable television in Minnesota.

In Minnesota, the crowd size would be in the range of 10-12,000 for a high school hockey state tournament game. He did volleyball, including women's pro volleyball, until it folded.

He called AWA professional wrestling on ESPN in his wrestling debut! "I did some ring announcing for 25-30 matches. We did them for ESPN, then we did the local show in the studio and I did play-by-play on the same matches. It was a great working boot camp for me because it got me to call stuff off the monitor, work on building my language, to get better at doing standups and interviews in the studio.

"The North Stars were looking for an analyst. I campaigned hard for the job. Their play-by-play guy Al Shaver, my idol, was my partner for the last three years in Minnesota. Al didn't move to Dallas and I stayed with Dallas for another 22 years."

Now that he's teaching, Strangis "tells them how to pack a backpack, what to put in their backpack. We work the first two weeks on schedules, showing up on time, how to manage your time and how to do homework. The good thing about this business is it's a deadline business, so you have to know how to manage your time. It's a homework business. They have to know how to research, where to look, how to cull information, how to find information, and how to be a dependable, responsible professional. I think if you're a dependable, responsible professional and somebody that does understand how to plan your time and show up on time, have your work done and be ready to go, that translates into any business you want to join for the rest of your life. These skills transfer over."

Ralph Strangis is eager for his students to do play-by-play of the 15 sports on campus. "They've got to get on the air and make mistakes just like the rest of us did. I'm excited about that."

Ralph's system of play-by-play

"I had my scorebook and what you might call spotting…but it's not really a spotting board in hockey. Everybody has their own system.

"My system was sort of a scorebook/roster book with line combinations in a different spot. The coaches change the line combinations so much, you can't even really go by that. To me, the real tool is preparation, is getting ready, is knowing those rosters cold, is handwriting everything out. I tried updating it on a computer program, but I don't remember it as well if I don't hand write it out. I have note cards for things that are not game specific. Like building-specific or event-specific. I do a lot of events now. I do the outdoor games for the NHL. I did their opening in Europe this year.

"I went to Prague, Berlin and Lausanne, Switzerland. I would prep for Berlin. I would prep for Lausanne, Switzerland and I would prep for hockey in the Czech Republic. I'd have all these notes. I'd prepare a hundred things and I'd only use ten but I don't know which ten, so I'd prepare all 100.

"*To me, the greatest tool I have walking into a booth is walking in being prepared. Having that homework done, knowing it cold, and sitting down being ready to go.* That's the whole thing to me. I preach that to these kids. If you don't like doing homework, do something else for a living. You have to be prepared. That's your number one thing. I have an iPad. and it tracks real time stats now. So, I'm always looking at an iPad during a whistle to see if there's a trend I can pick up. Like two guys coming in for a faceoff, see how they're doing during a game."

CHAPTER 18

SOCCER PLAY-BY-PLAY

Glenn Davis

Voice of Houston Dynamo

Glenn Davis took a different path to being the play-by-play voice of the Houston Dynamo of the MLS. He was a professional player, then a coach, then an analyst, THEN moved to play-by-play, He handles the Dynamo on TV in Houston and hosts the radio show "Soccer Matters." He is the owner of that show and founded it in 2002.

He got his break into broadcasting in 1994 on Home Sports Entertainment regional cable when a friend suggested him for the analyst role to the team's owner. Davis was hired without any formal broadcast training.

"I got there with Bill Land," (his play-by-play partner in 1994) said Davis. "I couldn't have had a better guy. Very understanding. He knew I was green. He knew I was a newbie. Very relaxed personality to work with. For me it's always about two people and the impression you make on a soccer match. You're judged as a pair. I not only became a great friend of his, but he's just an ultra-helpful guy. Encouraged me. Set me up beautifully. Here was a guy that was very experienced and he really welcomed me with open arms. That did make a big difference in the beginning. So, I've always tried to do the same thing with people I've worked with. I started as an analyst before transitioning to play-by-play. I think it was five years as an analyst."

Switching Seats

When Davis tackled play-by-play for the first time, he came at it from a different angle than a professional broadcaster who was schooled and trained extensively for the role.

"A little bit different to a degree," he said of calling the action from the play-by-play seat. "Obviously factual. Statistics. Making sure backgrounds and all the information was 100 per cent correct, so slightly different. I think the biggest challenge for me in the beginning, and I can tell you this with 100 per cent accuracy, is when you go from being an analyst to a play-by-play guy, these are two distinctly different roles. I would say in the beginning it was a little muddy, a little nebulous with me, because I still had the urge to break the game down and that was my analyst's job. I had to learn how to pull that back and set up my analyst.

"I feel with my playing background as a professional, once in a while I can slide something in there. But I always defer to my analyst. But I do remember in the beginning it took a little time to differentiate and make sure that I wasn't overlapping the two positions too much."

Soccer plays differently for a broadcaster compared to other sports. Davis, though, knew the sport inside and out. What he didn't know was the television and radio business. That came later for him. He didn't have a lot of assistance in the booth from the technical side. "We don't have spotters. You're pretty much reliant upon yourself as far as your game preparation. Obviously, you talk with your producers and everybody involved with the broadcast. You talk to coaches. I watch a lot of games. I always watch a game or two of the opponent before doing a broadcast. I have charts, general game notes, stadium, city, coaches, their backgrounds, records. All the basics on one sheet of paper. It's always there.

"Then I'll have all the charts on the different players, and those are usually done on a sticky, so when a substitution is made I can pull a guy from the bench and just tape it over, because I put the guys in the formation."

Relaxed Style

Glenn has a more relaxed style than some of the younger broadcasters working today. "My style is a little more minimal. I usually try to do some storytelling with the aid of the producer when there's a goal kick because you usually get 20 seconds there and you can get right into your story and get a shot of the guy or whatever. There are guys like me, usually a little bit older, who are more of a minimalist. And then you've got young guys who must be getting paid by the word, because they're nonstop.

"I don't like that, because it takes me away from the game too much. I don't want to be taken away from the game. I love the actual playing of the game."

Radio compared to TV

"Whole different way to do it. You certainly have to fill the space with words. Unless you're in Central America, where there was unbelievable crowd noise and I would lay out for a little bit, not long, but a little bit. Your layouts would be different there because you don't have pictures.

"Definitely more words, more description. Different. A tremendous exercise. But very different than calling a TV game. In a very fun way, actually."

Working with an Analyst

"That's where your knowledge of the game is very important. You can tell in certain phases of the game, with the rhythm of the game, how quickly the ball is being circulated. You really have to know when things are about to break. That's your knowledge of the game.

"When you see a buildup and all of a sudden, a rhythm change and there's one penetrating pass that puts three or four guys out of the game, a switch is flipped. This is the time when the analyst is out of the way and you've got to call the game action.

"That to me is where knowledge of the game becomes really, really important so that you're not in a story, you're not setting your partner up and asking him a question when the team's in an all-out attacking mode. Because those are the moments you're waiting for."

Preparation

"Every local newspaper. I've got my list of trusted sites and things, where you listen to people. I might go to another team's podcast and listen to the podcast to get a vibe of what's going on in those markets and with the teams. I talk to the other commentators. We have a nice thing in MLS where everybody's willing to share and trust each other, for the most part. I'm always helpful to the opponents' commentators. I think that's important. It comes with a lot of trust. At the end of the day you have to trust your conversations with coaches and players. I do like very much watching the game prior so I know their style of play, if it's a high tempo, pressing type of game I know I'm gonna have to be maybe even on my toes a little bit more because things might happen a little bit quicker with that style of game.

"Knowing the way teams play ahead of time and knowing it pretty well, you're able to lead your analyst into some areas where they might have a soft underbelly or areas where they can be taken advantage of. You're very aware of who the threats are and tactically the way they play the game."

Energy

"I know there were times there were three games in a day when I was doing them off a monitor, back-to-back-to-back. For the championship of South America. Great opportunities, but opportunities where you had to go in ultra-prepared because you were doing three games.

"In El Savador, there were a lot of back-to-back games. In a week when you're doing the World Cup early rounds, you're a doing a game every other day. The beauty of big tournaments like that is you do have months to prepare.

"You're looking at everything they've done, how they qualified, who their stars are, you're able to get some interviews from people in Europe. The networks sometimes help you with those."

Fueled by Passion

"I am incredibly passionate about the sport. I've been fortunate to spend my entire life involved with it. Passion for the game and responsibility too. You have a responsibility to the fans, to the organizations, to the networks to perform 100 per cent to the best of your ability. I'm a ritual guy, so this is the closest thing for me to actually playing a game outside of coaching if I had gone in that direction further. You love game day, you have a ritual, you exercise, maybe take a nap, have a coffee here, stop at your favorite place on the way to the stadium. I just love all that. I love working with my partner, too, because it's a team. It's fun."

No Voice Training

"What I did do the first year after I had done a little indoor soccer was think, 'Wow, I like this.' I enjoy the analytical side of it, because I started as an analyst. I said, 'Well, you've gotta learn about TV,' because I didn't really know about TV, learning how to work with a camera. My timing was pretty good, because Bill Land helped me with that really well.

"A lot of times, you know the replay is coming after certain things, so that was easy to pick up on."

Never Too Late for Education

"I went back and took some classes at U of H. Radio-TV production, where we had to do our own little piece and do on-camera bits and work with other students. I thought that was a good idea. I did a lot of reading, focused on other play-by-play guys, watched other play-by-play guys in all sports.

"I never wanted to be the show. Sometimes you run into people who think the broadcast is about them. I've probably done games with 80-90 different people in my career.

"I could tell you the names of ex-stars that the minute they got in the booth I was like, 'They're not gonna last long.' I was usually right. I would always try to have a conversation with them and ask if they wanted to make this a career. I had a number of guys who just weren't out of their ego yet, just weren't out of their playing careers, and weren't fully 100 per cent into trying to be the best broadcaster they could be. Not just because you happen to have soccer knowledge or if you happened to play in a World Cup or MLS or overseas. There's a lot that goes into this. It took me a lot of years to piece it all together, understand everybody's role in the truck, all those things."

Glenn Davis has called eight Men's and Women's World Cups for ESPN and Fox, two Olympics for NBC and NCAA Men's and Women's national championships.

CHAPTER 19

COLLEGE VOICES

Courtesy Ralph Barrera/AMERICAN-STATESMAN

Craig Way

University of Texas
2005 National Championship Football Game
Texas 41, USC 38 in overtime

"**All the dreams, all the hopes for the national championship come down to this play! Fourth down and five. Texas at the USC 8. Three wide receivers, Young from the shotgun. Back to throw. Vince looks. Under pressure. He'll tuck it in and run.**

"**Vince to the 5 – TOUCHDOWN TEXAS! TOUCHDOWN VINCE YOUNG! He's done it again! Vince Young has given the Longhorns the lead with 19 seconds to play in the game!**"

Craig Way was crushed when Pilot Point High School, the number one football team in the state in its classification in 1982, got upset in the third round of the Texas state playoffs. In 1983, Pilot Point again was eliminated in a classic playoff game. In '84, it happened a third straight year. He desperately wanted to work a championship game and didn't know if it would ever happen.

As a student at North Texas State, Way had to sell $25 sponsorships for underwriters to raise $200 in broadcasting costs in order to convince the public radio station to let him broadcast the games in 1982.

He didn't feel like the king of Texas high school football broadcasting at that time, but now he's called over 100 football state championship games on TV or radio and over 200 total state championships, including basketball and baseball. Way was inducted into the Texas High School Football Hall of Fame in 2016 as a special contributor.

After hosting High School Scoreboard Live on television Friday nights, Way frequently crawls into bed after 1 a.m. Often his alarm rings at 5:30 a.m. Saturday, beginning a college football day for the voice of the Texas Longhorns that might include a trip to Lubbock or Waco for another broadcast. Exhaustion can grab him by Saturday nights late in the season if the Longhorns have a Saturday afternoon tilt.

Way is devoted to the scoreboard shows because he was the original host of a radio scoreboard show on KRLD in Dallas that led to the TV program in 1996.

Way hosted High School Scoreboard Live from 1996-2000, had a three-year hiatus and then rejoined the program in 2004 and is joined at the hip to its success.

He's known for his knowledge of every high school mascot in Texas, among other things. He can make about 14 or 15 of the 18 yearly shows regardless of his Longhorn duties. He's been the voice of the Texas high school football championships since 1995 for Fox Sports Southwest.

He's done high school football on either radio or television continuously since 1982. Way did Austin Westlake games in 2001 and a Thursday night game of the week in Austin 1996-2012.

When North Texas State traveled to Austin to play Texas in 1983, did the thought cross NTSU student Craig Way's mind that he would love to be the voice of the Longhorns some day? "Never. Never occurred to me. That never entered my mind. I knew I wanted to work somewhere – in fact, for a while the dream at one time was to be Bill Mercer at North Texas State (now North Texas University), since Mercer planned to retire in another decade or so. Maybe I could be the Voice of the Mean Green, I thought."

He made his way to Texas because his father was transferred from North Carolina to Dallas. Craig was on the air at age 14 as the sportscaster for his high school's 30-minute newscast from its own studio every morning before school. He was part of a production with three studio cameras in the mid-1970s.

The University of Texas job evolved from Way's work at KRLD in Dallas. The Southwest Conference Radio Network was in full swing in the 1980s. At that time, Frank Fallon of Baylor and Jack Dale of Texas Tech would combine, for example, on the same broadcast for both teams. The SWC used the two play-by-play broadcasters of each team.

Way was hired by Host Communications and the Southwest Conference as studio anchor in 1988 based on his work at KRLD.

He did pregame and halftime reports for many different games on the network in 1988 and '89. In 1990, the network broke up, and the only conference schools that stayed with Host Communications were Texas and Houston. But Host brought in other properties by satellite.

That meant that Craig was now the studio anchor for Texas, Houston, Army, Navy, Pittsburgh, Florida State and Alabama games all at the same time! "I would just be finishing up my postgame for Florida State-Georgia Tech in the eastern time zone and I'd say, 'Stay tuned – the Seminole calls are coming up next on the Florida State football network.

"Then the producer would say in my ear, 'Stand by – you've got a halftime for Alabama' and Eli Gold would say, 'Craig Way is standing by in our Tank Talk Studios in Dallas.' There was only one studio! I'd have a pregame at 9:45 in the morning for Army and Rutgers, and when I'd get done with that, I'd have a halftime from Annapolis with Navy playing Lafayette. It would start in the morning, and when Andre Ware was playing for Houston with those four-hour games it would take me deep into a Saturday night!"

Way filled in for Bill Schoening in 1991 when Schoening had a conflict on a Texas-Texas A&M game, not knowing that he was being auditioned as Schoening's partner for the next year. In 1992, Way and Schoening began a run of 10 football and 9 basketball seasons together on the Longhorns' network. Way took over the play-by-play when Schoening left for the San Antonio Spurs. He has also done women's basketball and softball.

He called the 2006 Rose Bowl national championship win for the Longhorns, College World Series baseball titles in 2002 and 2005 and the Final Four in 2003.

"Once I got the opportunity to move into the booth for Texas, the people in Austin were familiar with me because the Texas affiliate by then was KRLD, so they had heard me." Brad Sham had come from KRLD to do

Texas play-by-play prior to Craig's arrival.

Although Way is well established as the voice of the Longhorns, his association with high school football remains strong throughout the far-flung state of Texas. "To this day, I'll go into some towns – Waco and Lubbock, among others – there's people that come up to me and chat with me there and they don't think of me as the Texas guy. They think of me as the high school guy because of the television show and doing the state championships, that sort of thing."

He's as qualified as anyone to compare broadcasting at the high school and college levels. "A lot of the craft elements are the same, and that goes to preparation. Doing all of your prep work and visiting with all of the people that you need to visit with, during the week talking to coaches and talking to student-athletes, it's still all about the preparation. That part is universal. It doesn't matter what the level is. I've always maintained that for doing football and basketball, it gets a little easier in terms of the prep the higher the level is. The reason is the information available to you and presented to you. For high school, a lot of times you're acting as your own SID (sports information director).

"So, you'd better be doing your homework - unearthing from the coach not only who the starters and the backups are, but also who could step in if somebody gets hurt."

The UIL has 12 state high school football championship games a year. How does Way accumulate his information for those games?

"It still comes down to how willing the coaches are to give you the information that you need. Sometimes at the larger high schools, the coaches can't be bothered or they're not paying attention. Sometimes the smaller schools will tell you everything about that kid. You always cringe when you get that roster and it has a number and a name and a position and it might have a classification and that's it. No height or weight. That's when I pick up the phone and call for it."

What should students know about what they need to do to be successful? "I tell them first of all, identify what you really want to do. If you really want to do play-by-play, that's great, but don't be afraid to diversify. You're going to need to be flexible enough in the assignments you do and the level of things that you do, and oh, by the way, how much you're getting paid. Don't be afraid to work and work for little or in some cases no money. When I was the play-by-play voice of the Crum Bobcats in basketball and the Ponder

Lions for three years, I never got a dime out of that. It was all about the experience of getting those games on the air and calling those games. That was the thrill of the deal."

Craig Way has been in the midst of an explosion in technology during his career. What has it meant to sports broadcasting? "There are far more opportunities now than in the '80s or '90s because of streaming and web broadcasts. There are opportunities out there. It may not be as glamorous as a guy wanting to do play-by-play and imagining to be me. The better you get at it and the more you work, the opportunities come down the line. You've got to be patient. You've got to be willing to grind at it."

2016 double overtime game vs. Notre Dame

"Third and goal Texas at the Notre Dame 3. Swoopes to take the snap from under center. D'Onta Foreman out on the field. Now Tyrone looks to the left side. Notre Dame had to rush Sean Crawford onto the field.

"Now Swoopes, perhaps changing the play call, will drift back into the gun on third and goal. Tyrone with it, turns, he'll run straight ahead - TOUCHDOWN! Tyrone Swoopes – his second score of the night. And the Longhorns are back in front. They scored first here in overtime!"

Dave South
Texas A&M

Before retiring in 2020, legendary Texas A&M voice Dave South wrote a book. The title was *You Saw Me on the Radio.* Although that title came from a different experience, it also applies to his first personal experience with broadcasting. South grew up lying on the floor listening to the radio at age 6 and 7. "I grew up on the radio," says South. "We didn't have a television until I was about 12 or 13." He attached himself to the Arthur Godfrey Show and Don McNeil's Breakfast Club. "I think that it helped a great deal in creating my imagination, and I used that so often in things that I would do."

Big Night on the Town

South and his mother and father went to downtown Wichita Falls Thursdays because his dad had afternoons off and the stores were open at night.

They grabbed an early bite to eat at home and his parents went shopping while he entertained himself by standing on the sidewalk watching through a plate glass window while a radio station disc jockey did his show.

"He would nod at me, and I got to be a regular every Thursday. One night I kind of smiled and asked to be buzzed in, and he invited me into the control room. He would explain all that was going on in that radio station. He would show me how the board worked, show me the teletype and the production studio. I just kind of fell in love with radio. I had no intentions of staying in that, but I just liked it."

But he was hooked. South funneled cash from his paper route into broadcasting equipment. He purchased two turntables, a control board and two tape recorders. He converted half his closet into a studio and started playing disc jockey. He taped his show and played it back for his mother later. She critiqued his work. He was 12. His friends dropped by and joined the show. He read commercials and news stories.

By his sophomore year in high school, his mother thought he was ready to go on the air. She drove him to the station and made him go inside. He sat in the car in the parking lot for a while until he built up enough courage.

There was one man in the station, just before closing time. South said he would like to work there. The man told him to sit in front of an old reel-to-reel Ampex tape machine. He was handed some news copy and read it into the tape recorder. After he finished, the man was rewinding the tape and preparing to leave for the day. Just before the tape was rewound completely prior to removing it from the machine, the man said, "You know, I've got time to listen to this right now." He listened for a few minutes and turned back to the boy. He asked, "Where have you worked before?"

South did not answer for a moment, ruling out telling him that he'd been working in his closet! Then he said, "I've just been practicing a lot." That was a good enough answer to get him a weekend job. Eventually it turned into a lot more work.

Little did Mrs. South know that she had just urged her son away from her preference for him, a job teaching history, and into a broadcasting career.

South had moved to Waco in the late '60s, and he came under the influence of a mentor, Frank Fallon of Baylor. "Frank was a great teacher, and that's what everybody needs in this business. You've got to have somebody to guide you through all of that, especially early on," explained South.

Fallon got him an audition with the Exxon Radio Network, getting him started in college broadcasting. Fallon was the original voice of the Houston Oilers and he was offered a job by the Astros, but he loved Baylor and wanted to stay there. "I've said many times that everything I do right is because of Frank," credited South. "And the things that I'm not so good at is because I didn't listen to Frank enough. If I hadn't had him, I'm not sure I'd have ended up doing what I did for all of those years."

The book title *You Saw Me on the Radio* came from the image listeners have of a broadcaster through his or her voice. "I had heard this broadcaster in Waco with the best voice I had ever heard in my life. It was just a tremendous voice, and I had this image in my mind of what he looked like. I figured he was about 6-6 and probably had played NFL football. I loved listening to the guy," said South. "I had to go the station one time to pick up some commercial copy, and when I did I walked up behind him and he started talking and there he was. That guy was probably less than five feet tall and maybe weighed a buck-30.

"So, I was really fooled by that image in my mind when I saw what he actually looked like. So, I started wondering what image I projected in people's minds with my voice.

"I was in San Antonio one time with R.C. Slocum (Texas A&M head football coach) and this little lady walked up to me and said, 'Somebody said you're Dave South.' I said, 'Yes ma'am, I am.' She said, 'No you're not. I don't believe you.' I said, 'Why don't you believe that I'm Dave South?' She said, 'Because I had this image in mind that you were short, fat and bald-headed.' Was that the image that I projected? That was when I came up with the title for the book cover."

Aggies Calling

The Texas A&M job came along when South was headed north. He had decided that sales and management was the direction for his career. He was managing a radio station in Waco. It was his dream job and he "had fallen in love with sales. I loved the process of getting into a sales presentation and then getting a yes." Exxon lost the rights to the A&M broadcast to a higher bidder. "I told them I wasn't coming back, because I had the ambition of owning my own radio station some day." In the spring of 1985, the man who had been selected to broadcast Texas A&M football left to take another job. South met with football coach Jackie Sherrill and they meshed. South told Sherrill he would do the games for one year and then move back into management. One year turned into 32 years of Aggies football. He was an athletic department employee as well and handled the corporate sales.

One of Dave's most memorable games was the Big 12 Championship football game in St.Louis in 1998. "We shouldn't have won that game, but we did. So many different things happened. Randy McAllen was supposed to be the starting quarterback. He was hurt. He couldn't play in that game. "Branndon Stewart was moved into the starting role, and the backup quarterback was actually Shane Lechler, who had a great career as a punter in the NFL.

"He had been a quarterback in high school, and they had to prep him to be the starter in that game against Kansas State. Well, Stewart was hurt. He went down on a great hit by one of the Kansas State players. He had to be assisted off the field. With that, Lechler went in and punted and then went to the sideline and I looked down and Ray North, who was our quarterback coach, was helping him take off his punting shoes and put on his quarterback shoes. I remember after the game I caught Ray out by the bus and I asked, 'What was going through your mind when you were helping Shane put those shoes on?'

"He said, 'I looked up at the scoreboard and I said, 'God, don't let it be 100-0!' As it turned out, Branndon Stewart was able to go in on the next series and didn't miss a down in that game. Years later, we were playing at NRG Stadium in that preseason against Arizona, I think, and Shane was at the game. I invited him up to the booth for the pregame show and interviewed him. I told him that story live on the air. As far as Ray North saying don't let it be 100-0, he said, 'I don't blame him.' I said, 'Why not?' He said, 'Because, as we were putting on my quarterback shoes, I looked at him and I said, 'Coach, don't call any passing plays because I can't remember them.' So, as a result, he didn't have to go into the game and we ended up winning. The other side of that was that if Kansas State wins that game, they're gonna play for the national championship in January. We ended up winning in overtime and there was a play-by-play clip in the game that they have ended up playing ever since in the pregame on the PA in our football games at Kyle Field."

Big 12 Championship Game

"There's no tight end. Jay Holder is exposed here on this right side. With a man in motion, now they snap it. Gonna throw here to Parker. At the 20, at the 15, at the 10, the 5, he is almos...HE GOT A TOUCHDOWN! HE GOT A TOUCHDOWN! HE GOT A TOUCHDOWN! HE GOT A TOUCHDOWN! HE GOT IT IN! HE GOT IT IN! HE GOT IT IN! HE GOT IT IN! OH, DOCTOR! They are mobbing him! Sirr Parker – it's a 32-yard pass. The Aggies have won the Big 12 Championship in overtime against KSU!"

"The memorable game, though, would have to be the game after the collapse of the bonfire when the Aggies beat the Texas Longhorns. Everybody at A&M at that time was hurting. It was really a very depressed time at A&M. We lost 12 young people. We needed something to help with the healing process. I had never in my life prayed that the Aggies would win a football game. God's got other things that are more important than winning a football game. I've always prayed for good sportsmanship on both sides and have good sportsmanship in the stands and keep everybody from any type of injury. That game, however, I prayed, 'God, let us win this football game.' I think a lot of people did. We won that game right there at the end. Brian Gamble, who was a linebacker for us, recovered a fumble and he was down there on his knees holding that ball in the air and there was an iconic shot of him that one of the newspapers took. Anybody that sees that picture and knew what was going on, you couldn't help but start crying. That game, more than any other game I ever did, meant more to me."

November 26, 1999

"And they're coming up the middle – he's been stripped of the ball! Who's got it? A&M's GOT THE BALL! AGGIES GOT THE BALL! 23 seconds to go! A&M's got it!"

Dave South is retired, living in College Station. He and his wife have traveled many miles in recreational vehicles, including making road trips in RVs to A&M road football games when he was working. Dave is involved with charitable projects in his retirement. As for his book, *You Saw Me on the Radio*, proceeds go to the Wounded Warrior Project. Former Marine Matt Bradford, who was blinded and lost the use of one arm and both legs while serving overseas, spent some time sitting next to Dave on broadcasts of Kentucky basketball. Dave found out that the Marine had a lifelong dream of broadcasting Kentucky basketball. Not only did Dave get him one of the best seats in the house when the Wildcats played the Aggies both at College Station and Lexington, Kentucky but also Dave put him on the broadcast.

As Dave writes in his book, he used to keep score of baseball games when he was 10. Then he would go into his bedroom, look out the window into the backyard and pretend he was broadcasting the same game. He said he had an audience of one – his dog.

He adds, "If you go to the book, it's the next to last chapter that I share my testimony because Jesus Christ is the most important thing in my life, and past that is my wife and family."

Yogi Berra, New York Yankees
"Baseball is 90 percent mental. The other half is physical."
and,
"When you come to a fork in the road, take it."
Jerry Coleman, baseball broadcaster
"Kansas City is at Chicago tonight, or is it Chicago at Kansas City? Well, no matter, as Kansas City leads in the eighth four to four."
Byrum Saam, baseball broadcaster
"Good afternoon, By Saam, this is everybody."

CHAPTER 20

Bayonets and Tanks

Mike Capps
Voice of the AAA Round Rock Express

Opening Day, 1991 – Few people in Mosul, Iraq were aware of the start of the baseball season. The war correspondent for CNN had been living in a tent near a hillside, borrowing batteries from Swedish medics to keep his flashlight working so he could read baseball books at night. He had packed a dozen books on baseball for his eight-month stay covering the Gulf War. In June, he was staring down a bayonet at a member of the Iraqi Republican Guards. Two truckloads of soldiers had surrounded his group on his last day before returning home. He started the day thinking about being with his family in Texas soon. Now he thought he might never see another Opening Day. Then two U.S. planes, A-10 Warthogs, swooped in and buzzed the Republican Guards, scaring them off.

Mike Capps would live to see many more opening days, thanks to the Warthogs.

Opening Day, 1993 – An exhausted Mike Capps was walking away from the scene of devastation outside Waco, Texas. There were more than 70 dead inside the Branch Davidian compound. Capps was a vital narrator of the shocking development during the 10 hours of CNN's live coverage. He was one of 300-400 journalists on the scene about 300 yards from the compound, which had gone up in flames fanned by 35-40 mph winds. Capps had been sent to the scene 51 days earlier and was captive to the ongoing coverage demands of the network.

A self-proclaimed religious leader named David Koresh told his followers they should be ready to die in the battle with the U.S. government. In the compound, the Branch Davidian group had stockpiled many weapons and they were ready for war. The FBI was talking with Koresh and giving him time to change his mind and leave the compound so they could take his weapons and set free some members of his group if they wanted out. The FBI knew Koresh was willing to die, and they decided to send in troops when Koresh was not cooperating. Mike Capps' live narration of the military tanks with battering rams knocking down the walls of the buildings was captivating. "Cappy, this is yours. This is your baby. Just roll with it as long as you need to go," the CNN producer told him. He narrated about 20 minutes of action as the tanks punched holes in the buildings.

"Bonnie, for 15 minutes we've watched this M-60 vehicle – this combat engineering vehicle – make large holes in the side of this building and pump tear gas in there. At times, as you well know, tear gas can be incendiary. Apparently this is what's happened. Now we have a very large-scale fire breaking out on what must be the south side of this building. There are some amazing pictures here. Fire has broken out. Let's just stay with this and watch it if we can."

"This is a roaring fire, and I don't know if there are any fire trucks here. I haven't seen any fire trucks come up. This fire is really burning out of control here."

The buildings in the compound were destroyed and few of the people inside were alive at the end of the day. The long standoff ended and the journalists would be headed home soon. Capps walked away from the scene as he had walked away from military battles halfway around the world.

As he passed good friend Dan Rather of CBS News, Rather and his producer put their arms around Capps and the anchorman said, "I've been watching this, and it was spectacular." Shortly after that, Peter Jennings of ABC News passed him and called out, "Mike, Mike!" He grabbed Capps' hand and shook it furiously while gushing about his work on the air. Jennings had tried to get Capps promoted to ABC in New York when he was deputy bureau chief for ABC News in St. Louis. Numbed by the event he had witnessed, Capps could not appreciate the compliments. He had one thought as he continued down the road: "I missed Opening Day." He took home a Cable Ace Award for his efforts.

A Friend on the Inside

Some 51 days earlier, Capps arrived on the scene and ran into a friend who had just joined the FBI six months earlier on the little street into the compound. The friend said, "I'm going to tell you something, because I love you and I trust you. This is a liar's convention. We've got the Bureau of Alcohol, Tobacco and Firearms, and ATF ran the raid and created a mess. No telling how it's going to turn out. It could be a nightmare." He added, "They're gonna have a news conference every day at 10 a.m. When it's over, you and I are gonna meet behind the building and I'm gonna tell you what's true and what's not." Capps was able to develop more FBI contacts as days passed by. One night at midnight, Capps' phone rang. It was an FBI contact who urged him to gather up his crew and head for the compound.

He tipped him off: "There's going to be a raid at dawn." He mentioned what vehicles would be used. Capps hit the Internet.

"There was enough internet then that you could get information on vehicles, what they could and couldn't do and how many people we had in them. That turned out to be really helpful during the ten-hour broadcast."

CNN had around 25 employees on the scene, rotating them through shifts of 17 hours on and seven off. There were 3-5 correspondents on duty.

Early Training

At age 12, Mike Capps visited the newsroom at KRLD-TV in Dallas the day after the assassination of President John F. Kennedy. The station's coverage of the events that day had a lasting effect on the youngster. "I don't know if a small-town hick kid passed away that day, or if a newscaster was born," said Capps.

Capps had visited Bill Mercer's minor league baseball booth when he was even younger, and he was attracted to the profession. Mercer was the first voice of the Dallas Cowboys and also worked for the Texas Rangers. Capps also was a news junkie.

The infielder at Hill Junior College had high hopes of playing professional baseball. Legendary scout Red Murff took time to scout him, and they became friends. Years later he did some scouting for Murff and wrote a book about Murff, the man who scouted and signed Hall of Famer Nolan Ryan: *The Scout: Looking for the Best in Baseball.*

The military draft was taking thousands of young guys like Capps and sending them to the Vietnam War. Capps failed a computer class at Hill JC and his mother was worried that he would be fitting into a uniform other than a baseball uniform soon. Capps needed a job. He and his two 19-year-old buddies were in the job market, but they weren't too marketable.

One step ahead of Uncle Sam

Then an idea came to Capps after he took a journalism class in 1970: get work at a radio station so they could get credit for a class project and improve their grades! He coaxed his friends to come with him to a nearby radio station and ask for work. They met with the owner, who said, "Get out of here!" when he heard what they proposed. Capps did not accept that answer as rejection, but continued the conversation. He attracted some interest from the owner with his promise of sports expertise on the air. But at what price? Capps proposed a volunteer approach. He says about the negotiations, "Free got us there." The owner said, "Can you fill two hours?" Their answer was, "Oh yeah, yeah!" Capps committed his skeptical friends to doing a Saturday sports show.

They were too stunned at being given the opportunity to have a plan for filling two hours of air time to realize that they had no experience in doing a show. What they discovered, thanks to some advice from a friend, was that motorists on their way through the area to see high school and college football games in Houston, Dallas, College Station, Austin and other cities were listening to the station. The trio bluffed their way through some high school scores from Friday night at the start of the show. Then they started discussing the Saturday college schedule.

"Thanks for Calling"

When the clock was ticking slowly and they were running out of ideas, they invited callers to join the show and discuss their favorite high school and college teams. To their delight, people called the show and discussed the games. After that show, Capps was convinced he should be a sportscaster.

The next move for Capps was to Huntsville, Texas to attend Sam Houston State University. Motivated to succeed in sports, he called the general manager of the radio station there and asked about job openings.

By chance an employee had just left the station and there was a slot open for a newsman and play-by-play broadcaster for high school baseball and basketball. The salary was a princely sum of $1.75 per hour. That was a big boost from free! Capps got two and half years of experience from that job.

Onward

After graduating from college, Capps attracted an offer from a radio station in Port Arthur, Texas as a newsman. Continuing his dual track of news and sports, he added weekend TV sports in neighboring Beaumont. Next stop? KPRC-TV in Houston for six years of news duty until the station fired 17 people in a major reorganization. Next? KSD Radio in St. Louis, Missouri. Fired again. Next? Back near home next to WFAA-TV in Dallas-Fort Worth for ten years of reporting and serving as bureau chief and executive sports director. His boss Marty Haag, senior vice president of news for Belo Media, was an admirer. "He was very persistent and aggressive on getting a story and one of the fastest we had on turning a story."

The attack dog mentality assisted Capps in helping to break the story on SMU football recruiting violations that led to the "death" penalty of banishment from playing football for two years. In the midst of that decade, he returned for a year to St. Louis as ABC News Deputy Bureau Chief.

Steering his career path again to sports broadcasting, Mike moved through three minor league play-by-play jobs in three years starting at age 45. In 2000, at age 48, Capps made his way to Round Rock, where he's found a home as the original Voice of the Express.

As the Round Rock team progressed from AA to AAA status and attracted large crowds, Capps was in lockstep with the team because of his own progress as a broadcaster.

Despite often leaving his house at 4 a.m. for a flight to the West Coast or the upper Midwest, Capps continues to set up his own equipment and do his own producing and engineering. He missed five games in 20 years. He is a two-time Minor League Broadcaster of the Year.

Capps has filled in on some major league broadcasts, including some work on ESPN. He was at the microphone for the Houston Astros June 12, 2019 at Minute Maid Park when he made this call:

"Tony Kemp stands in. Two aboard. Still 2-1, Brewers. That's slapped to left field. Back it goes! Racing back Gamel. Back, back…that ball is in the corner! One run is in. Here comes Chirinos. He'll score. A two-run double by Tony Kemp and a 3-2 Astros lead! That ball hit the corner just to the left of the 362 mark out in left center field right next to the scoreboard. Kemp with RBIs number 11 and 12 and double number

six!

The dream of doing major league baseball regularly has never died for Mike Capps. In his news career, Capps interviewed four U.S. Presidents: George H.W. Bush and George W. Bush, Jimmy Carter and Ronald Reagan. He also covered the bloody overthrow of a dictator in Haiti. "Being me is a pretty cool thing, just being able to smile every day when I pull in that parking lot," explains Capps.

CHAPTER 21

PRIME TIME EXTENDED

There are sportscasters who spent most of their lives in "normal" jobs. For various reasons, they had to keep sportscasting on the back burner until their lives could make room for their long-lost dream. Two of them are profiled in this chapter.

Brad Greenwaldt
Central Minnesota High School Sports

Have you heard of a basketball broadcaster who keeps his own statistics on points scored, rebounds, steals and blocked shots? Meet Brad Greenwaldt of Raymond, Minnesota. He began broadcasting later in life than most when his children's school, Central Minnesota Christian School, asked if he would be interested in doing play-by-play of its YouTube basketball and volleyball broadcasts. "I jumped at the opportunity to have that chance," said Brad. The salary? 0. "Personally, I wish I would have done that sooner, but it just wasn't in God's plan for myself or my family."

Greenwaldt was immediately interested. He was 36. He has a full-time job as safety director for a trucking company, training employees and getting permits for trucks with oversized loads to travel around the country. He was officiating basketball and   volleyball, but had not thought about broadcasting.

"I know the rules inside and out and I keep great stats. I pride myself on that," said Greenwaldt, who grew up in a small town in central Minnesota working on his family's dairy farm.

G   He was intensely interested in the major sports but played sports   mostly with his cousins for fun. "I did listen to the broadcasters because you could learn so much from them," said Greenwaldt.

"I realized that I could learn a lot about the game and apply some of the things they were talking about to my own game even as a high school player."

He got a business degree and started his career in restaurants and hotels, marrying early and raising three children. All of them became athletes. "I do find that I have a lot of passion, not only for broadcasting, but just for being around a sport," Greenwaldt explained. "It's been crazy to come from literally small-town America and my kids come through small-town America too. To be able to help my kids through it, talk my kids through it, it's been great."

No Training

Without any formal broadcast training, how does a broadcaster approach the job later in life? "It was really unknown and nobody had a script laid out for me. I said, 'Let's just do a game and see what happens,'" recalls Greenwaldt. "Then you get into the gym and you start calling a game and you realize that there's a lot of homework that's got to get done. If you want to do a good job at it, you have to put in your time and get something to talk about, because it's more than just the game, especially when they have video of it. There is a lot of prep time that goes into making that broadcast good."

For a family man with a full-time job, something has to give when play-by-play is a sidelight with no salary. Sleep is what gives! Rising at 5:30 a.m. and working until 3:30, Brad stays up late for his prep. And he hits the broadcast location running before a game to cram in some game-day prep work. While the junior varsity team is warming up, "That's when you talk to the varsity coach or even parents.

"At the high school level, sometimes the best thing I can talk about is what besides basketball, if I'm doing basketball, does this child do? Is he in band? Is he in choir? You talk to different parents for that information."

Greenwaldt compiles all the pertinent stats on his computer and has them readily available for the broadcast. He does that work usually the day before the game. "I save a lot of the stats on a Google Doc sheet and I have a laptop in the booth with me for home games."

He has five pages of information printed at his broadcast table. But all of his roster information is in his non-computer memory! "I probably spend an hour and a half to two hours at home getting all the numbers crunched and sheets printed out.

"When we first started, we had 10, maybe 15 people watching. But at the end of that first year, I told people, 'We're gonna make it better next year. We're gonna do some homework.' Then you listen to some of these other broadcasts and you hear the kind of things other broadcasters talk about. Then you start applying those things."

After diving into deeper preparation for the next year's schedule, Greenwaldt saw a difference in the broadcast. "All of a sudden we've got easily 100 people watching and all of a sudden people are saying, 'That was fun to listen to.'" Now people know the name of Brad Greenwaldt in other communities, which he calls "completely humbling."

He explains, "If people can feel that you're having fun, they'll have a better time listening to it. The better stories you have, the better you're going to be, so it's all in that prep work."

Who's the Boss?

Without a supervisor, how does a volunteer play-by-play broadcaster improve? "If people say 'Good job,' I want to know what made it a good job. Whatever they enjoy, I want to do more of that. Everything I do isn't great, and I appreciate all feedback.

"I'm just some dad who enjoys games and it's turned into this. I'm even considering doing this as a fulltime job." The YouTube audience has grown to more than 1,000 homes for some broadcasts.

Shaquille O'Neal, asked if he went to the Parthenon in Greece:
"I don't remember what clubs we went to."
Former Indianapolis Colts Coach Ron Meyer
"It's not like we came down from Mount Sinai with the tabloids."
Joe Theisman of ESPN on Sunday Night Football
"I don't think genius is a term that applies to football coaches. Geniuses are guys like Norman Einstein." (sic)
Yogi Berra, New York Yankees
"Nobody goes to that place any more. It's too crowded."

Ron Soanka
Portland. Oregon-Vancouver, Washington
High School Sports

This is the story about a man who desperately wanted to be in broadcasting so badly that he sent resumes to every radio and TV station in Washington, Oregon, Idaho and northern California. He worked on that project five days a week, eight hours a day for months. He got one response from a radio station in southern Oregon but failed to get the job because he didn't have enough news experience.

Ron Soanka calls himself a "whole different breed" of sportscaster. He started at age 43! He was unsure of what his career would be in high school. He moved from Hawaii to the Pacific Northwest. He had a job with Pacific Northwest Bell phone company in 1977 as an operator.

A friend who was doing play-by-play asked him to listen to a talk show in Portland, Oregon. Ron liked the show and became a regular caller. The host of the show liked his comments and invited Ron to join him on the show live. It went well, and Ron enjoyed himself immensely. Shortly afterwards, "The sports director grabbed me and asked how I would like to have my own show," recalled Ron. He was offered 4-6 a.m.! He took the offer, although his sleep would be limited to three hours a night.

Three months later, a high school color commentary offer came his way. Then another. In 1995, he did his first game in the Greater St. Helen's League Conference. Eventually he took over play-by-play duties. That was the start of a long run with high school sports.

Mixed in with his high school broadcasting, he did two years of local college basketball, both men's and women's, and was also sports information director at Cascade Christian College.

He did play-by-play for a Cascade College national tournament game in 2020 at Branson, Missouri. The broadcast was widely viewed on large screens on campus.

Chris Schenkel Influence

Soanka was influenced by Chris Schenkel, the longtime ABC-TV play-by-play voice of college and pro football and basketball, Triple Crown horse racing, bowling and golf. He distinctly recalls an interview with Schenkel in which Schenkel shared getting a letter from a viewer.

"The thing that I remember most of all was that he was known as the Voice of the Cotton Bowl." Schenkel got a letter from a woman who had been blind since birth. She wrote that she loved his broadcasts because he painted a picture of what she couldn't see.

"I can see in my mind's eye what is going on," she wrote. Letters like that are the ultimate compliment for a broadcaster.

Broadcast coach

Soanka has become a broadcast coach now after 23 years of play-by-play. He critiques young broadcasters. "There are five or six things I share with everybody that I think are important, and that's the lead one," said Soanka about the Schenkel story.

Soanka works for Eli Sports Network in Vancouver, Washington. At one time in his career he was broadcasting close to 115 games a year. "The simple fact is that there's a very large company in the United States called the

NFHS Network, and we happen to be the leading satellite company to that out here in the Pacific Northwest. It's a subscription service, and you can watch games from any city in the United States."

NFHS bills itself as the nation's leading producer of high school sports. For a yearly fee or a monthly fee, subscribers can follow their favorite high schools if those schools are members of the service. The schools do not pay a fee to belong – in fact, they get a check from the organization based on the number of subscribers who watch.

Full Description on TV

Although subscribers can watch the games on their computers, Soanka stresses to his announcers that they still have an obligation to paint that picture. Why?

"Somebody may be sitting in front of their computer watching a game and maybe it's time to fix dinner. Now they've moved to the kitchen and they're listening, but they can't see the game. Now you've got to get the paintbrush out. Give them the formation.

"Let them know where the three-point shot came from. Are the outfielders swung to the left, swung to the right? Are they deep? Are they shallow? All of this they can't see now, so you have to fill in the blanks. You have to get your canvas out, take your paintbrush out and paint by number."

Message

"I think in presenting one strong message that I would like to leave with people who are getting interested in this is to learn to paint the picture as quickly as you can and make sure that you do it on every single broadcast from day one. You'll find that it makes your broadcast a lot easier to communicate, a lot more enjoyable, and you are the guy that can make that happen by painting the picture."

A three-man crew is standard for NFHS games. There's a play-by-play broadcaster, an analyst and a camera operator. Students can fill some of these roles. Soanka's Eli Sports Network has been affiliated with NFHS for six years. Through two cancer surgeries, Soanka has plowed through his career, fueled by his faith and his passion for sports. "The growth of this has been absolutely phenomenal," said Soanka. There have been almost 800,000 viewers for a weekend high school tournament.

"It's been more than I ever envisioned, and it's just by the grace of God that He opened all these doors and I got to do all these games and meet all these great people. It's been an absolute blast. I knew going in that you're not going to be rich.

"You can pay a couple of bills, go to a couple of dinners. But when you have a passion for it, you don't really care."

Common critiques for broadcasters

"In football, you want to let people know what the formation is. How much time is left in the quarter? Distance and down. Those are the meat and potatoes of a football broadcast. When you're on TV, you don't need to mention the player's uniform number.

"In basketball, just keep up with the pace of the game. One of the most important things is when a team is in what I call a 'Dr. Kevorkian game' and a team wins by 80. It's a little hard to concentrate and make it sound interesting. You really have to call on all your resources to keep people focused on the game and keep yourself focused on the game. You can get a little lost in the boredom."

Soanka calls his late-life career "indescribable."

He never thought it would be so successful and satisfying on the high school level. "To do it as long as I have – I thought five years, maybe ten years at the most. I never in my wildest dreams thought it could run more than 20 years. The cool thing about it is that I took some DVDs to my parents and they got to listen. They had never done that before."

And his grandkids got to listen as well. He's stayed in touch with former high school players who have come home after college and returned to start careers. He's had lunch with some of them and some have even become sponsors on the broadcast years after Ron broadcast their games.

CHAPTER 22

RADIO TALK SHOWS

Charlie Pallilo
Houston Talk Show Host

He's been anchoring Houston radio sports talk shows since 1990. Few broadcast professionals have approached that longevity in a major market in that niche. But how many people graduate *summa cum laude* from Syracuse with a double major in Broadcast Journalism and Political Science? Or make Newhouse Class Marshal as one of two such honorees at graduation for his college within the university? Or are nominated for Rhodes scholar?

Charlie Pallilo would rather not supply those details about his life, but it will be obvious as you read his comments in this chapter that he speaks on the air better than many write.

A New York native, Pallilo grew up attached to Marv Albert because of Albert's mastery of delivering nightly WNBC-TV sports reports in New York City while handling play-by-play of the New York Knicks, New York Rangers, the NFL, college basketball and boxing. Of course, Pallilo followed Albert to Syracuse. He and Mike Tirico were classmates and eventually shared an apartment. He learned the history of Syracuse- trained broadcasters

Marty Glickman, Dick Stockton and Bob Costas in addition to Albert.

The Newhouse School of Public Communications and university-owned radio station WAER were major attractions for Pallilo and others who hoped to follow in the trail of the top names. The student station also offered opportunities.

"My first football game broadcast was Syracuse's last game of my sophomore year," recalled Pallilo. He also was cleared for basketball play-by-play work as a sophomore.

He recalled the same memories as Robert Ford's of many students doing play-by-play from the stands at the Carrier Dome, bringing odd looks from some surrounding students. But, as Pallilo explained, "You didn't want anyone bleeding over into the background of you calling the game on your cassette when someone was going to be listening to it. You'd see at least a handful of guys around you doing the same thing."

It was very competitive. "There were only so many air shifts. Maybe at times it was overly competitive or cutthroat, but it was also a good introduction to a challenging business, a tough business to crack. And you can't just show up and start calling big games just because you want to do play-by-play. I thought it was a tremendously healthy and challenging environment. "Of course, it went pretty well for me at the time in school. My last year I was the sports director at the station (WAER). You're there because you get selected by the professional management. But then you're also a boss of peers – fellow college students. That in itself was just a tremendous experience for me, from handling people and delegating responsibilities and having them make tough decisions and critique other people's air product when I certainly wasn't my own finished product."

Pallilo also coordinated broadcast and travel schedules for the students who were "cleared" for play-by-play. "If the cliché is college is supposed to be the best four years of one's life, I'm happy to throw in if not the greatest four, it was on the super short list." Students were rewarded by calling basketball games before 32,000 at the Carrier Dome.

Syracuse was a university that attracted potential employers because of its reputation. "Across the entire industry, there is a path there. There are connections to be made. In some fields there would be on campus recruiting. Locally, each of the television stations would take on a number of the students spread out over the course of the year. Other than after the freshman year, you didn't go home for the summer."

That's because there was work in Syracuse for broadcasting students that could help them with valuable experience. "Of course, in this era, maximizing versatility has never been more critical."

Pallilo headed for a job working for a Syracuse grad at Morgantown, West Virginia after getting his master's degree in 1988. He was set with that job before graduation, joining a former broadcast student. He covered an undefeated West Virginia University football team until they lost a national championship, then covered a basketball team that enjoyed a 22-game winning streak. But when KTRH in Houston showed interest, Charlie quickly decided to move to the larger market because he desired major league sports activity year-round.

"Coming out of school, if I was going to draw it up it was absolutely going to be play-by-play," said Pallilo of his career wishes. "I don't know how to sound somewhat immodest with this, but I was pretty good. Loved it. Not because of a face made for radio, arguably I loved radio. It was where my experience was and I felt the craft of play-by-play being the eyes and the ears – and probably enhanced by getting to call some very high profile, big atmosphere games, 'This is great. This is fantastic.'   The opportunity to come to Houston from Morgantown was very simple, to get to a top ten market at age 22.

"But that took me off the play-by-play track...Once the talk show stuff kicked in and I grew with that, that was just the track that the job went on, and for the most part it worked out pretty well...I guess I'm one of all kinds of examples that you can't always predict your finish line, but if you get out on a course you really love
running, it can work out any number of ways."   Here's some advice from Charlie Pallilo to future broadcasters:

In Houston during Charlie's career, he has adapted to many changes in the business. "The multiplication of shows from two to four," Charlie answers when quizzed about radio talk. "The volume of material out there. The internet has changed things dramatically. No more stacks of media guides and encyclopedias in studios or offices. It's all on line and all kinds of people now can circumvent the whole thing and create their own platforms, whether it's podcasts or blogging or websites…There's just a much broader spectrum now in terms of content than there was 10-20-30 years ago."

Multimedia reporters/writers such as Tom Verducci and Buster Olney have branched out from writing to television. Their versatility is notable. Pallilo reminds us, "The more bets you have on the roulette wheel, the better chance you have of hitting on one."

As a serious sports observer who has been immersed in his craft, Pallilo has seen more trends created by the information highway. "In the mid '90s, I could have told you the top five guys in the NL batting race, but now we're in an era when people don't have to remember anything anymore," he observed.

"For someone coming along now – and it is such a competitive business – so many people want in who are able to get in and thrive. In media, if bombast works for you, that's an individual decision to make."

As for Charlie Pallilo, the facts and his studied opinions have made him one of the Houston market's top sports communicators.

SIGNATURE CALLS?

Broadcasters can spend hours trying to come up with "signature calls" that will be their own personal stamp in a broadcast. At this point, after 100 years of broadcasting, finding a distinctive call that hasn't been used can be exhausting and unproductive. Here are some signature calls associated with great baseball broadcasters:

Harry Caray
"It might be…it could be…IT IS!

Ernie Harwell
"He stood there like a house on the side of the road."

Milo Hamilton
"Holy Toledo, what a play! Put a blue star on that one!"

Dave Niehaus
"Get out the rye bread and mustard, Grandma. It's grand salami time!"

Bob Elson
"Good night, Irene!"

Vin Scully
"You can almost taste the pressure now."

Red Barber
"He's running like a bunny with his tail on fire."

Chapter 23

Perspective

Deputy Press Secretary Peter Roussel with President Ronald Reagan (White House photo)

Peter Roussel

Peter Roussel, former special assistant and deputy press secretary to President Ronald Reagan, fulfills the Philip G. Warner Endowed Chair in the Department of Mass Communication at Sam Houston State University.

He had thoughts of becoming a sportscaster when he graduated from the University of Houston in 1965 with a bachelor's degree in radio and TV, but he ultimately wound up a press spokesman for President George H.W. Bush before he became President (1969-73) and had a similar role at the White House for President Ronald Reagan (1981-87). In the latter assignment, one of his various duties included occasional briefings of the White House press corps.

On Roussel's first day in the Reagan White House he was assigned to handle media relations for the historic appointment of Sandra Day O'Connor as the first female Associate Justice of the United States Supreme Court.

Technological Explosion

From his time in college 55 years ago to now, there's been an explosion of technology. "The student of today has the benefit of technological advances that those who have gone before didn't have," says Roussel. "That's a notable difference, because it gives a student access today to so many forms of information, including job sources. In the past, we had to really scramble to find things out. It might take days. Today, all you have to do is click a button on an iPhone or on a computer and there you go, I tell students who are graduating, 'Look, you have a big advantage over when I was a student looking for employment. We didn't have computers to tell us where the jobs were. We had to go out and find them on our own.' The student of today, I think, is blessed with some great technological advantages."

Read Indeed!

> **These days Roussel offers this mantra for success: "READ, READ, READ! If you'll do that - and continue to do that - you'll be on the way. Try it." And he reminds: "Even though it's easy to email out resumes today, an interview in which the applicant effectively presents oneself will, in most cases, be the determining factor in whether or not an offer is made."**

Roussel decided not to pursue sports broadcasting after his experience as a student broadcasting University of Houston baseball games on KUHF Radio. He didn't think his voice was good enough. "So that kind of steered me toward print journalism and the written word," he explained. He suggests students constantly be alert for opportunities in their chosen field.

"In school, whether it's high school or college, students should constantly be on the lookout to volunteer for situations that relate to what they ultimately want to do career-wise. Volunteer just to be there, even if just to get their coffee for the staff, whether it's in a broadcast booth, a television or radio studio, a newspaper – wherever, so you can see how it works and learn about the process."

Doors Opened

Some different doors opened for Peter Roussel after turning away from sports. He became press secretary for George H.W. Bush in the years before his Presidency when Bush was U.S. Congressman and U.S. Ambassador to the United Nations. His initial tour of duty in the White House occurred when he was staff assistant to President Gerald Ford (1974-76).

During the years Roussel served as a spokesman for President Ronald Reagan, he had to be responsive to reporters who were already legendary, such as Helen Thomas (UPI) and Sam Donaldson (ABC News). He has remained an ardent sports fan while keeping his focus on the current generation. Frequently students seek his advice on getting jobs after college.

"Today, Sam Houston State University graduates who major in Mass Communication are getting jobs in communications-related fields – broadcast, film, public relations, journalism. Is it easy? No. But getting that first job wasn't easy for me, either. The key is to believe in yourself and don't let discouragement prevail."

Small Steps

"Some students want to begin their careers in a major market. Instead, I suggest they begin in a smaller market and learn their craft there. I just think it's very hard for a student nowadays to start in a major market.

"I'm not saying it can't be done, but it's challenging. If you talk to most people in the business now, they'll say that. They'll refer them to start in a smaller market."

You'll hear that advice over and over when you ask broadcast veterans for their thoughts. Many of us start in small markets. Salaries are low. The hours are strange. You are assigned tasks that surprise you and cause you to think they have nothing to do with your career goals. Most of us need time to learn, time to make our mistakes. If that happens at a 1,000-watt radio station, it's not going to cost you your job in most cases. But it makes you better.

By the time you reach a larger station, those earlier mistakes will have caused you to learn how to eliminate the same missteps in the future.

Roussel picks it up from here: "Another emerging aspect of this is the volume of competition in sportscasting. Nowadays you have many athletes who are going right from the playing field to the broadcast booth. That's great, but that's also one less slot that someone else could fill.

"Today there are many more outlets, what with cable, internet, social media and podcasts, for people to pursue communications-related careers. But it's very competitive now. That's something that hasn't changed. Hey, it was competitive when I started out!"

"No" Means "For Now"

"I certainly had my share of rejection as I sought that first job, enough that I got discouraged and thought maybe I should pursue another career," said Roussel. "But then I said to myself, 'No. Wait a minute. You ARE good. You CAN make it. You've just got to hang in there and have confidence in yourself and keep knocking on doors until somebody gives you a chance.'"

Roussel points out that many job-seekers hear a similar response from potential employers to whom they have applied. "They'll say, 'You just got out of college. You don't have any experience. Come back in two years when you have experience.'

"And then you say to yourself, 'Well, how am I gonna get that experience if you won't give me a chance?' I heard it and just about everybody hears it when starting out. You then have to decide that you do have the ability to succeed and stick with it. I think if you're willing to do that you'll eventually land that first job."

After his college graduation, with no job offers piling up, what was Peter Roussel's approach, one that finally got him noticed and the offer of a position at an advertising agency?

"People say good advice deserves good listening. I suggest tuning in when a source for whom you have high regard is offering helpful advice." He points out that his late father, Hubert Roussel, who had a lengthy career as a newspaper columnist and fine arts critic for the *Houston Post*, was often a source of such advice for him.

"After graduation and a few temporary jobs, I finally managed to get an interview at a large Houston ad agency. The reality was that I hadn't had any advertising or public relations courses and wasn't quite sure as to exactly the range of services they provided their clients, other than TV and radio commercials. As I was soon to discover, they not only did that – but a lot more."

Turn the Tables

"Before going to the interview, I mentioned to my father that I felt a bit uneasy and somewhat intimidated that I would be going to an interview without much knowledge of their business," recalled Roussel. "He looked at me for a long moment, then exclaimed: 'Intimidated? The heck with that, You go in there and put that guy on his heels!'

'How can I do that?' I countered. 'I hardly know anything about their business.' My father took a deep breath, harboring patience for a son he was about to educate. Then, in a tone of assurance, he said: 'It's simple. Interview him.' It was advice I never forgot. I didn't hesitate to use it and I got the job."

As for your future, a four-year college may be too expensive for you. Another option is attending a junior college for two years while living at home to save money on housing, then entering a university with a degree. If that's your choice, check to see what classes in broadcasting might be available in the community colleges you consider.

A college degree is a sign of discipline and academic achievement. But in particular, a sports broadcaster is cut from a different cloth than a teacher or IT specialist. As former ESPN producer and coordinating producer Gus Ramsey remembers, "I saw plenty of production assistants whose first job out of college was at ESPN, whose heads were spinning, who didn't know terminology, who didn't understand some basic stuff. It was pretty obvious that there was a lack of preparation for people who want to get into the business."

Broadcast Schools

Other educational options are broadcast schools, such as Full Sail University's Dan Patrick School of Sportscasting. Patrick is an Emmy award-winning former ESPN sportscaster. He also has recruited ESPN staffers and other broadcast professionals in the educational sessions. Full Sail University, located in central Florida, features state of the art television studios. Students are educated in various aspects of sportscasting, including storytelling and play-by-play.

Full Sail has an agreement with Rollins College to provide play-by-play broadcasters for sports events on campus. Gus Ramsey, the program director of the Dan Patrick School of Sportscasting, had his own talent coaching business before joining Patrick's team. Schools of broadcasting bring a focused approach to this specialized field and also offer a few courses in mathematics and other fields as well.

There is a bachelor's degree from this broadcasting school, and that makes it unique among schools of its type.

The Dan Patrick school was launched in January of 2018 and produced 23 graduates by early 2020. The program on campus lasts 20 months. The online course takes 29 months. There are 32 classes offered, 15 of them created by Ramsey and his staff dealing specifically with practical sports broadcasting work. There are no textbooks.

Is a high school graduate suited to this type of jump start into broadcasting at an early age? "It scares me a little because when you get the high school kids, that means they're out of here when they're 20," says Ramsey. "It's a tough business. I don't know that I would have been ready for it at 20. I was by 22. One of our first grads came to campus from San Francisco. He was in our first graduating class and he got a news reporter job in Bakersfield, California. He just turned 21 two months ago. He's already done 50-75 live shots. He did 16 in one day because he covered a shooting on a Greyhound bus and stations all along the California coast wanted live reports, including San Francisco and Los Angeles."

Although the Dan Patrick experience exposes students to many seasoned professionals and coaches, it does not offer a specific course in play-by-play. There are seminars in play-by-play with opportunities to interact via Zoom with some of the top play-by-play broadcasters.

Practice for Live Shots

"One of our classes is how to do a live shot," says Ramsey. "We put them through the paces in that class. We'll send them out to the parking lot to do a live shot. Someone's standing near my car. I get in my car and honk the horn, because that's going to happen while you're doing live shots. We'll simulate a press conference outside the classroom. We'll tell them, 'All right, you've gotta go back to class and you're gonna be live in two minutes.'

"We make them all stand side by side, because sometimes you're covering a big story and there is no spacing. There's no social distancing for live shots! You may be within three feet of the next person.

"You need to get used to talking while someone next to you is talking. The first time we did that I was playing the role of the Sixers' coach after they lost that series to the Raptors on that fluky shot that bounced on the rim and went in. One of the kids left the press conference about halfway through to go back to the class. When I got back to the class I said, 'Why did you leave early?' He answered, 'Well, I got the information I needed.' I said, 'Well, what if after the last question I announced that I was retiring?' He said, 'Oh.' We're constantly coming up with different scenarios that, between myself and my instructors, we know are gonna happen to them. That's why we don't use textbooks. Because you're not gonna find that in textbooks."

Tirico or Not?

As with any profession, young people bring tremendous enthusiasm and idealism through the front door. Some of them see themselves as a future Mike Tirico or James Brown, only to realize after a few years that their dream is fading quickly.

Some pivot toward a different type of pursuit in sports. Some move into media relations with a professional or college sports organization. Some become executives. Others gravitate toward the technical side of the business, such as producing or specializing in a statistical service. Gus Ramsey has seen plenty of that. "As much as we want to groom sportscasters, it's far more likely that we're just grooming people to work in this business from the jump," says Ramsey. "That's gonna be those entry level positions where you just know, it's production assistant kind of stuff.

"Even now, if you get a job in Lubbock, Texas as a weekend sportscaster, you're doing your own writing, you're doing your own editing, you're doing your own shooting. You're spending more time doing that stuff than you're actually on the air. We're taking that approach and trying to make people as well rounded as possible." That's a realistic and sound approach for a student as well. Learn as much as possible about the various facets of the profession. It's thoughtful to prepare skills other than play-by-play expertise. Writing, learning how to operate a videotape camera and editing video can all be extremely helpful.

Even if that career in front of a camera does materialize, having an understanding of how the technical side of the operation works can bring you a deeper realization of what is needed of you by the cameraman. His concerns will include the position of the sun and the background in the shot. If you have an eye for that, the two of you can work well as a team.

Artists love to learn from "The Masters," such as Van Gogh, Degas and Renoir. Sportscasters have similar aspirations when they get a chance to hear from national names such as Dan Patrick, Jim Nantz and Jon Sciambi.

The credibility of these broadcasting giants is captivating to a student. When one of them instructs a student or a class, it carries much more weight than reading a textbook from twenty years ago. Other areas of specialization in the Dan Patrick School of Broadcasting are Gaming and Virtual Reality.

Networking

An important part of this profession is networking. If you get a chance to meet a top professional, it's helpful to try to strike up a friendship if possible. Then make your pitch to watch that person at work some time, in the studio or elsewhere. In lieu of that, perhaps that person will critique your tape and offer some helpful career advice. It's important to pursue this angle and try to start networking with people you respect. There may be an internship with that person or someone else he or she knows.

Most of the jobs in this industry go to people who have done some networking before they are hired. They are often hired by people who have worked with them before or worked in the same market and competed with them, gaining respect for their work. One conversation can lead to a job, surprisingly years later in some cases. Broadcasters shop tapes of their work freely and often use their mentors to help them get jobs.

Although these "audition tapes" are edited versions of their best work, the people who receive them understand that they must do far more digging than watching a few minutes of somebody's "best of" tape. This is where networking, or relationship building per Jon Chelesnik, becomes important.

A program director, sports director or whoever does the hiring usually chats with several people in different markets who are familiar with the work of the job applicant.

The subjective nature of the profession leads to many differences of opinion, but the broadcaster can benefit from many personal and professional contacts who can serve as sources for job openings.

STATS ON WHEELS

Years before the Internet, Pittsburgh Pirates broadcaster Lanny Frattare could be seen pushing a trunk on wheels along the hallway leading to his broadcast booth. When asked what was inside the trunk, he replied, "The team record book." In my 37 years in the booth, no other broadcaster went to such great lengths to transport his team's record book from ballpark to ballpark. Most teams have their most important team records on the back pages of their media guides. The Pirates lined up a cadre of interns who could be seen in their huge home broadcast booth sitting behind the broadcasters. Evidently their duties were keeping scores of other games for the score updates on the air and, most likely, updating the team record book!!! Very impressive.

Chapter 24

HISTORY

The North American sports market was valued at nearly $72 billion before the COVID-19 pandemic hit in 2020. Media rights alone for sports events carry an estimated $20.9 billion. *Forbes* reported, "As money pours into media rights, naturally the amount of television and digital coverage increases as more content is needed to sell commercial inventory against." That creates "thousands of new jobs across the sports media spectrum, from broadcasting, analysis, content production, and everything in between." Unfortunately, some of those jobs were lost during the pandemic and it's going to take time before we know how many will return.

The art form began in 1921, two years before Calvin Coolidge's presidency began. Baseball on radio. On KDKA in Pittsburgh, 26-year-old Harold Arlin used a telephone as a microphone and used a scorecard on a wooden plank. There were a few hundred radio sets in Western Pennsylvania. Graham McNamee was one of the first baseball broadcasters, and he became a star as radio sets multiplied in the country. He went on to broadcast 12 straight World Series and NBC's first Rose Bowl.

In the century since that major technological advance, the essential elements of the radio play-by-play voice are the same. The broadcaster has always been charged with describing the action, reminding listeners of the score and giving background and entertaining stories. But so many other technological developments have turned the world into a far different society.

Television came along; then color television really enhanced the picture and the realism of televising sports. More cameras were added; slow motion replay created a need for a good analyst to explain the nuances of the game from a player's standpoint. Graphics added a much more statistical slant to the telecast. The ability to isolate each camera into a replay machine gave the producer and director carte blanche to feature any aspect of a play they selected. Electronic digital media forms made it possible to cue up a play instantaneously. Audio blossomed into a world of many microphones throughout the stadium, digitally enhancing what the viewer could hear. The sounds of a pitcher grunting as he released a pitch brought realism into our living rooms. A baserunner sliding into a base highlighted the speed, quickness and impact of a game. The moves of a football wide receiver could be examined and understood much better.

Sports on television with digital signals has made it so enjoyable for viewers that staying home is the first option for many fans.

The year 2020 was unprecedented in the world during the pandemic. People were starved for sports, but all they could watch on television or listen to on radio for months was an occasional rebroadcast of a historic game. While the pandemic swept through the world, sports leagues waited cautiously for the approval of health authorities to resume their seasons. As August arrived, there was activity in the MLB, NFL, NBA, MLS, NHL and on the college campuses. It was indeed the most unusual time in the lives of executives, players and fans.

Testing protocols were instituted and schedules were set, but provisions had to be made for larger rosters and adaptations in case the COVID-19 virus claimed many athletes.

Some athletes chose to sit out their seasons for various reasons. Many broadcast employees were unemployed or furloughed.

ESPN college football and baseball announcer Tom Hart:

"I think the sports broadcasting world is in danger of losing some very talented people. I have a positive outlook that we're going to have a college football season, but I think it's going to look different than any other season we've ever seen. Get comfortable being uncomfortable."

"There's a lot of pain and uncertainty in the industry right now," said LSU television play-by-play broadcaster Lyn Rollins.

To the Next Generation

Unlike a sculptor, artist, assembly line worker, carpenter or many others who have something tangible to show for their work at the end of the day, the sportscaster's work is quickly gone. The words disappear into a microphone and are soon forgotten, except for a few highlights now and then. But it's a great profession.

From all of the broadcasters who left their advice on these pages to all of you: Have fun, and we hope you fulfill your dreams!

Curt Smith, *The Voice:* "If a Voice is good enough, lasts long enough, and has an easy familiarity, he becomes an extended member of the family."